The Psychology of Emotion

FOURTH EDITION

The Psychology of Emotion

FOURTH EDITION

Theories of Emotion in Perspective

K. T. Strongman

Department of Psychology, University of Canterbury,
Christchurch, New Zealand

JOHN WILEY & SONS
Chichester · New York · Brisbane · Toronto · Singapore

Other Wiley Editorial Offices

John Wiley & Sons, Inc., 605 Third Avenue,
New York, NY 10158-0012, USA

Jacaranda Wiley Ltd, 33 Park Road, Milton,
Queensland 4064, Australia

John Wiley & Sons (Canada) Ltd, 22 Worcester Road,
Rexdale, Ontario M9W 1L1, Canada

John Wiley & Sons (Asia) Pte Ltd, 2 Clementi Loop #02-01,
Jin Xing Distripark, Singapore 129809

Library of Congress Cataloging-in-Publication Data

Strongman, K. T.
    The psychology of emotion : theories of emotion in perspective /
K.T. Strongman. — 4th ed.
        p.   cm.
    Includes bibliographical references and indexes.
    ISBN 0-471-96619-3 (paper : alk. paper))
    1. Emotions.   I. Title.
BF531.S825   1996
152.4—dc20   96–20324
                                                            CIP

British Library Cataloguing in Publication Data

A catalogue record for this book is available from the British Library

ISBN 0–471–96619–3

Typeset in 10/12pt Times by Dorwyn Ltd, Rowlands Castle, Hants
Printed and bound in Great Britain by Bookcraft (Bath) Ltd., Midsomer Norton, Somerset
This book is printed on acid-free paper responsibly manufactured from sustainable forestation,
for which at least two trees are planted for each one used for paper production.

For my family

Between the emotion
And the response
Falls the shadow

T. S. Eliot, *The Hollow Men*

Contents

Preface

The publishers regard this book as the fourth edition of *The Psychology of Emotion*. While it is a pleasant experience to have a book move into a fourth edition, I am not sure that I agree with them. The previous editions have been characterized by a close interweaving of theory with the results of empirical research. The first edition was behavioural in orientation, the second cognitive, and the third cognitive but also with a somewhat wider reach. This progression reflected the progression that had occurred in the study of emotion over the years between 1973 and 1987.

Matters have moved on even more. The interplay between emotion and cognition has become even more important and psychologists who are interested in emotion are becoming more aware of the work of philosophers, sociologists, anthropologists, linguists and historians. Numerous specialized books on emotion have appeared, many of them very impressive. There are thousands of journal articles, Handbooks are appearing, and theories of emotion have proliferated. Meanwhile, of course, psychology in general and the other social sciences have also been developing, such developments in turn affecting the way in which emotion is studied.

The upshot for *The Psychology of Emotion* is that what was once a possible endeavour, that is to present an overview of theory and empirical research on emotion, is no longer possible. Perhaps that is an exaggeration; it is possible, but not in the number of pages that any reasonable publisher is likely to permit. A Fourth edition therefore had to be a little different from the other three.

The subtitle of this book then is *Theories of Emotion in Perspective,* and theories of emotion is all that it contains. There is little mention of empirical work and certainly no detailed descriptions of it. There are a number of reasons for taking this approach, not the least of them being a positive reaction to the Theories of Emotion chapter which appeared in each of the previous editions of the book.

However, more importantly than this, there is an enormous number of theories of emotion, dealing with the subject from a plethora of perspectives. No other area of psychology has this characteristic, and it is not possible to gain a considered understanding of emotion without engaging hard with basic theoretical issues. The aim of the book then, is to set out these issues, to canvass most of the emotion theories of the present, and some of the past, to spread the canvass more widely than psychology, to make some informed judgements about the relative merits of the theories, and finally to extract whatever common themes there might be.

The result of reading *Theories of Emotion* should be that readers know a considerable amount about emotion, a fair amount about theory construction, and something of the interplay between the various social sciences. Whether it also means that the readers would be able to *define* emotion any better than they had been able to before reading the book is another matter. Their definitions though would certainly be better informed and they would be unlikely to leave out anything of importance.

In putting together a book of this sort, there are numerous people to whom one is grateful. Many of them must go unnamed; several generations of post-graduate students for example, whose stimulating discussions have helped to maintain one's zest for the topic. They say they don't much like theory, but once they are engaged with it, it is another story. As in a previous Preface, I thank my good friend and colleague Brian Haig. We speak much about the nature of theory (although not only about this) and I owe much of my under-standing of theory appraisal to him.

As ever, I very much appreciate the support that comes from my family in endeavours such as book writing. Thelma, my wife, is always supportive in every way, and keeps me as level-headed as is possible, putting aside her own academic concerns to do so. Lara, my daughter, although at a distance, makes sure that my feet stay on the ground, and rapidly pricks any potential bubble of pomposity. And, finally, Luke, my son, can think about theory more penetratingly than his father; I look forward to our discussions.

1

An introduction

A treatise on emotion theory should begin with a consideration of what makes a good theory of emotion. If one were setting out to build a theory of emotion, what would one necessarily include, what issues would *have* to be dealt with? Although these are perfectly reasonable questions, they do not delve quite far enough. In order to make judgements about what is a good theory of emotion it is important to have some understanding of what makes a good theory in general, or, if not in general, at least in the science of psychology. This, then, is the starting point.

There have been many penetrating analyses of the characteristics of good theory, but to re-iterate these would be to go too far. It is enough to mention a few that might be considered particularly significant in the context of the present endeavour.

Any theory should not only provide a cogent summary of some aspect of the world but should also have reasonable explanatory power. In the world of emotions, does a particular theory explain things that other theories do not? Does it explain things better than other theories? Related to this, is a theory expressed in a language which is (logically) consistent?

Of course, it is often not these two characteristics which are put first in any consideration of the value of a scientific theory. Frequently, pride of place is given to the degree to which a theory leads to testable predictions. Of course, this is an important characteristic of theory evaluation, and should be taken into account, but it is not *the* most important. Nor, in the view of the author, is it a necessary aspect of good theory.

Arguably of more importance than the capacity to generate testable predictions, in an area as complex and fraught with difficulties as emotion, the worth of a theory might depend more on the extent to which it generates new ideas, or provides new ways of looking at things. If a theory prompts a critical re-evaluation of thought, which in turn might lead to the sort of theory from which testable predictions jump out, then it has been worthwhile.

Finally, when considering theory on this broad front, and particularly in an area as wide-ranging as emotion, there is the question of the focus of the theory. Is it general or is it more circumscribed and critical. There might be a cogent and useful theory of emotion in general or of fear or guilt in particular. There might be a theory which is concerned solely with the links between emotion and memory or with emotional expression and recognition, for example. Or a theory might have far broader concerns, for example with the links between emotion and culture. Both types of theory have their place, but it is important that the extent of a theory's domain be made clear. Again, this is a general quality on which it is important to judge the worth of a theory.

What a theory of emotion should do

With these more general concerns as a background, the foreground is taken up with emotion theories themselves. What should they accomplish if they are to be judged as worthwhile, as *good* theories? A useful way of attempting to answer this question is to consider the views of some of the more recent emotion theorists.

Lazarus (1991a, 1991b) lists twelve issues that any theory of emotion should address. They are: (1) definition, (2) the distinction between emotion and nonemotion, (3) whether or not emotions are discrete, (4) the role of action tendencies and physiology, (5) the manner in which emotions are functionally interdependent, (6) the links between cognition, motivation and emotion, (7) the relationship between the biological and sociocultural bases of emotion, (8) the role of appraisal and consciousness, (9) the generation of emotions, (10) the matter of emotional development, (11) the effects of emotion on general functioning and well-being, and (12) the influence of therapy on emotion. In fact, that those who write about emotion agree with the importance of these issues can be seen in their coverage in almost any text that has appeared on emotion in recent years. There are also one or two other issues that are typically mentioned, although they are not considered by Lazarus. They will be returned to later.

In order to deal with all these matters, Lazarus argues that any theory of emotion must put together the numerous eliciting conditions and mediating processes of emotion. To bring this about, such a theory has to make propositions of various sorts. For example, there must be statements based on emotion seen as a dependent variable. So the causes of emotion should be addressed, from personality to environment, from culture to appraisal. Other propositions should derive from emotion viewed as an independent variable, ie, the effects of emotion. Moreover, from Lazarus's perspective, there must be propositions about specific emotions. Naturally, these must be consistent with the general propositions and must depend on decisions about what particular emotions to include. This, in turn, depends on whatever is the initial definition of emotion, thus bringing the theoretical endeavour back to its starting point.

To take a slightly different approach to the question of what any theory of emotion should take into account, it is instructive to consider Oatley's (1992) stimulating contribution. In a book which is avowedly Aristotelian in approach and reliant on a cognitive science perspective, he lists seven postulates which form the basis of Oatley and Johnson-Laird's (1987) communicative theory of emotion. This will be dealt with in detail later, but for now the areas of the postulates will be listed. They concern: (1) the function of emotions, (2) discrete emotions in which there is a bridge between folk theory and scientific theory, (3) the unconsciousness to the individual of the causes of emotion, (4) the interpersonal communication of emotion, (5) emotions as dependent on evaluations of events to do with goals, (6) basic emotions, with distinctive physiology, and (7) the ability to simulate the plans and understand the emotions of other people.

The sort of theory which Oatley espouses might be from a particular viewpoint, but it is nevertheless very far-reaching. Clearly, its propositions overlap with the sort suggested by Lazarus, but they do no more than overlap. They have a different emphasis. Oatley proposes that there are two types of test to which the sort of theoretical emphasis he suggests might be put. His point, although self-directed, has a more general application. The Lakatos (1978) sort of test is that a theory can deal with more of the evidence that is considered relevant than any competing theories. The Popper (1962) sort of test is that there can be derived from the theory specific predictions, which should cast doubt on the theory if they are not supported.

Considering Oatley's views on what should be accomplished by a theory of emotion also suggests the possibility that perspectives on this will depend to some extent on the breadth of the theory. It might be reasonable to suppose that *any* theory of emotion should be broad enough to include most or all of the facets of emotion which are typically studied. There should be room for matters physiological, behavioural, cognitive and experiential. Consideration should be given to the development of emotion, to its abnormal or pathological aspects, to the fact that it is primarily a social phenomenon, and so on. However, in spite of these theoretical moral imperatives, not all emotion theorists take such a broad approach. Some put most of their eggs in only one theoretical basket. Naturally, this has implications for what *their* type of theory might be expected to achieve.

It is perhaps instructive to take an extreme example. Denzin (1984) takes an entirely social phenomenological perspective on emotion. This means that any study of emotion must be from within and concerned with the lived emotion, it must be situated in the natural world (of lived experience), and then to search for the meanings of emotion quite independently of the propositions and methods of natural science. Following phenomenological description there must be interpretation, any and all such interpretations being restricted to the lived experience of emotion.

Denzin goes on to list various criteria for judging phenomenological interpretation. The results of any interpretations are then put into a context, a putting of emotion back into the world. Finally, and somewhat ironically in the present context, Denzin points out that the goal is not to test theory, but rather to make descriptive interpretations. In short, any social phenomenological approach to emotion must involve "deconstruction, capture, reduction, construction, and contextualization" (Denzin, 1984, p10). As should be obvious, such criteria for this type of study bear little resemblance to those which might be suggested for the appraisal of emotion theories within the framework of natural science. As will be seen much later in this text, however, they begin to be relevant to some of the more recent approaches to emotion, within a post-modern framework for example.

A problem that follows from this type of analysis is whether or not there should be an insistence on any theory of emotion having to cover all of its facets rather than being restricted to one or other of them. This will depend on one's viewpoint. On the one hand, anything goes, and anything that is relevant theoretically, however narrowly it might be aimed, is useful. On the other hand, some might argue that a full understanding of a topic as broad as emotion will only devolve from theoretical perspectives which are equally broad. The present view is that the narrower perspectives are useful and can be placed within a broader context by others.

The remainder of this book

As should be obvious by now, the aim of this book is to give an overview of theories of emotion and to consider their worth. The structure of the book is simple. The many theories of emotion, and there are at least 150 covered here, can be categorized according to their particular emphases. The major emphases are: phenomenological, behavioural, physiological and cognitive, developmental, social and clinical. Each of these will be dealt with and the main theories within each will be summarized and a concluding evaluation made.

There are also the theories from which, in one sense all of the others derive—the historically early, background theories. There are theories which deal only with specific emotions, such as anger or anxiety, and there are theories in which emphasis is placed on the individual or the environment or even more broadly the culture. And of course, there are ambitious theories in which the attempt is made to do everything. Again, all of these approaches will be considered, theories summarized and evaluations made.

Consideration will also be given to theories of emotion which have their origin outside psychology in related disciplines such as philosophy, history, anthropology and sociology. Finally, the themes to which all these theories give rise or which may be said to run through them will be abstracted and discussed. Moreover, recent theories of emotion which cut across a number of disciplines will also be canvassed, those stemming from social constructionism or from the post-modern approach to social science for example. At this point, if it is possible to draw conclusions they will be drawn.

2

Early theory

Emotion theory had its origins in philosophy. At the end of the nineteenth century and the beginning of the twentieth century, psychologists, and others, then began to be interested, as their own discipline developed. The aim of this chapter is to provide a brief overview of the earlier theories, some of which still have a mild influence today. Although this will give an historical context for the remainder of the book, it can easily be omitted by any reader who either has the context already or who believes it to be unnecessary.

Early philosophical theories of emotion

Both to provide a sort of baseline and a little for the sake of completeness, any account of the theories of emotion should go back further than William James. This is especially so when emotion is considered to be more than a purely psychological phenomenon, as is the case here. The aim in this section then is to paint an outline of some of the early philosophical views of emotion but with a few broad brush-strokes. Far more complete introductory overviews of the philosophy of emotion are given by Lyons (1992) and Solomon (1993).

To begin where most philosophical accounts of anything begin, Plato seemed rather to look down on emotion. Reason, spirit and appetite made up his tripartite soul, so emotion had no central position. If anything, Plato saw emotion as something which confounds, interrupts, gets in the way of or otherwise detracts from human reason. Solomon argues that Plato placed emotion somewhere between spirit and appetite, but it is clear that he viewed it as base. Amazingly, this view is still prevalent in everyday folk theory about emotion. We are expected to curb our base passions, even though few other than evangelical preachers would use such language any more.

For Aristotle emotions were much more interesting facets of existence. He viewed them as being accounted for by a mixture of higher cognitive life and a lower sensual life. Predating much of modern cognitive psychology, Aristotle saw at least some of our feelings as arising from our views of the world around. He also saw emotion as being linked with pleasure and pain, and listed various specific emotions such as anger, fear and pity.

Aristotle also made an interestingly complete analysis of anger, which he based very much on the idea of a 'slight' and also stressed the importance of revenge, a behavioural component. According to Solomon's (1993) analysis, Aristotle's account of emotion should be seen within an ethical framework. Viewed in this way, emotions such as anger are in some cases justified and in others not.

Although Aristotle's ideas on emotion clearly strike chords today, they did not last for long at the time. Lyons (1992) believes this was because the theologians who followed tried to transform Aristotle's ideas back into Plato, which of course had very little role for emotion. The second reason why Aristotle's account of emotion fell into disfavour according to Lyons also happens to be the reason for the eventual development of many new ways of looking at emotion—namely, the seventeenth century rise of a science based on observation and experiment. In effect, Aristotle's cognitive account of emotion had to wait to be revived until the new science could embrace cognitions more generally.

Following Aristotle, it was Descartes' conceptualization of emotion that was to predominate until psychological theories started to be generated at the end of the last century. Descartes' name is almost synonymous with dualism, there being a physiological body and a mind which somehow also doubles up as a soul and mediates a decidedly non-corporeal consciousness. Within this framework, Descartes placed emotions uncompromisingly in the soul and made them a solely human affair—animals only have bodies.

As with Aristotle, Descartes' account of emotion was essentially cognitive. Foreshadowing much of what was to come from psychology, Descartes had a place in emotion for physiological changes and behaviour but also for mental processes such as perception, belief and memory. But the experience of emotion and hence its essence or core takes places in the soul. The information about the world is carried to the soul via the pineal gland, the soul makes its deliberations and then sends messages back to the body, again via the pineal gland, about what to do. However, the most significant aspect of this is the conscious experience that is occurring in the soul. Animals might be able to react bodily as though experiencing emotion, but the *experience* is actually impossible for them. After sending messages to the body, the soul then produces "... a final mirror-image feeling of all that is going on" (Lyons, 1992, p299). This is the emotion.

As Solomon (1993) points out, for Descartes emotion was one type of passion. Passions are not like 'clear' cognitions and are rather hazardous to judgement. Emotions are particularly difficult in this way, even though it is possible for reason to have an effect on them. So, from this view, it is possible for us to manipulate our emotions, to some extent, even though they tend to obscure proper judgement. Like many who have followed him, then, Descartes had a somewhat confused view of emotion, although he did place it in the soul and therefore as amongst the higher, more interesting capacities of human beings. His primitive passions of wonder, love, hatred, desire, joy and sadness are not base and animal-like but particularly human.

Darwin

Darwin had an important influence on the early understanding of emotion, as he had an important influence on many things. His contribution is nowhere better summarized and commented on than in Fridlund (1992), on which what follows largely depends.

In very brief summary, in *The Expression of the Emotions in Man and Animals* (1872), Darwin suggested that emotional expressions have not evolved, they do not depend on natural selection. Instead, he argued that they are either simply dependent on the way in which the nervous system is wired or possibly are remnants of old habits. What Darwin sought to achieve was, as part of his general thesis, to place humans on a continuum with the other animals, based on his documentation of emotional expressions across a range of species. He also sought to point out that the facial expression of emotion is not really an expression at all but merely something which goes along with the emotion; it has no communicative function. This might have been an interesting point to make at the time, but more recent thought has clearly shown the usefulness of seeing emotional expressions as having a communicative function.

Fridlund (1992) points to two developments which cast more than doubt on Darwin's views of facial expression. "... the rediscovery of Mendelian inheritance led to the refutation of Lamarckian use-inheritance mechanism for hereditary transmission" (p128). The second development was that of adaptationist accounts of signalling behaviour. So, ironically, Darwin's own insistence on natural selection led to the downfall of his non-adaptationist accounts of expressive displays.

Replacing Darwin's views of expressive movements are accounts in terms of information in which "... the ecology of social interaction is shaped by coevolution of displays of social intent with the vigilance for them" (Fridlund, 1992, p130).

McDougall

McDougall's theory of emotion (1910, 1923, 1928) depended on some basic biological considerations and on an attempt to distinguish between emotions and feelings. He believed that the capacity to approach beneficial goals is fundamental to psychological functioning and that all behaviour stems from seeking food or from escaping or avoiding noxious stimuli. He argued that what we term emotions occur as adjuncts to these basic processes, arising from the way in which we perceive our environment and our various bodily changes.

Although McDougall believed that just two feelings, pleasure and pain, modify all of our goal-directed behaviour, he also recognized the cognitive nature of human beings. This gives them expectations, allows experiences to be fused and sets up unusual concentrations of feelings. It is this cognitive aspect that sets humans apart from other animals and allows a more complex life than would be afforded by the simple alternation of pleasure and pain. Through everyday use these complex feelings have come to be known as the emotions, although these are not 'real' emotions.

As further background to his theory of emotion, it is also necessary to mention the emphasis McDougall placed on instincts, which he believed to provide the impetus for all thought and action. One of the many facets of McDougall's instincts is that of emotional excitement, which he argued is reflected in discreet visceral and bodily changes.

He also implied that perception triggers emotion. So, for example, an organism might perceive a threatening stimulus which would provoke it both to flee and to feel fear, the entire process reflecting a basic instinct. However, he is not clear about how the instrumental and emotional aspects of such reactions become connected and did not ever say much about precise bodily reactions of cognition.

McDougall's theory of emotion depended on the view that throughout human evolution goals became more specific and goal-directed behaviour became more specialized. This resulted in more precise and particularized bodily adjustment. The experience of these two types of strivings gave the quality of 'primary emotion'. If two or more of these main bodily reactions conflict, then experientially the result is the secondary or blended emotions.

McDougall made some points of comparison between complex feelings (which are not emotions) and emotions proper, whether primary or secondary. (1) 'True' emotions are what make each impulse distinctive and have no effect on later strivings. By contrast, complex feelings are conditioned by success or failure in our strivings and hence colour any subsequent similar impulses. (2) Real emotions appeared before humans on the evolutionary scale, whereas complex feelings are restricted to humans because they depend on cognitions. Emotions are independent of cognition. (3) Each primary emotion is long-lasting; it is "an enduring feature of the mental structure of the organism" (1928). Again, by contrast, complex feelings are not entities like this; they simply reflect ill-defined and unblended ranges of experience and feeling. Each emotion is associated with desire and so, unlike complex feelings, conflicting desires may produce blends of emotion. These subtle distinctions are not easy to catch, so it may help to compare the everyday experience of the 'true' emotions of fear and curiosity with the 'complex feelings' of anxiety and hope, although this is not the place to do it.

James–Lange

The James–Lange theory is probably the best known of all theories of emotion, if for no other reason than that it has generated a controversy that has lasted over 110 years. Perhaps because of this it has also acted heuristically and stimulated other theories and much research. As is well known, the theory was put forward at much the same time by James and Lange (1884 and 1885, respectively), although James was its main exponent.

James limited his field to emotions which have 'a distinct bodily expression'. His aim was to distinguish between mental processes which have no obvious physiological concomitants and those in which straightforward and hence easily observable changes occur. He characterized, rightly, the everyday (now, folk psychological) way of theorizing about these emotions as being: (1) we mentally perceive something, (2) this produces a mental affect (the emotion), and (3) this produces some bodily expression. However, he argued for the converse of this:

> *the bodily changes follow directly the PERCEPTION of the existing fact, and that our feeling of the same changes as they occur IS the emotion.* (1884, p189; italics and capitals his)

To put this in terms of an example, in terms of the everyday theory, rather than face some public performance to which we are unused *at this point we become anxious* and then have butterflies in the stomach tremble, stutter, and so on. In James's terms we face the public performance, have butterflies, tremble and stutter and *as a result feel anxious*. James was making a clear *volte face* on previous thought, the guts of his theory depending on the view that the visceral discharges associated with some external situation actually lead to the emotion as we know and experience it.

Support for this theory was based largely on introspection. The argument can be reduced to a few main points. James asserted that any sensation has extremely complex physiological manifestations and that these are all felt, some obviously, some more obscurely. We imagine some strong emotion and then try to push from consciousness all feelings of the bodily symptoms associated with it. If we do this successfully, then in James's terms there will be nothing left; the emotion will be gone. He cited many examples of how everyday situations lead to these complex, strong bodily feelings (seeing a child peering over the edge of cliff for example) and argued that his case is supported by the idea of how easily we can classify both normal and abnormal behaviour according to bodily symptoms.

The James–Lange theory can be most easily summarized as in Figure 1. The main points of the theory are that afferent feedback from disturbed organs produces the feeling aspect of emotion. Any cortical activity which comes from this feedback is the emotion itself. It should be remembered that James not only emphasized the role of the viscera in emotion but also gave a similar role to the voluntary muscles. This laid the groundwork for a search for bodily patterns in emotion and for theories which stress the significance of facial expression in emotion.

James (and Lange) produced the first fully psychological theory of emotion, one which assumed the existence of discrete emotions, which themselves have an instinctive basis and are separable from certain feelings. So, for example, in James's conception stimuli which come from colours and sounds lead to non-emotional feelings and on a pleasantness/unpleasantness dimension, but also

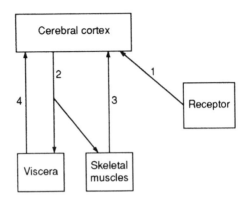

Figure 1.   Diagrammatic representation of
the James–Lange theory. Arrows show
direction of function

nonemotional feelings of interest/excitement from intellectual activity. This
type of point, as well as James's theory in general have continued to influence
theoretical developments in emotion to the present day. There is an inherent
untestability about the James–Lange theory which has proved a consistent
irritant. On the other hand, in stressing the importance of the viscera and of
facial expression it has had far-reaching effects.

It is worth remembering Izard's (1990) point that psychologists remember
James for stressing that emotional experience follows behaviour. Izard re-
minds us that the most important part of James's theory was the view that
emotion is feeling, that without feeling it does not exist. Although many
contemporary theorists nod in the direction of James, Izard believes that
those who stress motivation owe him a great deal whilst behavioural scientists
have virtually ignored James's core beliefs.

Cannon (Cannon–Bard theory)

Cannon's views on emotion were put forward firstly in reaction to those of
James and secondly in order to propose an alternative theory (1915, 1927,
1931, 1932). Cannon made five major criticisms of James's theory. (1) The
artificial production of visceral changes does not seem to lead to emotion. (2)
There is (or there was at that time) no evidence for visceral response patterning in emotion. (3) Visceral organs have little sensitivity; any feedback from
them could hardly be used to differentiate emotions. (4) If the viscera are
separated surgically from the nervous system then emotional behaviour still
occurs even though no visceral responses can be made. (5) The viscera react
slowly. Emotion could occur only at least one second after external stimulation. At times, subjectively, it seems to be faster than this.

It should be pointed out that some years later, Schachter (eg 1964) effectively argued against the first three of these points. He showed that the viscera appear to be a necessary although not a sufficient condition for the occurrence of emotion, although it is hard to be certain that emotion cannot occur without visceral involvement. Moreover, Mandler (1962) argued that Cannon's points (4) and (5) can be accounted for by the fact that after the initial formation of emotional behaviour it may then become conditioned to external stimuli, and therefore may occur before visceral change or without its intervention.

These points of criticism, plus other evidence suggested to Cannon that the neurophysiological aspect of emotional expression is subcortical, or more particularly thalamic. He argued that all emotions depend on a similar chain of events. An environmental situation stimulates receptors which relay impulses to the cortex. The cortex, in turn, stimulates thalamic processes which act in patterns corresponding to particular emotional expressions. Cannon believed that nothing more specific is required than that the neurons in the thalamus be 'released'. The nervous discharge from the thalamus has two functions, to excite muscles and viscera and to relay information back to the cortex. In Cannon's words:

> the peculiar quality of the emotion is added to simple sensation when the thalamic processes are aroused. (1927, p119, italics his)

So, when the thalamus discharges, we experience the emotion almost simultaneously with the bodily changes.

Cannon's theory is represented in Figure 2. He brought into regard the importance of the thalamus to emotion and produced some anti-James arguments which seemed cogent at the time. However, the particular significance of Cannon's theory lies in its emphasis on the neurophysiology of emotion. As will be seen in Chapter 5, this has culminated in some recent theorizing about emotion which is amongst the most sophisticated to be found.

Papez

After Cannon, Papez's (1937) theory of emotion was the next to have a physiological basis. He emphasized the connection in lower vertebrates between the cerebral hemispheres and the hypothalamus, and between the cerebral hemispheres and the dorsal thalamus. According to Papez, these interconnections, further elaborated in the mammalian brain, mediate emotion.

Papez's theory depended on the simple view that emotion implies behaviour (expression) and feeling (experience, subjective aspects). Expression depends on the hypothalamus and experience on the cortex. Interestingly, in humans Papez believed that the phenomena of emotional expression and experience can be dissociated from each other.

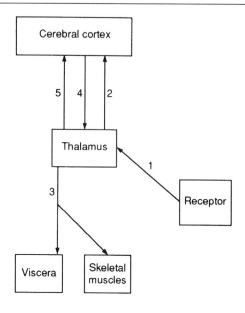

Figure 2.   Diagrammatic representation of
the   Cannon–Bard   theory.   Arrows   show
direction of function

Without going into neurophysiological detail which is now very dated, it is enough to say that Papez's theory depended on much neurophysiologising. However, it was put in such a way as to account for the apparently different origins of emotion, for emotion felt and emotion expressed, and for the emotional colouring which can be present in apparently nonemotional experiences.

Duffy

"For many years the writer has been of the opinion that 'emotion', as a scientific concept is worse than useless."

This compelling sentence begins Duffy's 1941 paper (but see also 1934, 1962). For Duffy, emotion is something to be explained away rather than explained, and she attempted to do so with a behaviourally oriented activation theory.

Duffy had the view that emotional phenomena are separate aspects of responses which actually occur in continua. She saw this as in contrast to the typical use of emotion to refer to the extreme end of a continuum of behaviour, but one which anomalously involves a distinct non-continuation between emotion and nonemotion.

Duffy hypothesized that states of emotion must involve changes in energy level, for example excitement representing a higher energy level and depression a lower energy level. The energy level itself is dependent on the stimulus. It increases either when we are blocked or when a block is removed. Further, energy decreases only when a goal is so well blocked that we give up altogether.

She widened her argument by pointing out that all behaviour is motivated, without motivation there being no activity. In this expanded context, emotion simply represents an extreme of motivation, or energy. She then asked how do we know when behaviour is extreme enough to be called emotional? And of course, by her own argument there is no criterion by which to judge this, because emotion-producing behaviour is no different from other behaviour. All responses are adjustive, adaptive responses.

The second common characteristic of emotion according to Duffy is that it is disorganising (cf Leeper, 1948). She argued though that this is a function of behaviour at high or low energy levels, rather than of emotion. Disorganization can be found at energy levels not high enough to be regarded as emotional. This represents emotion as the hypothetical inverted-U function that relates arousal to performance.

Duffy also dealt with the common conception that our conscious experiences of emotion seem to us to be different from our conscious experiences of everything else. This involves awareness of the relevant environmental situation, bodily changes, and of a set for response in the situation. She argued that these same factors make up any nonemotional state of consciousness as well.

So Duffy breaks down all behaviour, including emotion, into changes in level of energy, organization, and conscious states, and puts each of these on a continuum. Finally, she argues that it is meaningless to try to study emotion at all, because it has no distinguishing characteristics. Instead, any response should be considered according to its energy level, how well it maintains goal direction and the environmental situation in response to which it occurs. Duffy's is a theory of non-emotion and has been so far overtaken by more sophisticated theorizing as to make it as hollow as she attempted to make emotion. Almost all theories become dated, but there is a sense in which Duffy's has become almost nonsensical. It has historical curiosity value but little more.

Conclusions

This chapter has been no more than a first skirmish with theories of emotion, simply in order to provide something of an historical perspective to the remainder of the book. Of course, in the history of thought, and no doubt not merely Western thought (with which this book is concerned) other scholars (and many poets) have given consideration to emotion, and have even had their theories about it. However, the theories briefly described in this chapter were chosen because they have helped to generate some of the main shaping forces behind current theories.

It would not be particularly useful to evaluate the theories so far summarized in any of the terms mentioned in Chapter 1. In contemporary terms they do not have enough significance to make this worthwhile. However, it is easy to see the themes which emerge from them.

Between them, the early theorists of emotion began to consider the origins and development of emotion and the distinction between emotion and non-emotion. They started to deal with what exactly is the emotion that we experience. They thought about where it might be sited physiologically and began to deal with the nature of its physiological aspects. They recognized that emotion has its behavioural, expressive side and that it can be seen as functional in an evolutionary sense. Moreover, it is possible to see in these theories the beginnings of the debate about the origins of emotion lying in biology or social interaction.

Above all, and this is to anticipate the remainder of this book a little, it is in the early theories, that a particular type of tension is first manifest—namely, the difficulty of giving an account of emotion which does not have a definite cognitive component.

3

Phenomenological theory

'Phenomenology is that empiricistic philosophy which asserts that the givens of experience are configurational entities having a unique integrity of their own and are, therefore, not reducible to sense contents or to any other elemental structure.' (Turner, 1967, p60)

Turner's definition is of the philosophical foundations of phenomenology as conceptualized by European philosophers such as Husserl (1913). He argued that our thoughts and feelings have a purpose and that this purpose must come from the 'essential' person. A thought or a feeling is about something, it reaches out; in other words, it is *intentional*. Husserl believed that our senses give us a direct knowledge of the world, but suggested that the intent in our perceptions might distort this reality. Such distortions could take many forms, from something such as racial prejudice through to the effects of simple visual illusions.

Modern phenomenological psychology developed from this foundation. It is the study of consciousness and experience, an individual's perception of the world being the crucial aspect of psychological investigation. It is implied that each of us perceives the world in a unique way, although there might be common elements in our experiences. *And it is these perceptions that determine the way in which we react or the way in which we behave.* Phenomenological psychology might be empirical but it is a very different sort of empiricism from that of the behaviourist or that of the cognitivist. It rests on a different set of assumptions about human functioning.

Phenomenological psychologists are concerned with what a person is experiencing here and now, at this moment, in this place, in their present state. Such experiences can to some extent be manipulated by controlling prior experiences. The data of experience though are necessarily subjective; they are personal reports of conscious processes, or of experiences. Interest centres on the content of whatever reports the person makes, experiences or conscious processes being given a casual role in determining behaviour.

Apologists who stress this approach (eg Giorgi, 1970) argue that it gives the psychologist a specialised unique way of dealing with a specialised unique set of problems. Psychology is set apart because its object of study is human beings, human beings have consciousness, and this should therefore be the proper and foremost concern of psychologists.

It follows from this that psychologists should be concerned with the functioning of the whole person rather than isolated processes such as learning or memory. From the phenomenological perspective, we have choice, free-will to choose what to do next. So phenomenologists should deal with real-life needs, problems and motivations of fully functioning people. As part of this, psychologists may well have to make value judgements, rather than to eschew them as modernist science would have them do (see Chapter 14 for more discussion of this).

The type of question prompted by a phenomenological approach to emotion is concerned very much with whether it is possible to generate a good theory from this angle. Can it be anchored to the real world, does it summarize what we know, does it lead to predictions, is it internally consistent, does it have heuristic value, and so on?

Stumpf

Reisenzein and Schönpflug (1992) provide an interesting overview of Stumpf's (eg 1899) theory of emotion which was based in introspective psychology although is pertinent to current cognitive-evaluative theory. Stumpf maintained that mental states are intentional and can be divided into the intellectual and the affective. He further divided the affective category into (1) active affective states (nonperformative desires, motivational desires, and volitional states—intentions) and (2) passive affective states (for and against evaluations of various states of affairs). Stumpf also saw a two-part relationship between beliefs and evaluations. (1) Beliefs cause evaluations, and (2) evaluations are directed at the same state of affairs as the object of the belief. So, these are a casual connection and a semantic relation.

According to Reisenzein and Schönpflug, Stumpf believed that emotion can only be defined through emotionally relevant judgements, so non-cognitively caused evaluations are not true emotions. Stumpf argued that his theory accounted for intentionality in emotions, their differentiation and discrimination, their dependence on beliefs and desires and their modifiability.

Reisenzein and Schönpflug believe that Stumpf's theory has implications for theories of emotion that stress noncognitive bodily sensations, facial feedback, centrally generated feelings, non-representational mental states such as arousal, mental qualities or action tendencies. They also draw attention to the relative lack of clarity in discussions of the nature of cognitive appraisals in emotion. They further point out that for Stumpf cognitions are amongst the defining features of emotions, a viewpoint that has an obvious relevance to far more recent theories of emotion.

Sartre

Perhaps not surprisingly given his existential philosophical background, Sartre (1948) was prompted to his theory of emotion by an over-generalization; this was that psychologists tend to think of consciousness of emotion as reflective, a state of mind. Even in 1948 there were a number of psychologists to whom this would not have applied, many in fact not even seeing the usefulness of an analysis of consciousness in any sphere, not just that of emotion. More substantively though, Sartre argues that an emotion such as fear does not begin as a consciousness of being afraid. Instead he believes emotional consciousness is non-reflective, emotional consciousness being a general consciousness of the world.

For Sartre, emotion is a way of apprehending the world, thus combining the subject and the object of emotion. To take an example, if a man believes that his partner is losing interest in him then he apprehends his every action in terms of what he should do about it. If his attempts fail then again his apprehension of the world is coloured.

As well as an apprehension of the world, Sartre also believes that emotion involves a transformation of the world (reminiscent of Hillman's, 1960, view). The argument runs that if paths to a goal are blocked or thwarted in some way, the person might try to change the world so that the path or some alternative path can be followed. If one cannot do this straightforwardly, then the world could perhaps be dealt with if it is changed. Emotion allows such a transformation to take place, its impetus coming from the impossibility of solving the problem, or removing the block, with whatever is already available.

To take an example, if someone has said something critical of me in a social context, I might be in the situation of wanting to be thought well of but having been criticised. I might not be able to sit quietly and accept this, but nor might there be anything I can say calmly in return—normal channels of social intercourse are blocked. So I become righteously angry, which transforms the situation into something to which I can respond.

Sartre then is emphasizing the qualitative change which emotion brings to an object. The body changes its relationship with the world, seeing it, through consciousness, with new qualities. The important characteristic of this transformation for Sartre, is that it is *magical*; of course, the world itself does not change.

Sartre gives many examples to illustrate his theory, including that of fear. It is usually considered to be rational to run away from the source of one's fear. But for Sartre, this is not rational. One runs away not to find shelter, security or protection, but because one cannot 'annihilate (oneself) in unconsciousness'. Both the fear and the running away make a magical change in the world to negate the dangerous object. By running away in fear one is pretending to be in a world in which the dangerous object does not exist. So, from Sartre's perspective, fear is consciousness magically negating or denying something that exists substantively and is dangerous. (In passing, it should also be said that running away from something dangerous may also serve the purpose of physically removing the danger.)

Emotion always involves a qualitative transformation of the world. At first sight, some behaviours appear to be emotion; Sartre gives the examples of the pretence of anger or joy. However, these are spurious or false emotions, because unlike real emotion they are not accompanied by a belief, although he does not make it clear how true and false emotions can be distinguished observationally. We use our will to give new qualities to objects in the world and then we believe that these are real qualities. So a real emotion is experienced; cannot be stopped at will or cast off because it is unpleasant. To be genuine an emotion must fill and overflow us. Interestingly, Sartre points to the physiological aspects of emotion as allowing the distinction to be made between true and false emotion; we can stop running but we cannot stop trembling.

Sartre argues that the body is two things simultaneously. It is an object existing in the world and it is something lived by our consciousness. Against this background, emotion is a matter of belief. Consciousness *lives* in the new magical world it has created, an emotional world, a new world with a new quality. Bodily, emotion is akin to a local disorder; it is consciousness that lives and realizes the emotion.

Emotions originate in a spontaneous debasement lived by the consciousness in the face of the world. It provides us with a way of enduring something which would otherwise be difficult or impossible to endure. However, Sartre makes the point that consciousness is not conscious of itself in emotion. If it were, then the emotion would be false. If I am aware of myself being angry then this is not true anger. In emotion, the consciousness is entirely absorbed by the belief, it knows only itself. Consciousness is in turn moved by the emotion and heightens it. We run faster and in so doing become even more afraid. So, emotions give a transcending quality to an object or situation, magical qualities that seem infinite

According to Sartre's theory, not all emotions are fully fledged. The more subtle emotions can give a brief glimpse of the unpleasant or the excellent. One might be overwhelmed by a vague sense of disaster or of something good just round the corner. In Sartre's eyes, the social world is full of such potential; it constantly nudges towards the magical.

In emotion, *everything* in the world is modified so giving the world a new quality. Everything might become horrific or beautiful. The view of the world we have when we are in an emotional state simply cannot be achieved in the everyday, deterministic, non-emotional world. From Sartre's perspective, when we are in an emotional state it is as if we were dreaming—the *whole* world is magically transformed and perceived in a different way. Emotion allows us to see an absolutely coherent world in which everything hangs together magically. For Sartre, emotion is a sudden plummeting of consciousness into the magical, giving a different mode of existence, a way of existentially being-in-the-world.

Buytedjik

Buytedjik's (1950) analysis begins with the nature of facts; science might be concerned with facts, but are feelings facts? If I say 'I feel angry with him' or 'I love her' are these factual statements? For Buytedjik, feelings are acts which are intentionally present, their meaning coming from what they signify. If we feel angry or feel that we are in love then this implies that we know the meaning that some situations have for us.

The phenomenological approach begins with the notion that consciousness is consciousness of something, and that we are also conscious of existing. So we are aware of being in situations in which we must respond, that is, we must have attitudes and feelings and make intentional acts. Feeling and emotion function to assure us of our attitudes in various situations, each situation having its own special feeling for us. A spontaneous response to a situation transforms it into a new world. Choice must be involved. Our emotional attitude towards a situation is confirmed by a feeling, although we choose to become happy in some situation in order to alter our feeling towards it.

Against this background, Buytedjik argues that emotion is *not* intentional, but it is like sensation or excitement. I am only conscious of myself. If I detest someone then I project myself as detesting and make further projections about the person. This is brought about by feeling. Such projection rebounds and takes on the character of emotion. Thus, we cannot experience emotion without feeling, but emotion is not intentional, it is the quality of our existence which occurs through feeling. Although feeling and emotion, according to this way of looking at things, are spontaneous and unintentional, we are able to alter our feelings by the situations we create with the words we use. We use language intentionally to modify, enhance or suppress our feelings.

Buytedjik uses the example of the smile to illustrate the understanding of meaning that a phenomenological analysis makes possible. He argues that a smile anticipates something in the future, representing a moderate excitement linked to the knowledge that this excitement will remain moderate in our intentional act. A smile is an easy physical act which indicates a relaxation on the threshold of something such as joy or elation. A smile makes a transformation of the situation that faces us whilst simultaneously confronting ourselves with this transformed world, that is, being aware of it.

In arguing for the value of a phenomenological analysis, Buytedjik points out that it is not introspection but is directed at experienced phenomena and towards acts such as thinking and feeling. In such a context, it is irrelevant whether or not the phenomenon being considered is real. Emphasis is on what is termed its *essential structure.* To ask 'What is guilt or anger?' is similar to asking 'What is a table or a chair?'. Causal relationships are not of moment here, but rather an exploration of the inner essential structure of the phenomena, in this case, of emotion. The aim is to make analyses of the experience of feelings in various situations, in order to discover patterns and invariances in our usual mode of existence. Described in this way, this type of analysis resonates with that which is coming from post-modern approaches to emotion (see Chapter 14).

Rapaport

Rapaport (1950) represents the psychoanalytic theory of emotion, beginning with the view that Freud was unclear about the topic. Although of course, psychoanalysis does not equate with phenomenology, there are sufficient similarities to include it briefly within this chapter.

As Rapaport sees Freud's view, emotions may be psychic energies or they may be the discharge processes which are associated with these energies. In either case, to understand emotion one must delve into the unconscious and into instinct. Unlike other accounts of emotion, the psychoanalytic is not concerned with possible sequences of emotional events. From this perspective, perception occurs and thereafter anything might happen; the emotion 'felt', the bodily process, both or neither.

Rapaport distinguishes between Freud's view of emotion and those of some of the so-called neo-Freudians. Freud saw affects as being *a* or *the* form of psychic energy or he sometimes saw affect as an implied attribute of other psychoanalytic concepts. By contrast, Brierley (1937) believed affect to be a tension phenomenon that leads to both an inner and an outer discharge. As Rapaport describes it, the conscious parts of increasing and decreasing tension accord with Freud's notions of pleasantness and unpleasantness. Federn (1936) brings in another dimension by stressing the importance of conflict theory. In this context, emotions follow conflict between drive cathexes, a cathexis being an amount of psychic energy which is associated with an idea.

Generally, psychoanalytic theories of emotion suggest that the substrates underlying emotion are unconscious and the emotions or affects may be psychic energies, discharge processes of psychic energies, and manifestations of instinctual conflict. This type of theory is not easy to understand nor is it easy to be convinced of its worth.

Pradines

To understand Pradines' theory of emotion (1958, also see Arnold, 1968) it is important to begin with his view of sentiment. He asserts that perception occurs both intellectually and through affective states, such states being both complex feelings and simple feelings of pleasure and pain. Sentiments involve complex mental images of possible pleasure and pain. Sentiment also has the power to break down feeling and to make the power to act autonomous. Sentiment is also a strong feeling because it is able to absorb strong energies aroused by the associations attached to perceptions. So, sentiment, according to Pradines, is a simple sensory feeling or a complex feeling following perception.

These sentiments are regulators of action; they guide us towards specific objects and in so doing are adaptive. Sentiments depend on the objective circumstances; this makes them agreeable because circumstances change. Sentiment itself is only as stable as the object to which it is attached. Pradines regards emotion as one of four ways in which sentiment can become disorganized—the others are through fixation, passion and inversion. Emotions disrupt in that they reduce sentiments almost to reflex; they are sentiments in extreme, explosive, crisis form. Any situation then may produce some sentiment in us without necessarily leading to an emotional outburst.

The final strand to Pradines' theory is imagination. Through imagination and belief memory images become more affective and active. Sentiments and emotions come from imagination, one being adaptive and the other maladaptive. Emotional reactions tend to squash the more gentle and adaptive sentiments. 'Emotion is a mental and motor disaster experienced by the subject who is its victim.'

Clearly, Pradines' experiential type of theory is unique in seeing emotion as solely maladaptive and hence negative. Sentiment is good and emotion is bad, in an adaptive sense. Perhaps in passing it is worth asking what might be maladaptive about happiness or joy. Pradines does not just seem to be equating sentiment with positive emotion and emotion with negative emotion, but if he isn't then it is fairly easy to find some positive and adaptive emotional reactions.

Hillman

Hillman (1960) bases his account of emotion on Aristotle's four causes, although he writes from a Jungian background.

1. *Efficient cause.* Stimuli which function as efficient causes, that is, which cause emotion, are in Hillman's view either representations, conflicts and situations, or those with a physiological basis such as arousal, instinct, constitution or energy. Also important to this conceptualization is the symbol, which Hillman characterizes as a mixture of inner and outer, conscious and unconscious representations. So a situation will arouse emotion if it is perceived symbolically. "Emotion is thus the symbolic apprehension of the subjective psyche ..." (1960, p253)

2. *Material cause.* Material cause is concerned with the *stuff* of emotion. Hillman's conclusion, reached through an Aristotelian type of analysis is that the material cause of emotion is energy. To be able to say that emotion is present, there must be gross bodily changes plus representations of these in consciousness. Simultaneously though, emotion *is* the body experienced in the here and now. The body is the stuff of emotion and the order of its energy is a person's homeostatic balance.

3. *Formal cause.* Whatever it is that defines emotion, that distinguishes it from everything else, is its formal cause. In Hillman's view, this is the psyche, emotion being the total pattern of the psyche, which comes from a combination of expression and inner states.

So far, then, in emotion, Hillman has symbol and form corresponding to each other and occurring only when there is energy.

4. *Final cause.* Aristotle's conception of final cause is either the purpose or goal of something, or more simply its end point. Hillman reconciles these by suggesting that the finish of any emotional process is in itself an achievement; this is its purpose. This purpose or end does not have to be at the end in time, but can occur contemporaneously with the other three causes. However, it is the final cause of emotion that gives it its value, a value which comes about through change, particularly if it is a change which promotes survival or improvement.

The difficulty with this type of view, as is so often the case with emotion, lies in determining how emotional change can be distinguished from any other type of change. Hillman suggests this can be done with the idea of transformation. Emotion is the transformation of conscious representations in terms of symbolic reality; it is a transformation of energy, of the whole psyche. Other types of change are presumably lesser than this.

As will be seen much later in this book, the question of the value of emotion is significant. Although Hillman mentions value, he is not clear on the possible value of emotion. He suggests that true emotion always achieves its purpose, and so may be seen as always good. However, its results may be good or bad, even though the emotion itself must always be an improvement of some sort. It is difficult to know where one is in this thicket of ideas, particularly since the way into it is through the difficult gate of *true* emotion, which has to be distinguished in Hillman's terms, from abortive emotion, or deep feelings or even concentrated willing.

To summarize, Hillman's account of emotion depends on Aristotle's four causes. Efficient cause is the symbolic perception of the objective psyche, the material cause is the body's energy, the formal cause (essence) of emotion is the total pattern of the psyche or soul, and the final cause of emotion, that is, its value, is change or transformation, which is always good.

Fell

Fell's (1977) compelling analysis of the phenomenology of emotion depends on the idea of *pretheoretical* experience. This is concerned with the foundations of both science and knowledge more generally in that Fell sees the starting point for science as coming from a person who has a prior understanding of a familiar world. To be investigated there is a sense in which a phenomenon must already be known. Whatever psychologists might say of emotions such as fear, anger or happiness, they must first recognise what they are studying as being fear, anger and happiness.

Husserl provided the starting point for Fell's analysis, in placing human beings in cognitive situations that allow them to find the world patterned, organised and intelligible. This ability is there from the start and so allows us to make sense of the world intuitively, that is, immediately and directly. Amongst other things we can intuit emotion in this way and just see other people as angry, afraid or happy. A human emotion is a meaningful relation between a person and a meaningful environment. Behaviour and physiology are simply components in this.

Fell makes some interesting points of comparison between the phenomenological approach and the behavioural. One takes an external view-point and the other an intuitive. For one the environment is filled with rein-forcers, for the other it is filled with meaning. Observationally, emotions are responses, experientially they are feelings that make sense. Emotions might depend on contingencies but their power, according to Fell, hinges on what they mean or how they are understood. Emotions might have behavioural aspects but they are qualitative experiences.

The behaviourist is concerned with the prediction and control of emotion. By contrast, the phenomenologist is concerned with its description. An emo-tion is an amalgam of the observed and the experienced, of behaviour and meaning. Because emotion as a felt experience is difficult, perhaps impossible, to quantify and measure, does this mean that it is not real or does it mean that science should be supplemented by direct experience and understanding, or even that our conception of what is acceptable science is broadened? Fell implies that it is foolish to attempt to restrict what is real, to restrict knowl-edge to what can be observed. From his perspective, the objective scientist must have intuited and experienced emotions to know what is being studied. Pre-scientific experience should not be ignored.

A difficulty that Fell recognizes for his analysis is that if concern centres on pre-theoretical experience then how can a phenomenological *theory* of emo-tion be conceived? Or to probe further, is it possible to describe pre-theoretical experience without to some extent theorizing about it? A measure of sorts comes from consensual validation; do others agree with the descrip-tion or not?

According to this type of analysis, any phenomenonological investigation of emotion depends on a prior understanding of what emotion is and subsumes six possibilities: (1) emotions considered as meanings in a meaningful environment; (2) emotions considered as events by the person experiencing them; (3) emotions considered as 'making sense'; (4) distinctively human emotions and moods con-sidered from a perspective of how they are brought about by the intuitive under-standing which characterizes cognition; (5) consideration given to emotions which seem similar being qualitatively different in humans because of cognition; (6) a consideration of the way in which language might affect emotion.

Fell argues that the best way of deciding on the adequacy of the various theories of emotion is by returning to what he terms the original cognitive situation. Whatever a theory of emotion might suggest, a precondition for it is the preliminary or experiential comprehension of the emotion. Whatever the 'it' is that is being studied is specified by ordinary experience. This approach predicates any investigation on naive understanding; understanding or intuition is a necessary precondition for knowledge.

Fell stresses the importance of always returning to the original cognitive situation and argues that a phenomenological approach to emotion helps in this aim. Fell's final justification for taking a phenomenological approach to emotion is that it is so fundamental, a necessary pre-requisite, that nothing less would do. It sounds like a compelling argument when Fell makes it, but it is nevertheless an article of faith.

de Rivera

Since his *A Structural Theory of the Emotions* (1977), de Rivera has had an important influence on our understanding of emotion from a phenomenological perspective. Recently, he has turned his attention to the idea of *emotional climate,* his analysis of which again adds to our knowledge of the experiential side of emotion.

By emotional climate de Rivera (1992) is referring to "... an objective group phenomenon that can be palpably sensed—as when one enters a party or a city and feels an atmosphere of gaiety or depression, openness or fear ... I have in mind, for example, the climate of fear which existed in Chile during the Pinochet regime ..." (1992, p198).

de Rivera distinguishes between emotional atmosphere, climate and culture. An emotional atmosphere is a collective emotional response to a particular event, it is localised, and an emotional culture is enduring and relatively stable, part of the social structure and institutions of a society. Emotional climate is somewhere between the two, possibly although not necessarily enduring for a generation or two (considered societally) but responsive to factors such as religion, politics, economics and so on.

de Rivera is particularly interested in emotional climate within nations, and predicates his account directly on his structural view of emotion in general. He argues that emotions are not *in* people, but rather that they exist *between* people. So, against this background, emotions are *in* a society. He believes that a nation's emotions have the function of maintaining both political unity and cultural identity.

In a penetrating analysis, de Rivera exemplifies the concept of emotional climate with a number of examples and also considers the problems of measurement when dealing with what amounts to an amalgam of a nation's prevailing emotional experiences. An instance of emotional climate is that already mentioned, fear in Chile under Pinochet. He describes this type of fear as brought about systematically by acts of violence directed against the people by the government. Political control is maintained by the sense of isolation that this produces in the population. Repression gradually increases as everyone becomes less and less willing to express views on anything. It pervades all aspects of life, making it impossible to maintain ordinary behaviour, beliefs, attitudes or values.

Of particular interest to de Rivera is the relationship between emotional climate and political unity. He attempts to link such unity with the dimensions of emotional climate as he sees them, these being fear/security, hostility/ solidarity, dissatisfaction/satisfaction, despair/hope, depression/confidence, and instability/stability. For example, he believes that national unity can spring from a climate of solidarity, although this may or may not embrace a sense of security which allows the existence of difference. "To the extent that solidarity is based on enmity or on a respect for authority that is mingled with fear, there will be strong conformity pressures that will hinder expressions of ethnic diversity and true individuality" (1992, p215).

de Rivera, then, has taken a phenomenological analysis of emotion a stage further than it has been taken previously by extending it to the national level. His concept of emotional climate represents a cohesion between the individual experiences of emotion within a society or a nation as engendered mainly by political forces. It continues de Rivera's structural analysis of emotion in a particularly interesting way and at the very least points to a series of very serious influences that should be taken into account when attempting to understand the experience of emotion.

Denzin

In recent years, Denzin (1984) has provided what is probably the most thorough analysis of emotion from a phenomenological perspective, being concerned with the way in which emotion as a form of consciousness is lived and experienced. His is a social phenomenonological view since although he is interested in emotion as experienced, he places this experience very much within a social context.

"Emotion is self-feeling. Emotions are temporarily embodied, situated self-feelings that arise from emotional and cognitive social acts that people direct to self or have directed toward them by others." (1984, p49, italics his)

Denzin is suggesting that any emotional experience serves a double function: it refers to the self and it takes into account the other. Although an emotion might originate 'out there' it will always refer back to the self. Within a person's emotionality, the experienced feelings have three elements to their structure: (1) an awareness and definition, (2) a self-awareness of experiencing the feeling, and (3) a disclosing of the essential (moral) self through the experience. All of which provides a process rather than a static experience.

From Denzin's view, the self is centred in social interaction and is defined by reference to anything that is called 'mine' at a particular time and what that means to 'me'. Emotion is simply in the social situation and any and all emotions are dependent on social relationships. This is with respect to their feeling components, their interpretation, their vocabularies and even their individual and social history. Taking this a stage further, Denzin argues that we give emotion accounts to ourselves of our emotional experiences in terms of self-justifications. These two are grounded in social interaction and hence within the culture.

Denzin's theory places emotion squarely within social interaction, and in this bears strong similarity to de Rivera's views. Emotions as self-feelings must come partly from the appraisals of self that are made by others. Denzin describes a ten-point sequence of emotional self-interaction: (1) the person is interacting and interpreting, (2) an object of interaction comes within the phenomenological field, (3) this object is defined via self-feelings (say, anger or fear), (4) these self-feelings are checked through bodily reactions, (5) there is imagination by the person of how he or she appears in the eyes of others, (6) this is interpreted, (7) feelings build towards the other based on these judgements, (8) this feeling is incorporated, (9) there follows a feeling of moral self-worth, and (10) the process is summarized into a sort of emotional self-definition. Denzin describes this as the 'hermeneutic circle of emotionality'.

Denzin sees emotionality as a form of dialogue with the world. *"Emotionality is a circular process that begins and ends with the transactions of the self in the social situation interacting with self and other"* (1984, p58, italics his). Within this context, he regards it as important to consider emotions as social acts, the circular nature of the temporality of emotion, the significance of others, the reality of emotion and what, drawing from Sartre, he terms the circle of selfness. In this, the individual and others around together produce a field of experience which is shared by everyone involved.

Denzin believes that his theory takes emotions beyond cognitions, making them instead interactional processes. Understanding of emotion should then come from the study of selves and others via an analysis of self-feeling. Denzin's is essentially a sociological theory of the phenomenology of emotion which has clear and obvious import for an understanding of emotional experience, the phenomenological analysis of the consciousness of emotion. (See Chapter 13 for a discussion of other sociological theories of emotion.)

Stein, Trabasso and Liwag

Stein, Trabasso and Liwag (1993) put forward a theory which is concerned with the representation of emotional experience. It is built on four principles (1) It is knowledge-based and situated. (2) It rests on assumptions about human intentionality and about actions which are goal-directed. (3) Concern centres on describing processes that maintain goals so that states of positive well-being can also be maintained. (4) Appraisal and problem-solving are given central importance in emotional experience.

An essential aspect of their theory is that subjective states and bodily reactions are monitored by a representational system. The system allows value to be evaluated, a value system being viewed as basic to emotional behaviour; it is through this that the person is alerted to whatever can bring pleasure or pain. The system has three fundamental characteristics: it is both hierarchical and sequential, some goals may be given more value than others, and it is dynamic. It is also integral to the model that change can be detected in both the environment and in internal states.

Events that precipitate emotion can come from three sources: the environment, the actions of another, and memory of past events. During evaluation there must be an encoding and an assessment of the precipitating event. Moreover, they recognise that emotion is specific to its context, and often this context is one in which the individual is trying to understand the past and yet is oriented to future behaviour.

Stein et al's general model of emotional experience depends on the tracking of an individual's specific goals, particularly with respect to success and failure in achieving them. Any event can be evaluated as obstructing a goal, facilitating a goal or as irrelevant to any present goal states. There are also three possible outcomes of plans that might achieve a desired goal: a plan is available, a plan is not available, or no plan is known of. The model has it then that personal goals are critical to an understanding of any emotion. Differences depend on the particular events that bring about emotions and the particular plans that determine the success or failure of goal achievement.

Self, identity and well-being

There are a number of phenomenologically based theories that are more usefully linked under this heading than giving them their individual status. For example, Epstein (see 1993) is primarily a self theorist, but he is also interested in looking at the link between the self-concept and emotions and motives. He proposed a cognitive-experiential self theory (CEST) in which he asserts that all people automatically construct implicit theories of reality, in which there are subdivisions of self-theory, world-theory and connecting propositions.

Within CEST, emotions are viewed as both influencing and being influenced by a person's implicit theory of reality, and as playing an important role in the development of conceptual systems. Constructs are seen as developing around primary emotions which Epstein sees as organised and organising cognitive-affective systems. Emotions conceived in this way are cognitive-affective units that organise adaptive behavioural patterns providing a background against which a model of the self and the world can develop.

This is simply a taste of the way in which one theorist attempts to find a place for emotion in a theory of self. However, related to this is Haviland and Kahlbaugh's (1993) interesting analysis of emotion and identity. Although identity is clearly a concept which has an obvious place in an experiential or phenomenological analysis, it also reflects a concern for what is socially constructed (see Chapters 13 and 14). Emotion and identity influence interpretations of each other.

Haviland believes that there is an innate set of emotions or emotion processes (and so moves away from a strongly social constructionist position).

For her, different emotions provide links between different stimuli and responses, perceived causes and effects, and the self and others. Emotions function, not just as responses to the environment, but also metaphorically to unite scenes, experiences, internal cues and thoughts.

From this perspective, emotion functions as the 'glue' of identity that magnifies and resonates to create experiences. Things emotional help us to distinguish the central and organizing parts of identity from skills or ideals. Haviland and Goldston (1992) mention two types of emotional magnification that can occur in constructions of identity. A single content issue (theme) may be 'emotionally elaborated', ie associated frequently with many different emotions. Diversity is important here. Alternatively, a single emotion may be 'content elaborated'. This produces scripts about emotion in which emotional experience is the primary link between different roles or scenes.

Haviland and Kahlbaugh analyse the place of emotion in various theoretical constructions of identity. They suggest that theories of identity have developed from the history of how emotion has been responded to, elicited, shaped and socialized. They argue that the role of emotions has to be examined in any theory or research into identity. They even go so far as to suggest that the emergence of identity that is emotionally integrative may have come only after the development of interest in emotion and motivational processes.

Diener and Larson (1993) speculate about the experience of emotional well-being, a matter which is again relevant to a phenomenological approach to emotion. They ask three basic questions about the structure of emotional well-being. (1) Given that emotions constantly fluctuate, does emotional well-being obtain across situations and time? (2) Should discrete specific emotions be studied in this context rather than large scale pleasant/unpleasant emotions? (3) What is more important to the experience of well-being, intense or prolonged pleasant emotions?

The various theories of emotional well-being do not provide fully fledged accounts of its origins. However, each suggests particular factors that may influence it. In summary these are personality dispositions, resources, social comparisons, personal aspirations and ideals, emotional training, and the end state of various psychological needs or motives.

Diener and Larson incorporate a number of the relevant theories into a cognitive-evaluative theory of emotion. Here the emphasis is on emotion depending on evaluations of events happening to a person, which may be influenced by the temperament of the person and early learning. The evaluations will also depend on the extent to which the events meet needs and goals, emotion giving people feedback on how well they are doing in this regard.

They draw a number of conclusions. (1) Pleasantness and unpleasantness over time contribute largely to people's evaluations of their well-being. (2) The process is influenced by events, physiological state, genetic temperament and personality factors. (3) Intense emotion is rare in daily life and so is not significant in evaluations of well-being. (4) People learn to adjust emotionally to changes in the circumstances of the resources available to them. (5) The general state seems to be one of mild happiness most of the time. (6) There is cultural variation in the emotional associations with well-being.

Diener and Larson believe that the type of conceptual analysis they make of emotional well-being will further our knowledge of emotions more generally. And it is essentially a phenomenological analysis.

Conclusions

Clearly, the theories considered in this chapter represent a very specific approach to emotion; they are primarily concerned with the nature of emotional experience. In this emphasis on *some* aspects of the subjective side of emotion, they have something in common with the everyday or folk theoretical approach. Inevitably, however, this means that in placing the emphasis as they do, much is left out. Phenomenological theorists of emotion do not have much to say about behaviour and physiology, and in some cases, even cognition.

To evaluate such theories in this context then, is immediately to see their disadvantage. They might be interesting and cogent with respect to emotional experience, they might offer a good summary of existing knowledge and they might have good heuristic value. However, they are inevitably incomplete, they cannot offer full explanations of emotion, and for the most part, it is difficult to derive testable predictions from them. This is the case in spite of the development of qualitative research methodologies.

Looking at phenomenological theories from the perspective of Lazarus's (1991a,b) various points about what a theory of emotion should accomplish, then they have to be found wanting. Generally, they are concerned with possible causes of emotion, but they have little to say about emotion either as a dependent or an independent variable. More specifically, the only points among Lazarus's list that they tend to cover are to do with definition, with discrete emotions, with effects on general functioning and possible therapeutic ramifications. They are concerned to some extent with the development of emotion and again to some extent with appraisal. However, of course, they are fundamentally couched in terms of emotional consciousness.

If one applies Oatley's (1992) suggestions about what should be accomplished by a theory of emotion to the theories summarized in this chapter, they can only be described as relatively poor on all of them. Certainly, in Oatley's characterisation of the Lakatos approach, phenomenological theories of emotion do not deal with more evidence than other theories. In fact, they are so restricted as to deal with rather less evidence than most. Alternatively, it is possible to apply the Popper type of test, namely, can specific (and hence testable and refutable) predictions be derived from these theories? It is probably fair to say that some predictions can be derived, but this is hard to do. Moreover, some of the predictions that can be derived are difficult to test.

Perhaps the fairest test to apply to phenomenological theories of emotion is that which Denzin (1984) argues to be appropriate. These are criteria which he judges to be important only for phenomenological interpretations. These will be listed below. In general, and perhaps not surprisingly, it may be said that most of the theories in this chapter fulfil the criteria, to some extent, with those of Fell, Denzin himself, and to some extent de Rivera fulfilling them most readily.

Denzin's suggested criteria for applying to the efficacy of phenomenological theories of emotion are:

1. Does the interpretation of emotion illuminate, disclose and reveal lived emotion? 2. Does the interpretation rest on thickly contextualised, thickly described materials and on concepts near to experience? 3. Is the interpretation historically embedded and temporally grounded? 4. Does the interpretation reflect the emotion as a process that is relational and interactive? 5. Does the interpretation engulf what is known about the phenomenon? 6. Does the interpretation incorporate prior understandings and interpretations (...) as part of the final interpreted, understood structural totality? 7. Does the interpretation cohere? 8. Does the interpretation of emotion produce understanding; that is, do the elements that are interpreted coalesce into a meaningful whole? 9. Is the interpretation unfinished? All interpretation is necessarily provisional and incomplete, to begin anew when the investigator returns to the phenomenon. (1984, p9)

These criteria are included here in case the reader would find it interesting or illuminating to apply them in detail to any of the phenomenological theories. Clearly, though, from a broader perspective, they are less pertinent. As will be seen later, it be of little profit to attempt to apply them to behavioural or physiological theories, or even to cognitive theories of emotion.

Even though the phenomenological theories of emotion may fairly be said not to extend much beyond their own obvious boundaries, this does not mean that they are without value in our understanding of emotion. They are useful in that they overlap with everyday theories of emotion and they are useful in that they are used at least to make the attempt to explicate the subjective, the experiential side of emotion. Although this aspect of psychological functioning might not sit all that comfortably in the armchair of conventional science, it cannot be denied, and should not simply be swept under the chair.

If this somewhat liberal approach is taken, then it is perhaps important to see what of a more general nature can be learned from the phenomenological theories of emotion. Are there any general themes that emerge that might be instructive?

Perhaps it may be fairly said that even though the subjective does not equate with the cognitive, most of the emotion theorists who have chosen to emphasise experience have consistently included mention of cognitive factors in emotion. As will be seen throughout the remainder of this book, at a theoretical level, this is almost a necessity. Of course, such theorists have also drawn attention to the importance of an analysis of the role of consciousness in emotion and of the particular functions that emotion might serve for the individual. Again, as will be seen, these are themes that will be returned to time and time again.

Overall, the phenomenological theories of emotion, although interesting, are not the best of the theories to be found. However, they do have a function and they do add to the richness of our understanding of emotion.

4

Behavioural theory

Introduction

For the most part, research and theory into emotional behaviour has been focused on what is directly observable and measurable. Those who have taken this approach usually regard emotion as a response, or a large class of responses, basic to life and survival, rather than as a state of the organism. They sometimes bracket emotion with motivation. Their aim does not appear to be to say that emotional states of feelings do not exist, but simply to take the emphasis from these and put it instead on what is most readily (in their terms) open to investigation in the terms of conventional science. When viewed in this way, emotion can be defined in terms of the operations believed necessary to bring it about, an approach traditionally of importance to science, but which may seem somewhat restricted when applied to a concept such as emotion.

Looking at the development of the behavioural approach to emotion, its oddest aspect is that it has never embraced facial expression, although this is obviously behaviour. Facial expression, bodily movement and posture have become highly significant in attempts to understand emotion, but they have been taken into account by social psychologists working within a cognitive framework.

Those who have taken a behavioural approach to emotion have sometimes used some remarkably non-behavioural concepts such as emotionality and frustration and then attempted to give them respectability by the rigour of the empirical studies they have made of them. In so doing, they have taken away some of their meaning and unwittingly ensured that they no longer seem to be as pertinent to human emotion.

Times have moved on and the behaviourally inspired investigations of emotion and hence behavioural theories of emotion have become relatively quiescent in recent years. However, as with all approaches to emotion there is something to be learned from an overview of the major theories.

Watson

Watson (1929, 1930) put forward the first of the clearly behavioural theories of emotion, although he stressed things physiological as well.

An emotion is an hereditary 'pattern-reaction' involving profound changes of the bodily mechanism as a whole, but particularly of the visceral and glandular systems. (1929, p225, italics his)

Watson went on to distinguish between emotional and instinctive reactions, by suggesting that an emotional stimulus shocks an organism into a temporary state of chaos, whereas an instinctive reaction is not chaotic. For Watson, emotions are disorganising.

On the basis of his well-known although not particularly well-conducted work with children, Watson postulated that there are three types of fundamental emotional reaction—fear, rage and love (to use approximate words). He maintained that because of verbal confusion it would be better to label the three reactions X, Y and Z. X is caused by sudden removal of support from an infant, loud sounds and mild but sudden stimuli just as the infant is falling asleep or awakening. The result is breath-catching, hand-clutching, eye-closing, lip-puckering and crying. The Y reaction is caused by hampering movements, and includes screaming, crying, body-stiffening, limb-slashing and breath-holding. The smiling, gurgling and cooing that characterize the Z reaction is caused by gentle manipulation, especially of the erogenous zones.

Watson's main contribution to emotion theory was to offer this three factor view, which was to have later influence, and to emphasize behaviour rather than feelings or internal states. The three factor theory and the much quoted study with Raynor (1920) on the fear conditioning of Little Albert, laid the foundation for the building of later behavioural theories of emotion.

Harlow and Stagner

Harlow and Stagner's (1933) theory owes much to Watson, but also owes something to Cannon; it is behaviouristic and yet makes a distinction between feelings and emotions. They suggested that emotions are based on unconditioned affective responses (also seen as central physiological traits experienced as feelings). Any emotions then occur through becoming conditioned to these responses. the original unconditioned affective state is then modified in two ways—the range of eliciting stimuli is widened and the force of the original response is dampened.

Harlow and Stagner extend their theory in four fundamental ways. (1) They suggest that emotions may reflect conscious states other than simply feelings. (2) Feelings are controlled thalamically and sensations cortically. (3) They argue that emotions are not innate, rather that there are unconditioned responses from which emotions develop. The innate part is the 'four fundamental feelings tones, pleasure, unpleasantness, excitement and depression.' (4) They distinguish between emotion and feeling in a way which was a precursor to much more recent thought, by suggesting that in emotion there is cognition about the outside situation. Thus we are born with the capacity to feel but have to learn the various emotions.

Again, presaging later thought, they argue that the emotion labels that we attach to various experiences simply reflect our cognitions of the external situation and the meanings that these might have for us. Any name which comes to stand for an emotional state arises from social conditioning. So, for example, they viewed fear and rage as basically the same state. But if the situation that causes the state is one of threat and it is appropriate to attack we call it rage, whereas if it is appropriate to run we call it fear.

In summary, Harlow and Stagner suggest that there are innate, undifferentiated, basic feelings, emotions being the conditioned form of these which we learn to refer to in particular ways. The feelings, the emotional conditioning and the social learning of labels are mediated both cortically and subcortically. So, although their theory was essentially behavioural and based on conditioning, they had room for feeling, for physiological mechanisms, and of particular interest, for cognition.

Amsel

Like many of the other behavioural theorists of emotion, Amsel is not concerned with studying emotion directly, but rather is interested in how certain aspects of it impinge on whatever other behaviour is ongoing when it occurs. Amsel's work (eg 1958, 1962) in this area was almost solely concerned with the frustration effect which he defined operationally as an increased vigour of responding that occurs when an animal experiences non-reward where it had previously experienced reward. Clearly, this is an emotional effect which alters what the animal might be doing at the time. Its similarities are obvious to the views of other behavioural theorists of emotion who stress emotion following changes in reinforcement conditions.

Amsel put forward a theory of frustrative non-reward to account for the frustration effect. It is worth describing this briefly in the present context because, although somewhat restricted, it is a theory of emotion within a Hullian framework. Most of the behavioural approaches to emotion have been made more against a Skinnerian background.

After reward, non-reward will elicit a primary aversive emotional reaction—frustration—which is related to the magnitude of the anticipatory reward. Amsel regards the components of such frustration as becoming conditioned to antedating stimuli, resulting in anticipatory frustration. If this is so then the decrement in instrumental behaviour which results from the withholding of, or absence of reward may be due to: (1) suppression effects of incompatible responses which are learned via anticipatory frustration, or (2) the acquisition of avoidance responses reinforced by a reduction in frustration-associated cues.

Amsel's theory contains three fundamental generalisations. (1) Frustration is defined solely by non-reward in conjunction with reward. (2) Anticipatory frustration is seen as being conditioned to specific stimuli within the environment. (3) Anticipatory frustration affects response strength by increasing overall drive strength (motivating immediate behaviour), by acting as a drive stimulus the reduction of which is reinforcing and to which other stimuli become conditioned, and finally by inhibiting overt behaviour

Millenson

Millenson's (1967) model (rather than theory) of emotion owes much to Watson and is also predicated on the technique of conditioned emotional responding (CER). He takes Watson's X, Y and Z factors and puts them within a CER context. For example, a conditioned stimulus (CS) leading to an unconditioned negative stimulus (S−) leads to anxiety which suppresses positively maintained operant behaviour and sometimes facilitates that which is negatively maintained. A CS leading to an S+ or to the removal of an S− invokes some form of elation which may enhance some operants. And a CS leading to the removal of an S+ produces anger which can increase both the strength of some operants and the frequency of aggressive behaviour.

Realising that anxiety, elation and anger do not exhaust the possibilities for human emotion, Millenson extends his behavioural analysis by making two assumptions. (1) Some emotions differ from one another only in intensity, joy and ecstasy for example. (2) Some emotions are basic (anxiety, elation and anger) and others are compounds of these. His reason for giving pride of place to these three emotions is that they cover all the logical possibilities for the presentation and removal of positive and negative reinforcers, this setting the occasion for emotion. Moreover, in their conditioned form they cover all the conceivable simple classical conditioning procedures.

From this, Millenson developed a three-dimensional emotional coordinate system, as shown in Figure 3.

The three primary emotions are seen as vectors and any other emotions depend on different intensities of the reinforcer which forms their basis. The emotions at the extremes represent extremes, and the fact that the vectors come together at one point suggests that as emotions become less intense or extreme so they become more difficult to distinguish behaviourally.

Millenson was aware that his model does not include all the human emotions, but argues that those excluded are simply mixtures of the primary emotions. A neutral stimulus can become paired with two or more primary emotions or with a US that embraces more than one primary reinforcer. He gives the example of a child stealing a cookie. The cookie is a CS for the S+ of eating it, plus a CS for the S− of punishment. In Millenson's terms, this combination is usually called guilt. As another example, a CS paired with a US that has both positive and negative characteristics produces conflict, of the sort that can lead to experimental neurosis. Or what we would normally term sorrow or despair or depression is the result of removing a generalized reinforcer, such as would be involved in the death of someone close or in the loss of one's job.

Finally, Millenson extends his ideas by commenting on emotional control and pathological emotion. From the behavioural viewpoint, he proposes that we use three methods of controlling our emotions. (1) Adaptation to the

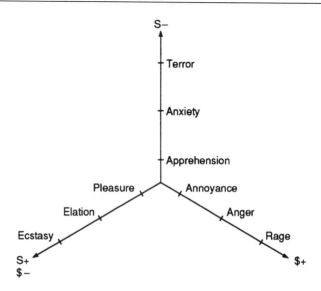

Figure 3.   Millenson's three-dimensional model of emotional intensity

continual presentations of emotion-producing stimuli—this leads to the building of frustration tolerance and to 'good' things losing their efficacy. (2) Masking respondents with opposed operants, keeping a poker face or a stiff upper lip for example. (3) The avoidance of emotion-producing situations.

Millenson's view of pathological emotion is straightforward but definitely oversimplified. He regards prolonged anxiety-producing situations as leading to neurosis and psychosis as due to the more extreme, normal positive reinforcers being either drastically disrupted or absent altogether. Would that it all were so simple.

Weiskrantz

Weiskrantz's (1968) basic behavioural view of emotion is that if reinforcers can be defined as stimuli which are consequent to responses, then emotion can be defined as responses which are consequent to reinforcers. This neat perspective draws together a number of the other behavioural approaches to emotion. Because reinforcers can be positive or negative and because it is often difficult to distinguish the effects of the onset of one from the offset of another, Weiskrantz defines responses widely and speaks of emotion as a *state* which includes many responses. He also regards respondents (in the Skinnerian sense) as the stuff of emotion.

Weiskrantz does not accept autonomic activity (including electroencephalograms) as indicants of emotion for three reasons. (1) Autonomic activity may not be a sufficient condition to infer emotional states—cognition may be necessary. Note that this is yet another emotion theorist of behavioural persuasion who brings cognition into things. (2) There are many problems and opposed viewpoints on the relevance of autonomic responding to emotion. (3) Autonomic and EEG changes cannot yet be well enough differentiated to discriminate between different emotional states.

Instead of autonomic activity Weiskrantz argues that in emotion respondents in general should be studied. He believes that in an everyday sense emotion often refers to alterations in characteristic *patterns* of behaviour. This implies, as do other behaviourally oriented theories, that the effects of emotion-producing stimuli are to make ongoing behaviour more or less vigorous.

In summary, Weiskrantz regards emotion as respondent behaviour and suggests that emotional states are reflected in changes in large classes of behaviour. He argues that to speak of emotional states has heuristic value as long as the situational context is not forgotten. Weiskrantz's view of emotion is clear, simple, based on few assumptions and draws together most of the other behavioural perspectives. One obvious difficulty with it however is that it does not give a clear indication as to how any behaviour or set of responses can be definitely labelled as emotional rather than non-emotional. This is particularly so since emotion almost always occurs in a social context. Here any one behaviour can act simultaneously as an operant, a respondent and a discriminative stimulus that sets the occasion for further behaviour.

Hammond

There is a sense in which Hammond (1970) provides one of the better syntheses of behavioural ideas on emotion, bringing together the Hullian and the Skinnerian traditions. Hammond regards emotion as a central state (CES) of the organism, which is elicited both by learned and unlearned stimuli. Both the unlearned and the learned stimuli may be the presence or absence of rewards and punishments. The learned stimuli signal the unlearned and acquire similar properties through classical conditioning.

Hammond's thesis, which is very much within a motivational framework, draws on Mowrer's (1960) idea that rewarding events lead to drive reduction and punishing events lead to drive induction. These are correlated with pleasure and pain and represent unlearned, motivating states. If a neutral stimulus occurs just before an incremental event it is a danger signal, and if it precedes a decremental event it is a safe signal. Further, the nature of the emotional state which results depends on whether the signal is turned on or off.

Danger signal: on – fear; off – relief
Safety signal: on – hope; off – disappointment.

A scheme such as this allows a straightforward way of specifying the development of the signals, with behaviour being measured simply as approach or withdrawal. Hammond altered Mowrer's conceptualisation somewhat:

(1) Stimuli predicting an increase in the occurrence of an aversive event lead to fear—excitatory.

(2) Stimuli predicting a decrease in the occurrence of an aversive event lead to relief—inhibitory.
(3) Stimuli predicting a decrease in the occurrence of a rewarding events lead to hope—excitatory.
(4) Stimuli predicting a decrease in the occurrence of a rewarding event lead to disappointment.

The obvious question to ask at this point, the type of question that clearly has to be asked of all the rather limited behavioural theories of emotion, is whether or not fear, relief, hope and disappointment, singly or in combination, exhaust the possibilities for human emotion.

Gray

Gray (1971, 1987) puts forward a recent and searching theory of emotion in the behavioural tradition. He views emotion as made up of three distinct systems each of which is grounded in relationships between reinforcing stimuli and response systems. (1) When *approach* predominates the reinforcing stimulus is a conditioned stimulus for reinforcement or non-punishment. (2) When *behavioural inhibition* predominates the reinforcing stimulus is a conditioned stimulus for punishment or non-reward. (3) When the *fight/flight* system predominates the reinforcing stimulus is unconditioned punishment or non-reward.

Gray produced this view of emotion through an analysis of innate fears and early conditioning and an initial distinction of emotional states in the everyday language. He takes the position that emotions are internal states that are mainly caused by external events, and distinguishes them from drives. Further, when the relationships between external events and emotional states become confused then pathological reactions result, including anxiety, neurosis, psychosis and depression.

When considering fear in more detail, Gray gives a searching analysis of the degree to which fears might be innate or acquired. He suggests that the stimuli that promote fears might be classed under four headings: those which are intense, those which are novel, those which stem from social interaction, and those which indicate special evolutionary dangers.

Gray's general behavioural theory of emotion then, rather like Watson's and Millenson's, is based on three systems which vary according to the type of reinforcing stimuli involved. It has relevance to both emotional development and to pathological emotion. (See Chapters 8 and 11 for further discussion of Gray's ideas.)

Staats and Eifert

Other than Gray, Staats and Eifert (1990) are the only psychologists currently espousing a behavioural theoretical approach to understanding emotion. They rest their ideas on the need to establish a *framework* for a theory of emotion which can encompass a wide range of aspects of the subject. Their aim is to produce a theory/framework which unifies existing knowledge, resolve conflicts and to include consideration of biology, behaviour, human learning, personality, psychological measurement, and abnormal and clinical psychology.

They define emotion in a number of ways, the first being as central nervous system responses that have been localized in particular parts of the brain. They distinguish such responses from peripheral arousal. However, they also define emotion in terms of its stimulus properties. "... when a stimulus elicits an emotional response in the brain, this produces at the same time a stimulus event in the brain ..." (1990, p544). Through this they see the central emotional response as mediating overt behaviour. They argue that there are both innate and learned aspects to the emotion–behaviour relationship. Moreover, they lump emotional experience, subjective, phenomenological and cognitive facets of emotion together with the idea that they are in some sense the experience of the stimulus aspects of emotion.

Staats and Eifert spend some time in their framework making links between emotion and reinforcement, perhaps not surprisingly, since in some form or another it is this which is stressed by behavioural theorists of emotion. In their view "... *the stimuli that serve as emotion elicitors in basic classical conditioning are the same stimuli that serve as reinforcers in instrumental conditioning*" (1990, p545, italics theirs). In this respect, their conceptualization is very similar to Weiskrantz's. However, extending this to the learned rather than the unlearned side of matters, they argue that any stimulus, as well as having emotional and reinforcing aspects, may also function as a directive (incentive) stimulus that promotes either approach or avoidance behaviour.

Whilst recognizing that much of human emotional behaviour and learning is mediated through language, they argue that this is achieved mainly through classical conditioning. The acquisition of language-based emotion then makes it possible for emotions to be aroused and acquired *cognitively*. They go on to make a thorough analysis of how emotion words can then function as reinforcers, particularly via the concept of self-reinforcement. They extend this further by discussing the incentive function of language but also extend their range to emotional stimuli other than words, music and pictures for example. For present purposes the details of this part of Staats and Eifert's framework for the emotions is not important. What matters is that here is the most recent behavioural theory of emotion, relying on both a Hullian and a Skinnerian background, stressing what are essentially cognitive concepts. For behaviourists, Staats and Eifert have constructed a decidedly cognitive framework.

They also emphasize the idea of the emotional state. They define this as "... a complex of stimulus events that elicit emotional responses that together exhibit an enduring, pervasive, profound character" (1990, p554). They go on to consider facets of the theory/framework concerned with individual differences and hence measurement, abnormal behaviour and clinical psychology, with specific reference to anxiety and depression.

Staats and Eifert regard their theory as being at a developmental stage, with supporting evidence for some of its aspects and a dearth of material relevant to others. For example, they consider the lack of any useful information on whether or not emotional words can be used in any effective therapeutic way. They argue that the particular strength of their framework theory (as they term it) is its heuristic value. Because it has multiple levels then it is capable of great theoretical elaboration, so they believe, and yet it has a unifying function. They argue that they have managed to place large amounts of usually diverse material within the one framework. This may be so to an extent, but their theory leaves many questions unasked and unanswered and although purporting to be behavioural relies heavily on a cognitive analysis. They term the theory the paradigmatic behaviourism theory of emotion, but it is hard to see how it can live up to this name.

Conclusions

Most of the behavioural accounts of emotion are deceptively simple, their problem being that they do not go far enough. They are far removed from the subjective experience of emotion and their proponents try, although they do not always succeed, to keep cognitions out of the action. This both detracts from the qualitative richness of emotion, and simply does not do it justice. It is clear that there have been a few theorists who have sought to bring behavioural analyses of emotion to the present. A number of the theories in this chapter seem curiously dated and yet, interestingly, it is those theorists who toy with more cognitive concepts which seem to have more to offer.

As should be clear by now, the major purpose of the concluding sections in each chapter in this book is to consider the extent to which the theories summarized in the chapter might be considered to be good theories. Relatedly, the aim is to abstract the significant common threads from the various theories.

In general terms, the power of the behavioural theories of emotion is that they provide straightforward (perhaps too straightforward) definitions and lead to clearly testable predictions. Their weaknesses however are that their relatively narrow focus does not allow them to explain all that there is to explain and does not leave them with much in the way of heuristic value. Exceptions to this to some extent are the theories of Gray and of Staats and Eifert, which are clearly the most far-reaching of the behavioural theories.

With respect to the broad criteria suggested by Lazarus (1991a,b) in the evaluation of emotion theories, the behavioural ones do well in suggesting the causes of emotion and in considering emotion as a dependent variable. However, again, the area across which they do so is quite strictly limited, the complex human emotions such as guilt or shame or envy being dealt with summarily, if at all.

In more particular, the behavioural theorists do well in characterizing discrete emotions, in giving emotion a motivational framework, in dealing with the generation of emotion, with emotional development, with its effects on general functioning and even to some extent with therapeutic ramifications. However, they are wanting with respect to considering the links between the biological and the socio-cultural (although Gray might be an exception here), at distinguishing between emotion and non-emotion. Although this latter criticism might seem odd given that such theories score well on definition, the problem comes when attempting to distinguish emotion from non-emotion behaviourally, in practice.

The strangest aspect of the behavioural theorists of emotion is that although to begin with they apparently eschew matters cognitive, most of them bring cognition into consideration at some time in some way. Sometimes this is via a consideration of the role of emotional state, and sometimes it is more directly. What such theorists do not do however is to describe the nature of any such cognitive involvement.

Thinking of Oatley's (1992) prescriptions for emotion theory, although the behavioural theories are clearly concerned with the functions and goals of emotions, and to some extent the basic emotions, they are severely limited in other ways. For example, they have little to say, perhaps almost by definition, about the possible unconscious aspects of emotion.

Similarly, they are not much concerned with any links between science and the everyday of folk-psychological approach and rarely, if ever, consider the interpersonal facets of emotion. The latter point is particularly surprising, considering that emotion is predominantly a social phenomenon, even though, according to some theories, it has its origins in biology. It is also surprising in that the social aspects of emotion could be readily investigated from a behavioural perspective.

Moving to Oatley's more general questions about theory, the behavioural theories of emotion are not noteworthy for their capacity to deal with more evidence, unless it is obviously of a behavioural nature. On the other hand, specific predictions can be derived from them straightforwardly. It should be noted though that such predictions tend to be very limited. When the behavioural theories become extended enough to suggest the making of broader predictions, or at least predictions across a broader area, (as with the Staats and Eifert theory for example) then the predictions become more difficult to derive.

Much as with the phenomenological theories, the behavioural theories of emotion are quite restrictive and therefore do not fulfil many of the criteria for good theory, even when considered en masse. However, it is possible to derive from them a number of general points which at least act as pointers to what might be possible and to what should be taken into account within a theory of emotion.

The behavioural theories tend to stress the view that emotion has something to do with a change in the vigour of behaviour. Moreover, although they are concerned primarily with behaviour, they frequently make mention of the state side of emotion. Finally, and to some extent ironically, a number of them find room for cognitive issues. It seems almost as if the theorists set out to provide *entirely* behavioural accounts of emotion but, along the way, and with some exceptions, find that this is impossible, and somehow drop into the cognitive in spite of their better judgement. As will be seen later, and often, they are not alone in this.

5

Physiological theory

Introduction

There is an enormous amount of empirical research into the physiology of emotion. The role and status of physiology in accounts of emotion has been of significance since William James onwards, and perhaps before that, to be fair on the earlier philosophers. The major aim has been to find the substrate of emotion in the central nervous system, the peripheral nervous system and the endocrine system. However, the search was mounted early to find what was assumed to be the physiological patterns that might underlie each discrete emotion, and the search continues.

Both to support such research and as a background from which to derive hypotheses and predictions, physiological theories of emotion have existed for an equal length of time. Or, when the theories are not solely physiological, they are at least about the role of physiology in emotion. It is difficult to get away from bodily perturbations; we feel them in ourselves and perceive them in others. They *must* be involved.

Of course, it is not surprising that any of the physiological theories of emotion rest on the belief that emotions have a biological base. At the complex human level, they might have socially constructed aspects, but even these are only additions to a physical/biological foundation. Similarly, it is also not surprising, given these introductory comments, that most of the physiological theories are also based on the belief that there are discrete emotions.

Wenger

Following William James, Wenger (1950) equates visceral responses with emotion, but also describes how these might function in a 'hypothetical robot'. He concentrates on behaviour but views emotional states as emotional complexes, which he saw as 'explaining' why we have no language which is adequate to describe emotion, a point which might be debated.•Wenger suggests further that perception of emotional stimuli depends on the pairing of conditioned and unconditioned stimuli, following which the arousal of the

ANS leads to visceral responses. These in turn lead to drive stimuli which Wenger regards as perceptions of visceral action. The end point in the chain is overt, muscular response and verbal report.

Although this is a very brief description of Wenger's theory, it was thought worth including because of its simplicity. It was put forward at a time when there was a dearth of psychological publications about emotion and helped to form a basis for subsequent physiological theories.

Young

Young's (1961) theory of emotion is decidedly idiosyncratic and as such rather difficult to categorize. However, because it relies heavily on arousal it has been included in this chapter.

Rather than speak of emotion, Young speaks of affective processes and an *hedonic* continuum. He sees affective processes as varying in sign, intensity and duration. So, if naive organisms show approach behaviour an underlying positive central affective process must be at work. Similarly a negative affective process underlies withdrawal. These affective processes can vary from maximal positive intensity to maximal negative intensity, shown by differences in choice, and that they can also differ in duration.

Young views affective processes as ranged along an hedonic continuum. Hedonic changes can occur in either direction, positive or negative, and from time to time may be in opposition. This way of looking at things led Young to suggest four types of possible affective change: increasing positive, decreasing positive, increasing negative and decreasing negative.

Young draws a distinction between affective and sensory processes, affording affective processes a motivational, regulatory role in behaviour. He offers a series of principles concerning affective processes. (1) Stimulation has affective as well as sensory consequences. (2) Affective arousal points the organism towards or away from a stimulus. (3) Affective processes lead to motives. (4) The strength of a recent motive is related to various aspects of previous affective arousals (eg duration or intensity). (5) Motives also depend on learning—affective processes determine what will or will not be learned, but learning itself is neurobehavioural change due to exercise. (6) Affective processes can be conditioned; we learn how to feel. (7) Affective processes regulate by influencing behaviour. (8) Finally, neurobehavioural patterns themselves follow a pattern or organisation which maximizes positive affective arousal and minimizes negative affective arousal.

Furthermore, Young suggests that affective processes have four main functions. (1) They activate. (2) They sustain and terminate behaviour. (3) They regulate behaviour. (4) They organize.

In the end, Young appears to be speaking of pleasantness and unpleasantness rather than emotion. These are affective processes arranged on an hedonic continuum which itself has an arousal function. To some degree, the affective processes accompany all behaviour, they work to a set of underlying principles and in their turn they influence behaviour.

Lindsley

Lindsley's (1950, 1951, 1957, 1970) theory of emotion is similar to Duffy's (eg 1962) in that it has arousal/motivation mechanisms underlying emotion, although it is expressed in neurophysiological rather than behavioural terms. The suggested mechanisms of arousal are the brain-stem reticular formation interacting with the diencephalic and limbic systems via the ascending reticular activating system. Lindsley also maintains that the limbic systems control emotional expression and emotional and motivational behaviour.

Lindsley regards emotion as being expressed in three ways: through cortical channels, visceral channels and somatomotor channels. Also, as with many of the primarily physiological theories of emotion, Lindsley's depends very much on the empirical research of the time, mainly concerned with EEG mechanisms of arousal.

Lindsley is a wide-ranging neural arousal theorist, his ideas embracing far more than emotion. He is also concerned with phenomena such as sleep and wakefulness, alerting, attention, vigilance and motivation. At the time he was first writing, the descending and ascending reticular formations were in the theoretical ascendency and in the 1950s there were few other competitive theories of emotion. Like Wenger's theory of the same era, Lindsley's is simple, although nevertheless pointing to obvious CNS areas of involvement in emotion.

Gellhorn

Gellhorn (1964; Gellhorn and Loufbourrow, 1963) begins by suggesting that the basis of emotion is the integration of somatic and autonomic activities, modified by neurohumours and hormones, into what he terms ergotropic and trophotropic activities. The former are work-directed and the latter are rest-directed. When one of the two systems is excited the other is diminished. Ergotropic and trophotropic effects can be brought about by the manipulation of the thalamic reticular system, septum, anterior hypothalamus and medulla, the continuous balance between the two supposedly reflecting emotional reactivity.

Gellhorn regards emotional arousal and the modification of the ergotropic/trophotropic balance as coming about through afferent impulses, internal environmental changes which act on visceral receptors or the brain-stem, and by direct stimulation of the brain-stem, the limbic system and some subcortical structures. All of the relevant physiological mechanisms are in with a fighting chance, including the possibility that similar effects may be brought about by hormonal change. He suggests in fact that when emotions are aroused, the ergotropic/trophotropic balance must be altered by both neurogenic and hormonal processes.

Interestingly, Gellhorn also argues that in human emotion there is increasing cognitive involvement, a greater part being played by the neocortex. In his speculation about the possible physiological basis of this, he recasts Schachter's famous results. He views the euphoria and anger apparently experienced by Schachter's subjects as reflecting increased sympathetic activity, increased cortical arousal, and increased ergotropic excitation. He then introduces the idea of 'tuning'. He argues that the hypothalamic ergotropic/trophotropic balance controls the 'group-character' of the emotion, but within this the specific emotion results from cognitive factors and experience. So, for example, if we consciously relax we cannot feel rage. In other words, we can be ergotropically or trophotropically 'tuned', thereby increasing the likelihood of whichever type of response. Gellhorn engages in considerable physiologising, but nevertheless does so in a stimulating way.

Bindra

Bindra (1968, 1969) has a neurophysiological theory of emotion and motivation, suggesting that both types of phenomena can be accounted for with one construct, the central motive state (CMS).

Rather than distinguishing between emotion and motivation, Bindra subsumes them under 'species typical', biologically useful actions. He suggests that such actions are the result of an interaction between environmental stimuli (incentives in his terms) and physiological change, a change which occurs in a common group of CNS neurons. This change produces a CMS, which is a functional change in neurons, needing both an environmental stimulus and a physiological change before it will occur. For example, for a hunger CMS to happen there must be internal, physiological changes plus external stimuli such as the sight and smell of food.

In Bindra's terms, a CMS is thought to increase the probability of a response to certain environmental stimuli by altering the effectiveness of the sensory input, which Bindra refers to as 'selective attention'. Or a CMS may alter the likelihood of a particular action by altering neural discharge to appropriate autonomic and somatic motor sites—'motor facilitation' or 'response bias'. Believing that this scheme is equally apposite to considerations of both emotion and motivation leads Bindra to suggest that many of the words of these areas can be replaced by common terms. The obvious one in this context is CMS to replace emotion or emotional state or motive and motivational state.

Bindra also believes that CMSs can be classically conditioned, their particular nature depending on factors such as the physical state of the organism and the conditioned and unconditioned stimuli that might be involved. Furthermore, Bindra asserts that the idea of the CMS is useful in resolving some enduring problems in the study of emotion. For example, at the time Bindra was writing it was reasonable to say that many theorists had suggested that emotion is disorganising and motivation is organising. Bindra argues that both emotion and motivation can be organized or disorganized, depending on when they are observed during individual development. A lack of experience with an environmental stimulus will lead to disorganized responding, for example. However, he also suggests that motivational patterns start early in development and occur frequently, whereas emotional patterns occur less frequently and involve more unusual situations. In this sense, he views motivation as organized and emotion as disorganized, although there seems to be little justification for this in terms of the CMS.

Fehr and Stern

Fehr and Stern (1970) emphasize the periphery in accounting for emotion physiologically, also arguing that the original James–Lange theory has much to commend it. James spoke of 'primary feelings', 'immediate reflexes' and 'secondary feelings'. Fehr and Stern maintain that primary feelings and immediate reflexes should be seen as hypothalamic discharges which inhibit the cortex and excite the ANS. It might be thought that secondary feelings are perhaps given by afferent feedback from the periphery. However, Fehr and Stern argue that this does not occur, suggesting that behaviour can be produced that looks like emotion but without visceral mechanisms being involved. Even so, afferent feedback may still occur in 'real' emotion.

Via considerable evidence concerning the effects of stressors, Fehr and Stern argue that the periphery should not be ignored when considering the physiology of emotion, and that the James–Lange theory was sound in its emphasis on the viscera. Although there's is not a far-reaching theory, these are valuable points.

Maclean

Papez (1937, 1939) suggested that emotional expression and emotional experience may be dissociated and that the experiential aspects require cortical mediation. From this starting point, MacLean (1970) argues that the limbic system integrates emotional experience, although the effector system is probably the hypothalamus. His reasons for this are that the limbic system has extensive subcortical connections and it is the one part of the cortex which has visceral representation. This also accords with the extensive olfactory functions of the limbic system. MacLean argues that olfaction is of prime importance in lower animals, from their food-seeking to their obtaining of sexual partners. He suggests that although the sense of smell may no longer be involved to the same extent in more advanced organisms, their emotional behaviour may be mediated by similar mechanisms.

So MacLean regards the hippocampus and amygdala as having special significance for the subjective, experiential side of emotion. He views all the structures in the limbic system as in some way involved in emotion, but without stressing any specific mechanisms that might mediate particular emotional patterns.

More recently, MacLean (eg 1993) has developed his thinking a little further, although still basing his ideas on the view that factors related to the evolutionary development of the limbic system helped to refine the emotional feelings that guide self-preservatory behaviour.

Although MacLean's is primarily a physiologically based view of emotion, interestingly, he lays great stress on subjectivity or the experiential side of emotion. He argues in fact that subjective phenomena are not only capable of being studied but are also essential to study in order to gain a proper understanding of emotion. He links six forms of behaviour (in humans and animals) with six affects. Searching/desire, aggressive/anger, protective/fear, dejected/ dejection, gratulant (triumphant)/joy, and caressive/affection.

Plutchik

Plutchik's psychoevolutionary theory of emotion has been developed over more than thirty years (eg, 1962, 1980, 1989, 1991, 1993). It could appear in many chapters of the present book, but seems most appropriately centred here since its evolutionary emphasis gives it a clear biological basis. Plutchik defines emotion as an inferred, complex sequence of reactions, including cognitive evaluation, subjective change, and autonomic and neural arousal impulses to action. The resulting behaviour affects the precipitating stimulus.

For Plutchik, emotion is multidimensional, the dimensions being intensity, similarity and polarity. Any emotion can vary in intensity (eg between pensiveness and grief), its similarity to any other emotion (eg joy and anticipation are more similar than loathing and surprise), and all emotions are polar (eg disgust is the opposite of acceptance).

The typical way of showing Plutchik's model of emotion is via the two diagrams shown in Figure 4.

Intensity is represented on the vertical dimension of the cone, whereas each section portrays a primary emotion. The cross-sectional view shows in particular the central area in which there is the conflict of mixed emotions.

Plutchik discusses the importance of the language used in any analysis of emotion. Normally, we use everyday language to consider emotion, but it is also possible to use a purely descriptive language based on behavioural observation, and a language based on the adaptive function of whatever the organism is doing. So, for example, we may experience joy or ecstasy, whilst behaviourally we are mating and functionally we are reproducing.

Taking his usual evolutionary perspective, Plutchik regards the functional/ adaptive language as the best for emotion, since adaptation varies along the same three dimensions as emotion. Adaptively speaking, an organism can protect, destroy, reproduce, deprive, incorporate, reject, explore or orient— four pairs of what Plutchik regards as opposites which can vary in intensity and similarity to one another. Plutchik prefers to see emotion simply as a bodily reaction of one of these types.

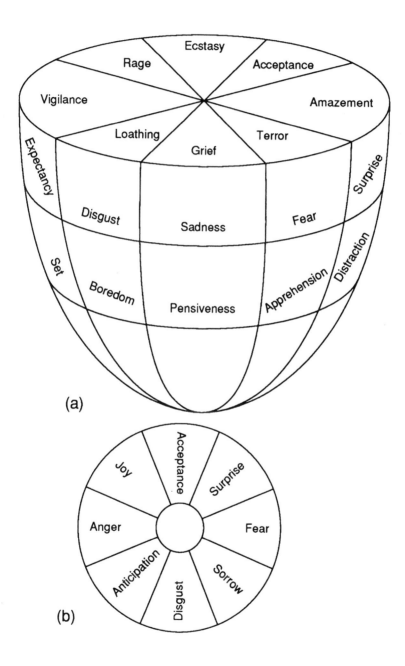

Figure 4. (a) Plutchik's three-dimensional model of emotion. (b) A cross-section through Plutchik's emotional solid. (Taken from Arnold, 1970)

Plutchik regards subjective feelings as sufficient conditions for emotion, but not as necessary; so a person may have an emotion but remain unaware of it. Similarly, physiological changes are necessary but not sufficient for emotion to occur. Physiological change may come about through exercise for example, in which emotion may not be involved.

Emotion to Plutchik is a patterned bodily reaction which has its correspondent underlying adaptive processes which are common to living organisms. Primary emotions are short-lived and usually triggered by external stimuli and there are often mixtures of physiological and expressive patterns. It is therefore only possible to infer discrete patterns of emotion approximately.

Plutchik develops this structural model of emotion into what he terms a sequential and a derivatives model. The sequential model suggests that events occur which are cognitively appraised with respect to their importance to well-being. Feelings and physiological changes follow this, the physiological aspects being primitive or anticipatory reactions to do with a range of functional impulses. There will be a final overt action, the result of all of which is to feedback into the system to maintain a homeostatic balance.

From Plutchik's perspective, some emotions are primary and others are derived; this implies that emotions are "related to a number of derivative conceptual domains" (1991, p53). So the language of mixed emotions appears to be similar to the language used in speaking of personality traits, and this in turn is related to the language of diagnostic traits and even ego defences.

From Plutchik's psychoevolutionary perspective, emotion has two functions: (1) to communicate information about intentions or probable behaviour, and (2) to increase the chances of survival when faced with emergencies. Emotion can be modified by learning, emotion finally being seen as mediating a form of behavioural homeostasis.

Rolls

Rolls (1990) offers a theory of emotion which is concerned with its neural basis, although rests it on a definition of emotion from the behavioural tradition—emotions being seen as states produced by instrumental reinforcing stimuli. He describes and classifies emotions in a way which is very reminiscent of Millenson (1967) and Weiskrantz (1968) and makes his initial analysis very much dependent on the presentation or removal of positive and negative reinforcers.

In refining this view, Rolls suggests that not all states produced by reinforcing stimuli are emotional. Emotional states are those which are normally produced by external reinforcing stimuli. He brings cognition into the matter by suggesting that *remembered* external stimuli which are associated with reinforcers can also lead to emotional states. Moreover, he gives cognitive processes the role of determining whether or not an environmental event is reinforcing. So an emotion is made up of a cognition that some event is reinforcing plus the mood state that results.

Rolls argues from this conditioning/reinforcement based, but nevertheless cognitive viewpoint that the type of brain mechanisms that underlie this type of learning are crucial to emotion. In particular, it is important to find brain mechanisms that are implicated in disconnecting inappropriate stimulus-reinforcement associations.

Before elucidating the neurophysiological part of his theory, Rolls suggests that emotion has particular functions, that have obvious survival value. (1) Emotion elicits autonomic and endocrine responses. (2) Emotion allows behaviours made in response to reinforcing stimuli to be flexible. (3) Emotion is motivating. (4) Emotion is capable of being communicated. (5) Emotion allows social bonding. (6) Anything that is positively reinforcing, that is that allows pleasant feelings, so that there are actions made to obtain it, has survival value. Similarly, from an evolutionary viewpoint, natural selection is likely to militate against the survival value of behaviour which is associated with unpleasant feelings and negative reinforcement. (7) Mood can affect the cognitive evaluation of either events or memories. (8) Emotion may help in the storage of memories. This may be through episodic memory being facilitated by emotional states, or an emotional state being stored with episodic memories, or by emotion guiding the cerebral cortex in setting up representations of the world.

The neural part of Rolls's theory of emotion, which he seems to view as basic, gives pride of place to the amygdala, the orbitofrontal cortex and the hypothalamus. He argues that the amygdala is concerned with the learning of stimulus-reinforcement associations. From Rolls previous line of argument this means that the amygdala must be involved in emotional learning. By contrast, he argues that the evidence suggests that the orbitofrontal cortex is involved in *disconnecting* stimulus-reinforcement associations. He sees this part of the CNS as being implicated in emotion by correcting inappropriate stimulus-reinforcement associations. Thirdly, the hypothalamus is involved through its connections with these two regions. This allows only particular types of emotional (and motivational) information to be dealt with there.

Rolls completes his neural theory of emotion by suggesting ways in which the CNS basis of emotional states might possibly affect cognitive processing. In this context, he draws attention in particular to the hippocampus and goes into some detail about how it might function in this capacity. In summary, he suggests the three possibilities that emotional states may affect whether (or how firmly) memories are stored, they may be stored as part of memory, or they may have an effect on the recall of memories or on whatever cognitive processing is associated with them.

Although dependent on a behaviourally based definition of emotion, Rolls's theory is squarely based on the neurophysiology of brain mechanisms, but also gives significant consideration to cognitive involvement.

Panksepp

Panksepp's theory of emotion is amongst the best and most thorough in the physiological or neurophysiological domain. (eg, 1981, 1989, 1991, 1992, 1993). His original aims, which are extending year by year, were to produce a neurobehaviourally derived taxonomy of emotions, to outline a scheme of how the emotions are organized in the brain, and to explore the implications of this type of theory.

The theory springs from the likelihood that mammals share emotional circuits in the limbic system, which provide what he terms 'obligatory internal dynamics'. It rests on five assumptions. (1) Distinct emotional processes are reflected in hard-wired brain circuits. (2) Humans and animals share primitive emotion processes. (3) Although there is a limited number of basic emotional circuits, mixtures of these plus social learning allow much more. (4) Neurotaxonomy can be considered through introspection. (5) The scientific understanding of emotion can be gained through the study of brain organization.

Panksepp also makes a number of proposals. (1) There are genetically hard-wired unconditioned responses made to life-challenging circumstances. (2) There is adaptive activation of inhibition of classes of related actions. (3) Emotion circuits change their sensitivities through feedback. (4) Neural activity can go on longer than the activities that give rise to it. (5) Activity in the emotion circuits can be conditioned to environmental stimuli through reinforcement. (6) The emotion circuits interact with the brain mechanisms of consciousness.

Panksepp suggests that there are four emotion-mediating circuits that pass between the midbrain, limbic system and basal ganglia. They are labelled according to the extremes of emotional experience they are presumed to mediate in humans—expectancy, fear, rage and panic.

Taking the example of expectancy, this is thought to be mediated in the medial forebrain bundle of the lateral hypothalamus. It is sensitized by homeostatic imbalances and linked environmental incentives and produces motor arousal for explorations and investigation for survival. Fear is mediated in the sites for flight and escape and occurs in response to potential harm. Rage sites elicit angry emotional displays and invigorate irritable or restrained behaviour. Panic sites bring about distressed calls and explosive behaviour.

Panksepp puts forward a convincing case for a neurophysiological basis for these four command systems. Anatomically, he suggests that they run from the mesencephalon through the reticular fields of the hypothalamus and thalamus to the basal ganglia and the higher limbic areas. Neurochemically, Panksepp believes the circuits to depend on single or multiple command transmitters. He argues for dopamine and acetylcholine having key functions in expectancy and rage and for the involvement of the benzodiazepine receptor and endorphin systems in panic and fear. The major brain amines, serotonin and norepinephrine are likely to be involved as well.

Psychologically, Panksepp stresses learning and reinforcement, with the view that emotionally neutral stimuli can gradually influence emotion circuits. The higher brain circuits may well assimilate some of the functions of the lower circuits, which may help to account for cognitive appraisal as having an important influence in the development of adult emotions. He also speculates a little about possible imbalances in the visceral brain underpinning various psychiatric disorders. For example, schizophrenia and depression would be found on the expectancy dimension and personality disorders and psychopathy on the rage dimension. Anxiety neuroses would be on the fear dimension and autism and obsession-compulsions on the panic dimension.

It is refreshing, that given the dependence of Panksepp's theory on biological science, he also stresses the importance of introspection. He argues that the conscious mind can see the dynamics of its subcortical heritage. Two possibilities for looking at the brain are as a generalized arousal state which promotes individual emotion through social learning, or as a system of hard-wired representations for every emotional nuance. Panksepp takes a middle course, with classes of behaviour going together, the basic control of each being in common circuits. These are genetically based but modulated by experience, perceptions and homeostasis, all of which would result in numerous specific behavioural expressions.

To summarize, Panksepp's theory of emotion suggests that there are brain emotion systems in the form of a limited number of translimbic command systems (in his more recent formulations, eg 1991, he includes a ludic system and also speculates about other emotions). That such states exist in animals is an assumption based on self-recognition and similarities in mammalian limbic systems. Panksepp believes that subjective experience provides a useful guide for categorizing and analysing emotive brain states.

Panksepp terms his preferred approach to emotion 'comparative psychoneurophenomenology'. This mixture reflects the way in which he would like to liberalize the manner in which emotion is studied—a view which is thoroughly endorsed here and which will be considerably extended in the final chapters. Panksepp argues for an 'as if' approach which should free an investigator to use words in a comfortable way. "In the absence of comprehensive knowledge of how such an emotional system (a brain system) operates, it should still be permissible to discuss the observed behaviours theoretically in terms of the operation of the putative underlying circuitries" (1991, p90).

In what might be seen as an illustration of, or even a vindication of, this view, Panksepp (1992) writes compellingly concerning the relevance of what he terms the neurobehavioural data to recent discussion of the nature of basic emotions. Addressing Ortony and Turner's (1990) significant concern with this issue, he persuades convincingly that in the matter of basic emotions consideration *must* be given to brain research. He does not gainsay the conceptual analysis made by Ortony and Turner (discussed at length in Chapter 7), but implies that it would be foolish to leave brain research out of the analysis.

Scherer

Strictly speaking, Scherer's (1993) cogent discussion does not offer a physiologically based theory of emotion. However, within his own definition and general *component process theory* of emotion (see Chapter 7), he puts forward some penetrating suggestions for the relevance of what he prefers to term neuroscience to our understanding of emotion.

> Yet, although the study of the neural substratum of psychological processes does not necessarily resolve functional questions, one can argue that more detailed knowledge of the *biological constraints*, concerning both structures and mechanisms, can help to select between different theoretical alternatives and to direct psychological research toward areas or topics that are crucial for our understanding of the phenomenon of emotion. (1993, p2)

Scherer emphasizes six important theoretical matters which he uses as the basis of evaluating the implications of neuroscience for understanding emotion. These are: definition, emotion–cognition relationships, appraisal, sequential and parallel processing, patterning, and what he terms entry points and intersystem feedback.

In his component process theory, Scherer defines emotion as what happens when the five components of all the subsystems of the organism's functioning are synchronized in reaction to some event (internal or external) which is of central concern. The components are: cognition, physiological regulation, motivation, motor expression and monitoring/feeling. His first aim then is to explore how a neuroscience approach might help to evaluate the worth of this or any other definition and theory.

Two possibilities are firstly to see different emotions as reflected in particular patterns of brain activity and appraisal, and secondly to look at dissociations between different components of emotional and nonemotional states through pathology. Further, there might be developed techniques in neuroscience that would allow the demonstration of various central subsystems in emotional arousal. Part of the neuroscientist's task would also be to attempt to demonstrate whether different emotions rest on the same or different substrate systems.

As Scherer rightly views it (and see Chapter 6) the emotion–cognition debate depends very much on the definition of cognition. Scherer's synchronization perspective allows him to consider cognitive processes very much as a part of the emotion process, and also as it is involved in subjective feeling, another component of emotion. He suggests that the neuroscience approach to these matters might move in the direction of attempting to find (that is, define) various central indicators that are involved in the processing of the different subsystems. If these could be defined, then there might be more precision about how cognitive processes and emotion interact.

Scherer's component process theory of emotion analyses the appraisal process through what he terms stimulus evaluation checks (again, see Chapter 7) and pays particular attention to whether such checks are made in parallel or sequentially. He argues that the neuroscience approach could help in this area in four possible ways. Firstly, there are neural network theory and parallel distributed processing models. Secondly, there is what is sometimes termed brain architecture, which as the name implies is concerned with the particular structure of features of the CNS. Here, Scherer draws attention to Le Doux's (eg 1987, 1989, 1992) work on identifying pathways involved in emotional learning.

Thirdly, there is multi-layered processing which points to the significance of the appraisal system depending on different levels of evaluation being available. Processing can then be changed according to the stimulus and the interpretative needs of the organism. CNS evidence can help here by showing what the biological constraints might be. Finally, there is the possibility of monitoring evoked potentials. This would give direct measures of what processing is going on centrally.

Scherer's component process definition/theory of emotion suggests that all the various modalities are involved in a highly integrated way in producing differential patterns for the various emotions. He argues that not only are there patterns but that the patterns of changes in the various subsystems should be closely linked. He points to most biologically/physiologically oriented emotion theorists espousing this type of view.

As a final matter of concern to emotion theorists that the neuroscience approach might shed some light on, Scherer points to the question of feedback between systems. He believes that the subsystems are all interconnected and are feeding back and forwards all the time. In his view this helps the establishing of synchronicity during an emotional episode or experience. To understand this he argues for a neural network modelling approach, tempered by whatever constraints are imposed by neural architecture.

In what is a very thoughtful and informative exposition, then, Scherer considers his own theory of emotion (almost as representative of others) within the approaches that might be taken by neuroscientists. He believes that the sort of evidence that would accrue from neuroscience would even help in the consideration of whether emotion is best seen from a universalist or a relativist perspective. To allow Scherer his own final word, he believes that emotion psychology should be involved in "Conceptualising the sequential multi-componential process that constitutes emotion episodes and operationalising the bonding of specific emotional experiences in the flow of consciousness. The neurosciences are well equipped to contribute to this daunting exercise" (1993, p35).

Cacioppo

The history of ideas about the psychophysiology of emotion began with James. There followed a plethora of research which was driven largely by the view that each discrete emotion would have its corresponding psychophysiological pattern of responses. Given that the ANS was clearly involved in emotion, and that an individual's *experience* clearly allows the various emotions to be distinguished, response patterning seemed likely. However, the search was largely fruitless, the view being that individual differences in emotional reactivity swamped any transperson patterns.

Cacioppo, Klein, Bernston and Hatfield (1993) provide a useful recent summary of the ideas on the *psychophysiology* of emotion. They place previous theories of emotion that have a role for peripheral physiological change into one of two categories. There are theories that suggest that discrete emotions stem from discrete somatovisceral patterns, and theories that suggest that such emotional experiences come from cognitive appraisals that arise from undifferentiated physiological arousal.

Consideration of the inconclusive and somewhat ambiguous nature of the evidence on the psychophysiological patterning in emotion leads Cacioppo et al to put forward what they term an organizing framework and a model of emotion. Various considerations lead them to suggest that it is more important to look for conditions and emotions in which there is differential physiological activity, rather than to look for invariant patterns.

Their *somatovisceral afference* model of emotions lists psychophysiological conditions in which "(1) the *same* pattern of somatovisceral afference leads to discrete emotional experiences, and (2) quite different patterns of somatovisceral afference lead to the *same* emotional experience" (1993, p137).

A stimulus undergoes a primitive evaluation; this determines approach/withdrawal and leads to physiological changes. Somatovisceral responses, although not necessarily occurring in this initial appraisal, may vary along a continuum from emotion-specific activation to undifferentiated activation. This is paralleled by somatovisceral sensory input to the brain. Then, in adults, there is further cognitive evaluation of the somatovisceral changes. This leads to discrete emotional experiences. This second stage of cognitive elaboration ranges, again on a continuum, from simple pattern recognition through to complex attributions and hypothesis testing. There is a time scale involved with greater cognitive elaboration requiring longer time periods.

The model has it that different patterns of somatovisceral afference can lead to the same emotional experience through pattern recognition, perceptual priming and pattern recognition or evaluative need plus cognitive labelling (Cacioppo et al see these as three distinct psychophysiological mechanisms). By contrast, they describe the same pattern of somatovisceral afference as leading to discrete emotions through two psychophysiological mechanisms: (1) somatovisceral illusions involving ambiguous afference and a primed emotion schema, and (2) cognitive labelling in which there is an emotionally undifferentiated perception of afference and an evaluative need.

Cacioppo et al regard their suggested framework as of heuristic value only at present. For the future they believe it to be important to find the variables that help to determine whether discrete, ambiguous or undifferentiated somatovisceral responses come from an emotional stimulus. Then it might be possible to begin to specify how discrete emotions are linked to particular ANS changes. This approach may be regarded as doing something towards bringing together the central and peripheral physiological theoretical approaches to emotion.

McGuire

Via an analysis of the history of research and ideas on animal emotion, including invertebrate emotion, McGuire (1993) makes some interesting observations on the future of biologically based views of emotion. He characterizes many researches and theorists as taking the process of evolution for granted and then attempting to fit the biological control of emotion into a linear model. Such researchers are keen to find the brain circuitry of emotion. The basis of this view is that certain, perhaps primary emotions, are hard-wired in the brain (ie they are genetically determined) and they occur when life is threatened. McGuire argues that simply because there are biological correlates of emotion does not mean that emotions are hard-wired. And in a similar vein, because an emotion has evolutionary advantage does not mean that it will necessarily be reflected in short term actions.

MacGuire argues for a wider definition of emotion than is typical in this area. "... a change in the internal system of an animal such that it is more likely to perform a particular behaviour" (1993, p163). He regards this definition as promoting the study of neural circuits plus their modulation, and genetic control mechanisms for emotions.

Neuromodulation is important in McGuire's view because, for example, not all emotions can be localized in specific neural circuits. Think, for instance, of the many functions that might be served by anger, or the difference between an emotional reaction and a mood. McGuire believes that neuromodulators can account for these differences. So, although specific neural circuits may be at the basis of particular behaviour, these circuits may be modulated by emotions. From this perspective, neuromodulators, prompted by emotions and moods, might increase or decrease the probability of behaviour, this certainly being a role which many theorists have given emotion.

In the end, McGuire adopts the rather strong position that the biologically based study of emotion should proceed through the modelling of *invertebrate* systems. He believes that this will lead to the finding of the neural circuits that underlie emotion, and to ascertaining the neuromodulation and genetics of emotion. After the invertebrates comes the mammals. While McGuire's argument is compelling, most theorists would probably not be able to resist extending their ideas to human emotion, which is of course their starting point.

Conclusions

Taken as a whole, the surprising aspect of the physiologically based theories of emotion is their breadth. It is particularly the more recent ones to which this comment refers. Some of the earlier theories are simply inadequate, doing little more than suggesting that emotion cannot and should not be conceptualized without recourse to its physiological aspects.

Again, as a whole, these theories do fulfil many of the general criteria believed to be useful in assessing 'good' theory. They summarize the existing knowledge, at least that which has a (neuro)physiological or biological base. They provide explanations, in some cases, intricate explanations, of emotional phenomena, although naturally, this is mainly at a physiological level. They lead to testable predictions at both the physiological and the behavioural levels. They are certainly focused and in some of their more speculative forms (say, Plutchik, Panksepp and Scherer) they have reasonable heuristic value.

Moving onto the more specific matter of emotion theory rather than theory in general, it is clear that the theories considered in this chapter paint a clear picture of the causes of emotion. These are placed squarely in the physical domain, largely although not wholly in the CNS. So, from this perspective emotion is seen as having a neurophysiological basis. Also, it is either implied or in some cases made explicit in these types of theory that emotion has a *biological* foundation and is of significance in evolutionary history.

With respect to emotion viewed as either independent or dependent variable, theorists who stress physiology are not so clear. On which side of the equation is it reasonable to place general physiological arousal, or the more specific actions of the limbic system or the peripheral psychophysiological responses? Are these the emotion itself, are they dependent measures of something else, or are they events that lead to other types of change that might be regarded as *the* emotion? Even in a well-conceived theory such as Panksepp's such questions are not easy to answer. Perhaps the complexities of emotion would suggest that from a physiological perspective, emotion is all of these things.

Working through the elements of what should be included in a theory of emotion according to Lazarus (1991a,b) again the physiological theories fare reasonably well. The best of them are good on definition, on dealing with issues of specific emotions, on distinguishing between and exploring the links between behaviour and physiology, and at looking at the possible interdependence of emotions. As might be expected, and almost by definition, they have a firm place for the biological, they have something to say about the generation of emotion although less about its development. And some of them consider the effects of emotion on general functioning, although not often straying into possible implications for therapy. However, an obvious exception to this amongst the better physiological theorists is Plutchik. His ideas on emotion both derive from and have implications for therapy in equal proportions to their derivation from 'normal' everyday life.

The physiological theories are less cogent on dealing with the distinction between emotion and non-emotion, having particular problems with the concept of arousal. Although they bring other aspects of emotion into consideration, or perhaps it would be better to say, although they explore some of the links between emotion and other types of phenomena, such as those of cognition and motivation, they do not go far in these directions. Relatedly, they are wanting in the areas of appraisal and consciousness, although it is again Panksepp who makes the best efforts in these directions. In particular, of course, the physiologically based theories of emotion are particularly lacking in sociocultural matters, but this is hardly surprising.

Considering the adequacy of the physiological theories of emotion from the suggestions about theory made by Oatley (1992), they are reasonably impressive on about half of the criteria. For example, they tend to be clear on the functions (biological, evolutionary) of emotion, about the matter of whether or not they are discrete (although they rarely stray into their folk-psychological aspects), and about whether or not there are basic emotions.

Turning the coin over, rarely is there mention of possible unconscious causes of emotion, and discussion about evaluations to do with possible goals is sketchy. More particularly, there is almost never mention made of anything interpersonal (even though it is obvious that emotions, however conceived, occur mainly in interpersonal contexts), and relatedly they make little reference to the simulated plans of other people.

More general though, from the broad Lakatos or Popper approaches mentioned by Oatley, the physiological theories do very well. The best of them are couched in terms which can definitely deal with more evidence. Also, the recent ones spring so obviously from a welter of empirically based data that they are expressed in such a way that specific predictions can be readily made from them. However, this is more obviously so when particular CNS functions or structures are under consideration than when they become more speculative about, say, the role and functions of experience.

Within the context then of the physiological theories, or at least the more recent ones, being judged to be relatively 'good' theories, in what directions do they lead our understanding of emotion. Of course, there is the obvious direction of the particular areas of the nervous systems that are involved, and the exact mechanisms of this involvement. There is also the related matters of the evolutionary history of emotional phenomena and their functions and of the extent to which it is reasonable to conceptualize emotions as having a biological base.

However, possibly of more moment in a general appraisal of theories of emotion, is the point that almost all of the physiological theories seem to have a place for cognition. Again, even though the theorists might set out to explicate emotion from a physiological perspective, sometimes, although not always, in spite of themselves, they end up speculating about the possible role of cognition. Sometimes, this is cognition considered as a part of emotion and sometimes it is finding a place for emotion as conceived physiologically, in its necessary interaction with cognition.

Clearly, the physiology of emotion has been with us for as long as psychologists have been grappling with the the nature of emotion. Somehow, it has been obvious from the start that bodily and hence neurophysiological reactions are involved in some basic way. Probably this is because psychologists are folk psychologists as well and they experience their own bodily perturbations. So, theories of emotion which can be described as primarily physiological have been frequent and influential. Which, then, is the best of them. In answer, attention has to be drawn to the enormous contribution to understanding made by Plutchik, and more recently by Scherer, admittedly in a theory which is broader than the physiological alone. But in particular a debt is owed to Panksepp who has gone farthest in a quite formal way to further our understanding of emotion physiologically conceived. His work displays an admirable blend of the empirical and the theoretical and he shows himself to be well aware of aspects of emotion that lie beyond the physiological but which nevertheless should be considered.

6

Cognitive theory

As this book progresses through the types of theory that represent various approaches or starting points, so the number of theories involved increases. With the cognitive approach, not only does the number of theories increase but to some extent their complexity also increases. From the frequent mention of cognition in the theories so far covered, that have quite different and even seemingly opposed starting points, this should come as no surprise. This is a point which will be returned to with steady, not to say monotonous, regularity throughout this book.

Perhaps it is because psychology begins in everyday life that it seems hard for a theorist to deal with emotion without making some mention of cognition. Perhaps it is simply obvious from a personal point of view that cognition is involved. Perhaps the recent upsurge in theories of emotion parallels the ascendency of cognition within psychology and the two have come to be linked. Whatever the reason, it is certainly the case that when discussing emotion, cognition is the most frequently mentioned 'other area' of psychology.

However, the particular point about the theories to be summarized in this chapter, is that those who have created them have given pride of place to cognition, and in some cases have almost left out other aspects of emotion entirely. Some have gone into the actual cognitive processes that might be involved in considerable detail. And some have become heavily involved in elucidating the nature of the relationship between emotion and cognition.

Even within the cognitive approach, the theories themselves, as will be seen, have taken a number of viewpoints. Some have regarded the basic problem as a study of whatever cues, either internal or external, allow us to identify and name our own emotional states. These are amongst the simpler cognitive theories. Some have assumed that cognitions cause physiological and behavioural change, it being important to study the one in order to gain knowledge of the others. The appraisal theorists fit into this mould.

Some cognitive theorists have considered emotion within a cognitive framework or have looked at emotion from a very broad perspective which nevertheless gives an integral part to cognition and to subjective experience (see

Chapter 8). Finally, the most profound theoretical discussions in this area have been led by those who have simply addressed the nature of the relationship between emotion and cognition.

Maranon

It is likely that a number of those who have studied emotion over the last few decades have thought in passing that it is possible that Maranon has had a slightly raw deal in the history of emotion theory. He is always quoted as the person who did the rather simple adrenaline study which, amongst other considerations, led Schachter to propose his two-factor theory of emotion, which in turn was instrumental in the upsurge of work on the links between emotion and cognition. Fortunately, Cornelius (1991) did not merely think this in passing but has done something to set the record straight.

Cornelius points out that not only did Maranon (1924) conduct the 'adrenaline study', he also proposed a two part theory of emotion. For him, the two parts were to do with (1) the body or physical, mainly consisting of the more obvious aspects of sympathetic arousal, and (2) the psychological, made up of the subjective experience appropriate to the situation which associates the bodily changes with a particular emotion. The experience of the emotion is stemming from the psychological state that is the context for the experience. As Cornelius points out, this would now be referred to as cognition. Maranon believed that true emotion will only be experienced when both components are present.

The similarities between Maranon's theory and Schachter's are self-evident: two factors, one concerned with arousal and the other with cognition, the cognitive allowing the person to understand the arousal. Cornelius points out further than Maranon also criticized James concerning his ordering of the processes involved in the experience of emotion. Maranon's suggestion was that an event evokes emotion, which leads to perception which leads to sympathetic arousal of which the person may become aware. Emotion ensues when the perceived arousal is joined with the initial perception.

The sole reason for including this brief section on Maranon is simply in accord with the spirit of Cornelius's (1991) article. Maranon should have his due and rightful place in the history of the links between emotion and cognition, not just for his adrenaline investigation but also for putting forward a two-factor theory of emotion rather sooner than Schachter.

Bull

Although Bull's (1951) theory of emotion is unusual in having a central role for motor behaviour, it also has a largely cognitive orientation. Bull argues that emotion is mediated by an attitude of preparedness to respond, to behave. This is an involuntary, motor attitude which leads to a series of incomplete but invariant movements. These possibilities for movement are built-in, dependent on neurally determined predispositions.

Although there is a motor readiness involved in emotion, there is also a mentally oriented awareness, this being the emotion as it is experienced. Emotion then becomes reduced by action, especially if the action happens to be consummatory. Bull regards emotion as occurring only when the individual is less than fully aware of readiness to respond. The alternative occurs when the individual is fully aware of the possibility of a complete sequence of motor behaviour, this leading to a feeling of purpose which precludes any experience of emotion.

Although Bull's theory of emotion stresses motor action, it also implies that consciousness or cognition sets limits on emotion. So, if a person realizes consciously the full implications of a sequence of motor behaviour, no emotion is possible. Alternatively, if the person is less than fully aware then the sequence of motor behaviour is fragmentary or incomplete and emotion is experienced.

Arnold

Arnold's (eg 1945, 1960, 1968, 1970a, 1970b) theory of emotion is a mixture of phenomenology, cognition, and physiology. It rests on the assumption that we can gain most understanding of brain function in emotion through cognitive analysis. Such analysis allows the identification of the physiological mediation of the process that runs from perception to emotion and action, as Arnold sees it.

It is with Arnold that the concept of *appraisal* took hold so firmly in the cognitive conceptualization of emotion. She suggests that we immediately, automatically, and almost involuntarily evaluate, with respect to ourselves, anything that we encounter. This leads us to approach anything we appraise as 'good', to avoid what is 'bad' and to ignore what is 'indifferent', unless some other appraisal intervenes. Of course, we may well re-appraise objects about which we have already made a judgement. Appraisal then is a process which complements perception and produces in us a tendency to *do* something. If this tendency is strong then it is called emotion, although from Arnold's perspective all appraisals have the status of affective experiences.

In most new experiences, memory underpins our appraisals. The exceptions to this come from 'simple' experiences such as taste or pleasure/pain. Anything new is evaluated in terms of past experiences, the new object or situation evoking a memory of the affect associated with the previous experience. Such affective memories are the relivings of our past appraisals, experiences which continually distort our judgements.

Arnold suggests that the final link in the appraisal chain is *imagination*. Before we act, the situation plus any relevant affective memories lead us to make guesses about the future. We *imagine* whether what will happen will be good or bad for us. So our appraisal then becomes dependent on memory plus expectation. Then we devize a plan of action which will allow us to cope with the situation; we choose what it is best to do. Remember that Arnold suggests that this whole, rather complex, process of appraisal may occur almost instantaneously.

Much of Arnold's theory is concerned with tracing hypothetical neural pathways that may mediate the hypothetical cognitive appraisal processes. However, she also distinguishes between feelings and emotions. Emotional action patterns arise from positive or negative appraisal of perceived or imagined objects, whereas feeling action patterns result from appraisals of something which may be beneficial or harmful for our functioning. Arnold nevertheless regards the hypothetical sequence of events involved in feeling as much the same as that involved in emotion. In a sense, to Arnold, feeling is a lesser form of emotion.

Arnold also attempted to distinguish between emotion and deliberate actions. To take an example of deliberate action, I might sit writing this summary of Arnold's views without much desire to do so. Any pleasure comes when it is finished, or perhaps from the particular stringing together of words, not from the rather mechanical progression of word-processing. This has no special attraction. If I were to express any emotion at all in this situation it would be because I had had a period of difficulty in expressing myself, or had just completed a fluid 2000 words, or had something else nagging at me that I would prefer to be doing.

Deliberate action of this sort Arnold believes to comprise most of our everyday behaviour, to involve so-called rational judgement, and to distinguish us from the animals. We judge situations both in terms of short-term, emotional consequences or possibilities, and long-term, more abstract goals. She also states that we often relinquish the former, although they are more immediately attractive, for the latter, which are better for us in the long run. However, the extent to which we do this probably depends on factors such as our background and personality. Animals do not have this capacity at all, only being able to make immediate, emotional appraisals. Arnold argues that in distinguishing between emotional and deliberate action patterns, she is separating emotion and will. This may be, but she is also maintaining the traditional rationalist doctrine.

Schachter

No coverage of cognitive theories of emotion would be complete without mention of Schachter. However, it is perhaps fair to say that his major contribution to our understanding of emotion came from a series of cunningly devized experiments and the interpretations they have led to, and their general heuristic value. Schachter (1959, 1964, 1970) has a cognitive/physiological view of emotion, suggesting that emotional states are determined mainly by cognitive factors. This rather simply put theory suggests that emotional states are characterized by general arousal of the sympathetic nervous system and that from state to state this may differ slightly in its pattern. We interpret and classify these states from the situation which we believe to have brought them about and from our typical mode of perception. In short, physiological arousal occurs and is given its precise direction by our cognitions of what brought it about.

This view led Schachter to put forward the three propositions for which he is perhaps best known. (1) If we are physiologically aroused but cannot explain why or what caused the arousal, then we will give this state a name and react to it in whatever cognitive way is open. Thus any *one* state could be labelled in many ways depending on the individual and the situation. (2) If we are physiologically aroused and have an entirely reasonable explanation of this available, it is improbable that we will entertain any alternative cognitive accounts. (3) The third proposition involves approaching the theory from the opposite direction. If from time to time we experience the same cognition, we will only describe our feelings as emotions if we are also in some state of physiological arousal. Schachter's basic view then is that emotions are controlled through a very close inter-relationship with and interaction between physiological arousal and cognitive appraisal—now usually known as the two-factor theory of emotion.

As mentioned earlier, Schachter devoted some time to a series of empirical investigations designed to test the three propositions that give form to his two-factor theory. Schachter's studies have been analysed and criticized extensively and it is not the present purpose to review this literature. However, it is worth making some points that devolve from it.

For example, Leventhal (1974) (see also Leventhal and Tomarken, 1986) sees it as a problem of *how* arousal and cognition combine in emotion. Schachter does not, for example, say when or how arousal contributes to particular states of feeling. His conceptualization of emotion allows cognitions three possible functions in emotional experience. They permit the interpretation of emotional stimuli, the recognition of arousal and the labelling of emotion.

Leventhal regards expectations as important determinants of emotional states. The more accurate the expectations, the more likely we are to become emotional. He also considers whether or not cognitions label arousal and so create subjective feelings. If this is so, then, he argues, feelings must be learned. He argues against this possibility by questioning how a young child can be capable of feeling anything before he knows the label for the feeling, if it is the label that promotes the feeling. This would only be possible if the situations are similar in meaning to those for which the child already has the labels.

Leventhal turns the argument round, in fact, and suggests that situations might be construed as similar because they generate similar feelings. An innate set of feelings generates meaning. This leads to a position in which cognitions can be seen as leading to particular reactions of the CNS and to distinctive bodily reactions, the latter being integral to feeling.

Cotton (1981) and Reisenzein (1983) make a very thorough analysis of Schachter's theory of emotion. From their critiques it is clear that only one of the propositions that derive from the theory is adequately supported. If an emotional state has an arousal attributed to it from an irrelevant source, it will be intensified. But there has been no study demonstrating that peripheral arousal is a *necessary* condition for an emotional state.

There appears to be support for a less powerful form of Schachter's theory. This is that feedback from arousal can have an intensifying effect on emotional states and this arousal-emotion relationship is mediated and/or modified by causal attributions about the source of arousal.

Generally, Schachter's theory of emotion has been very influential and has definitely focused attention on the cognitive aspects of emotion. It also may be said to have overstated the role of peripheral arousal and the links between arousal and emotion. As yet, however, the theory has not been entirely disproved, and may perhaps be one of those theories that can never be entirely disproved.

Siminov

A brief description of Siminov's (1970) rather simple theory of emotion is included here because of its similarity to Leventhal's (1974). It is an information theory approach and begins with a definition of what Siminov terms negative emotion:

$$E = -N \, (I_n - I_a)$$

where emotion equals need multiplied by the difference between the necessary information and the available information. Here, information refers to the possibility of reaching a goal due to a particular communication.

If an organism cannot organize itself appropriately because there is a lack of information the nervous system mechanism leading to negative emotions starts to act. Siminov describes this as having the following main implications. (1) 'Dominant' reactions occur—that is, previously neutral stimuli begin to be reacted to, and ineffectual activity (ineffectual with respect to any usual goals) is maintained. (2) The ineffectual activity leads to physiological changes typical of emotion. (3) The emotions have a strong physiological activating influence. If this mechanism becomes active, some habitual response must have been disrupted. The similarities of Siminov's views to Mandler's on interruption are obvious.

Siminov sees positive emotion similarly. If an organism's needs are satisfied it is emotionally quiescent, but a surplus of information over what is necessary for satisfaction leads to positive emotion. Such positive emotions endure as do negative emotions and may facilitate behaviour.

Siminov suggests that emotions can be classified by taking into account: (1) the strength of the need, (2) the extent of the information deficiency or redundancy, (3) specificity of the action aimed at satisfying the need. He believes that it is only when 'action at a distance' is necessary (ie defence or struggle rather than just pleasure or displeasure brought about by immediate contacts) that emotions proper are seen. He is viewing emotion from a standpoint which involves information theory directly and motivation by implication.

Leventhal

Leventhal's (1974) theory of emotion is based on information processing (but also see the discussion of Leventhal and Scherer under the cognition–emotion relationship elsewhere in this chapter, and Leventhal, 1982, and Leventhal and Tomarken, 1986). He argues that what he describes as this type of model of emotion must integrate four systems: (1) an interpreting system which turns on emotional reactions, (2) an expressive system, feedback from which defines the subjective quality of emotion, (3) an instrumental action system, and (4) a bodily reaction system which maintains the instrumental system. So, Leventhal is simply emphasising what many other emotion theorists have emphasized, that a theory of emotion must deal with how emotion is instigated, and must deal with its subjective, behavioural and physiological aspects. But he does this in information processing terminology.

Leventhal proposes a two-phase model of emotion. In the *perceptual/motor* phase the cognitions that promote emotion and expressive reactions are necessary for feedback to occur; in its turn, this feedback is necessary for subjective feelings. The process must involve the appraisal of meaning, something which is achieved by two types of decoder. The first is automatic and built in and the second sorts out discrepancies from a person's experience.

In this first phase of the model then, Leventhal is arguing for innate perceptual mechanisms which are sensitive to particular features of stimuli, the usual feature analysers of information processing models. These instigate feelings *before* expressive reactions can occur. These feelings are simply positive or negative rather than representing more precise categories of emotion. Later, more specific emotional discriminations occur, and involve feedback from the expressive and autonomic systems. All of this can occur automatically or deliberately, but contributes to subjective feeling only when automatic.

The second component of the model is concerned with *action*. The overactivity involved and any associated autonomic and visceral activity are clearly separated from feeling states. The action system might even detract from feeling—if one is aware of one's actions then one will be less aware, or even unaware, of one's feelings. However, his final point in this quarter is that if action and the feeling state that precedes it are closely associated then the action may enhance the feeling.

In a more recent form of the theory, Leventhal (1986) makes seven assumptions. (1) The study of emotion is best begun with the verbal report of subjective experience. (2) Emotional states are a form of meaning, so if cognition is meaning, emotion is a form of cognition. (3) There are several types of cognitive process. (4) Meanings develop in the perceptual processing system. (5) Emotion can interact with both perceptual and abstract cognition. (6) Meaning systems develop and change. (7) To understand mechanisms underlying emotion and cognition it is necessary to study specific meaning systems.

Following these assumptions, Leventhal outlines a hierarchy of three levels of processing. (1) Expressive motor. (2) Schematic or perceptual memory in which there is a record of emotional situations, experiences and reactions. (3) A conceptual or abstract memory for processing emotional experience and volitional behaviour.

For Leventhal then, above all, emotion is integrated with meaning systems. His perceptual-motor, cognitive theory is compatible with Bower's (1981, see later in this chapter) views of the links between emotion and memory. Both Leventhal and Bower assume that there is an emotion generator with emotion connected to specific cognitions. They also both suggest that emotion is experienced as a reaction to an object and as a reaction within the experience.

Within this framework, emotion acts as a meter of the internal condition and provides a capacity for particular types of action, awareness of which establishes new goals. It informs us of our state and the impact of this on the environment, through telling us about our feelings which are attached to perceptions and thought.

Bower

Bower's network theory of affect is best described in Gilligan and Bower (1984) and best evaluated in Singer and Salovey (1988). It is concerned with only one aspect of emotion, namely mood, and its relationship with cognitive processes.

It rests in a theoretically formal way on seven postulates:

(1) Emotions are centrally placed in a network of meaning, and are connected to everything relevant, from related ideas, autonomic activity, muscular patterns, expressive patterns and events. These units of emotion are *nodes* and are similar to cognitive nodes.
(2) Emotion matters are encoded propositionally with relevant events taking the form of subject–response–object.
(3) Activation of semantic network nodes promotes thought. Activation can spread from a stimulated node through to other associated nodes, be these conceptual, emotional or propositional.
(4) Nodes can be activated by internal or external stimuli.
(5) Activation described in (3) spreads selectively.
(6) Learning brings about new associations between nodes.
(7) When a network of nodes is activated together above threshold the result is consciousness.

Again, continuing the formal exposition of the theory, four hypotheses stem from the postulates.

(1) Recall is state-dependent, ie, memory is better when there is a match between the moods of learning and recall.
(2) There is thought congruity, ie there is a match between people's cognitions and moods, thematically.

(3) Mood congruity is important, ie, learning is better when the emotional tone of what is to be learned matches the person's mood.
(4) Mood intensity is important, ie, intensity of mood and learning show a positive correlation.

Singer and Salovey (1988) mention a number of qualifications to and expansions of these hypotheses. According to the network theory, state-dependent recall is facilitated by the discriminatory cues provided by context, the ideal being a match between learning and recall contexts. More particularly, *emotion* can function as a contextual cue, but is only of importance when contextual cues compete.

Sometimes, a mood will bias a search for memory of related material. This leads mood congruent memories to become more available and leads to recall, or thought, congruency. Further, on occasions when mood assists the learning of new material which happens to be congruent with whatever is already associated with the affect, there is mood, or encoding, congruency. This is accounted for by the idea of elaboration. If information is mood congruent then its connections to various nodes is more elaborate than if it is not congruent. This makes it easier to retrieve.

Increase in mood strength leads to more associated nodes being activated. In turn, this leads to an increase in consciousness of what is mood relevant. Interestingly, this proposed effect differs from positive to negative moods. A positive mood pushes attention away from negative and towards positive material, whereas a negative mood pushes in the direction of memories of failure, fatigue and the like and so gets in the way of dealing with any kind of external stimuli.

This is sufficient description to give an idea of the network theory of affect, dealing specifically as it does with links between mood and memory. For present purposes an evaluation of the evidence about the theory is not pertinent. Since the theory is expressed in terms which are so clearly linked to empirical prediction, it has generated a great deal of research which is well reviewed by Singer and Salovey (1988). They conclude that although there is considerable support for the theory, this support is not straightforward. For example, congruency in encoding has been consistently demonstrated, but it has been shown that the theory works better for happy moods and positive memories than for sad moods and negative memories. The theory may need some elaboration to deal with this, perhaps in the direction of considering motivation.

Oatley and Johnson-Laird

Oatley and Johnson-Laird (eg 1987) put forward a conflict theory in which emotions are seen as serving important cognitive functions. A significant part of their theory rests on the ideas of goals and plans. In this context, goals are symbolic representations of something in the environment that the organism is trying to achieve, and plans transform representations in sequences, so making links between the environment and goals. Their aim is to offer a theory which relates to theories of language and perception that are based on cognitive science.

They also regard emotions as essentially social affairs. Emotions do not only coordinate an *individual's* plans and goals but are also concerned with mutual plans. In putting forward their theory they want to account for subjective experience, bodily and facial changes, resultant courses of actions, diversity, variation, and links with other parts of mental life.

The Oatley and Johnson-Laird theory depends on the human cognitive system being both modular and asynchronous. Within such a system, emotions depend on two types of communication, propositional and non-propositional, the former being symbolic and denotative and the latter being simple and causal. Emotion signals, which are non-propositional set the system into a particular mode and maintain it there—emotion mode. "... The functions of emotion modes are both to enable one priority to be exchanged for another in the system of multiple goals, and to maintain this priority until it is satisfied or abandoned" (1987, p33). Where Bower has nodes, they have modes.

Oatley and Johnson-Laird list five basic, universal, human emotion modes—happiness, sadness, anxiety (or fear), anger and disgust. They argue that each of these emotional modes has an inhibiting influence on the others. They believe that the cognitive system has to be in one emotion mode or oscillating between two for an emotion to occur. Moreover, although an emotion mode is necessary for emotion, it is not sufficient. For adults, at least, a conscious evaluation of planning is also usually involved. This is based on whatever propositional signals arrive at the operating system. This in turn gives a meaning to the emotion mode, the result being the possibility of scheduling voluntary action.

They draw distinctions between emotions and enduring predispositions to emotion (temperaments), temporary predispositions, and instinctual actions.

So, the first prong of Oatley and Johnson-Laird's theory is that emotions co-ordinate a modular nervous system; they have evolved to do this. Their other prong is akin to Mandler's (eg 1976) major point, namely, that emotion occurs when plans are interrupted. They argue that there are distinctive and recurring junctures in plans when their likely success is evaluated. At these points, the emotion modes function to allow transitions to new aspects of planned behaviour. The importance of this is that emotion organizes plans of action to be made in complex and somewhat unpredictable environments. This capacity has developed as a biologically based answer to this type of problem.

The two prongs of the theory—that emotions are concerned with coordinating modular systems and signalling junctures of plans—combine in Oatley and Johnson-Laird's placing of emotions into the social world rather than leaving them in the biological world that determined them. Via a consideration of evolution and individual development, they stress the importance of the development of mutuality. From this perspective, social interaction depends on dealing with mutual plans in which cognitive systems can co-operate. This, they argue, depends on each person having a 'model of the self'.

Oatley and Johnson-Laird argue that the cognitive system has evolved in such a way that the mind is aware of itself. Further, this model has evolved from a mixture of language and culture. Only when this reflexive self is fully developed can the full set of complex human emotions develop as well. This development depends to some extent on the way in which we experience other people's reactions to us, the idea of a social mirror. So adult emotion has as an integral part the generation of self-consciousness when a social plan becomes problematic. Inner debates occur about the ambiguities that are inevitably involved. Everything becomes more complex because many of our plans are mutual and hence dependent on the complexities of language to set them up. They argue that much of this mutual planning is based on promise.

Finally, Oatley and Johnson-Laird turn their attention to complex emotions. Here, there may be a sequence of emotional states with one mode leading to another as various appraisals are made. Also, the start of any complex emotion may be quite undeveloped. Only after considerable reasoning might the fully complex emotion emerge. They believe that the basic emotions develop from universal biological mechanisms and that complex emotions develop from these. However, at this level there is great variation across cultures and persons.

Lazarus

Lazarus (1966, 1968; Lazarus, Averill and Opton, 1970) began his analysis of emotion by stressing the importance of cognitive factors, and more recently (1991), in something of a *tour de force,* produced a fully fledged theory of emotion.

Beginning with the earlier ideas, Lazarus also considers the significance of biological and cultural perspectives. He suggests that although concepts of emotion are important in describing and classifying behaviour, they are not necessarily of use in its explanation. There is an obvious comparison to be made here with the views of Duffy and Leeper. Lazarus argues that the concept of emotion has been hindered in its development, by awkwardnesses of description and classification. He terms emotion a 'response syndrome' because there is no one thing to which it obviously refers. This is a clear medical analogy.

Although Lazarus dwells on biological and cultural aspects of emotion, he finds them lacking. Biologically, he suggests that in attempting to account for emotion, there has been a move away from the periphery to the CNS and within this to the evolutionarily more primitive structures. Like cortical structures, these have undergone evolutionary change, and they also have an important part to play in cognition.

Lazarus also argues that culture can affect emotion in four ways. (1) Through the manner in which we perceive emotional stimuli. (2) By directly altering emotional expression. (3) By determining social relationships and judgements. (4) By highly ritualized behaviour, eg, grief. Rather than deciding whether to stress the biological or the cultural in accounting for emotion, Lazarus suggests that we can resolve the problem by taking an individual, cognitive perspective.

Appraisal is a core concept in Lazarus's view. We are evaluators: we evaluate each stimulus that we encounter with respect to its personal relevance and significance. This is cognitive activity with emotion as part of it. "... each emotional reaction ... is a function of a particular kind of cognition or *appraisal*" (Lazarus et al, 1970, p218, italics theirs).

He recognizes emotion at the three levels of behavioural, physiological or cognitive (subjective), sees each as important and believes that the pattern that might exist between them is a distinguishing feature of emotion.

Coping has also been an important part of Lazarus's views on emotion from the start. He argues that we have dispositions to search for and respond to particular stimuli, such dispositions shaping our interaction with the environment. Cognitive appraisal of these stimuli produces emotional responses. The stimuli constantly change and we continually cope with them; thus both our cognitions and our emotional reactions alter.

Lazarus suggests that there are two sorts of coping process. We may deal with threat or harm by direct action, the urge to which is an important part of emotion. Our success or failure in this fluctuates, which means that our cognitions and emotions also fluctuate. Then there is reappraisal, this being solely cognitive with no direct action involved. We reappraise from positive to negative or negative to positive, realistically or unrealistically. All information is appraised and reappraised and so we have intricate twists and turns in our emotional lives.

In putting forward his theory of emotion in more formal terms, and then explicating it with some style, Lazarus (1991) suggests that the best way to express the theory is via five metatheoretical themes.

(1) It is a *system theory*, suggesting that the process of emotion involves many variables which are organized interdependently into a configuration. The system variables consist of causal antecedents, mediating processes, immediate emotional effects, and long-term effects.

(2) There are two independent principles reflected in emotion. The *process principle* is concerned with change and the *structure principle* refers to stable relationships between person and environment that produce consistent emotional patterns within an individual.

(3) The *developmental principle* implies that emotion alters throughout life, from birth to later years. This is determined by both biological and social variables.

(4) The *specificity principle* points to the emotion process being distinctive for each emotion.

(5) The theory depends most heavily on what Lazarus terms the *relational meaning principle*. This suggests that "each emotion is defined by a unique and specifiable relational meaning" (Lazarus 1991, p39). For each emotion there is a core relational theme which is to do with with the harms and benefits that accrue to each person–environment relationship. The theory rests centrally on the process of *appraisal*, through which the meaning of the person–environment relationships is constructed.

According to the theory, decisions occur through appraisal which allow evaluations to be made of the various emotions. Lazarus believes there to be three primary appraisals, concerned with goal relevance, goal congruency and the type of ego-involvement; in other words they are concerned with motivation . There follow three secondary appraisals concerned with blame or credit, the potential to cope, and future expectations. The particular pattern of primary and secondary appraisals allows distinctions to be made between the various emotions. In its turn, coping feeds back and influences both appraisal and the emotion through its personal significance.

The relationship between the person and the environment promotes both appraisal and coping, a view which leads Lazarus to suggest that a new level of theory—relational meaning—becomes involved. "The task of appraisal is to integrate the two sets of antecedent variables—personality and environmental— into a relational meaning based on the relevance of what is happening for the person's well-being" (1991, p39). So personal interest and adaptation become crucial to emotion.

Lazarus goes further to suggest that if personal harm or benefit is implicated, then the emotion that results will include an innate action tendency. This, in its turn, provides each emotion with its unique physiological aspect. The coping process may be in accord with the action tendency, or may conflict with or even dominate it, but will also influence it and the physiological pattern.

Generally, it is instructive to follow Lazarus's theory of emotion over the 30 years of its development. Rather like the development of a person, it is possible to see the importance of certain core elements (such as appraisal and coping) as unchanging, but in the end they have matured into a substantial and complex theory which is likely to have a lasting influence.

Ellsworth

In an engaging article, Ellsworth (1991) not only summarizes her own theory of emotion, squarely based on appraisal, but also has some interesting points to make about the cognitive approach to emotion in general. The importance of Ellsworth's work is, amongst other things, that she attempts to unpack the appraisal process, to say what is involved in it, what it is made up of. In their original exposition, Smith and Ellsworth (1985) suggest that there are six dimensions of appraisal that distinguish between the emotions. These are: attention, pleasantness, certainty, anticipated effort, human agency and situational control. Ellsworth's (1991) concern however, is not with whether or not these are the correct or final dimensions of appraisal, but rather with the heuristic value and implications of the appraisal approach in general.

An appraisal approach to emotion has at its core the simple view that emotions result from sets of appraisals; we *feel* the result of a combination of appraisals. So, for example, this would suggest that even fundamental facial expressions might come about through elements that correspond to the dimensions of appraisal. She emphasizes the lack of identity in emotional expressions; similarity, yes, but identity, no. The same elements may appear in different emotions and the same emotion may be the result of a different range of elements. From an appraisal viewpoint, the expressions of a particular emotion resemble one another because they result from similar appraisals but differ because the appraisals are always slightly different.

Ellsworth also makes mention of cultural and individual differences. From a cultural viewpoint, appraisals could be the universal aspects of emotion. Moreover, appraisal theories also suggest ways in which any differences in interpretations of events or stimuli, that is differences in appraisal may lead to individual differences in emotional reaction. There may also be differences in appraisal style and individual differences in appraisal may also be affected by other individual differences, in, say, self-concept for example.

A further implication of appraisal theory as Ellsworth sees it is the drawing of attention to possible ways in which *emotion might affect cognition* rather than cognition affecting emotion. As well as appraisals leading to emotions, the emotions in their turn might affect future appraisals. For example, people who are typically angry might well be predisposed to judge situations in ways quite differently from those who are more typically sad.

Ellsworth considers in some detail the sequencing of emotion, and manages to put this in a very clear perspective with respect to the implications of appraisal theory. This bears on the Zajonc–Lazarus debate considered later in this chapter.

Ellsworth distils the three main approaches to the sequencing of emotion as follows:

(1) stimulus – interpretation – affect – behaviour (common-sense)
(2) stimulus – affect – interpretation – behaviour (affective primacy)
(3) stimulus – behaviour – affect – interpretation (motor feedback)

She points out that although in their details, theories are of course more complex than this, they do nevertheless suggest a rather stark view of sequencing. By contrast, appraisal theories, by unpacking the interpretation phase suggest that the sequencing may not be as sequential as has been thought. "As each appraisal is made, the body and the affective experience change. The sequence may be so rapid as to be perceived as instantaneous or it may be considerably more drawn out" (1991, p157). There are many more possible complexities depending on the nature of the appraisals, say from clear to ambiguous or variable. Moreover, very few events are entirely discrete, they alter and develop over time and so therefore do the appraisals. Through all this complexity, Ellsworth's view is that feelings come both first and last. Furthermore, and interestingly, Ellsworth makes the point that if a person cannot make a particular appraisal or type of appraisal through a lack in the cognitive capacity, then the emotions that would result from it cannot be experienced.

In the end, Ellsworth points out that she does not argue that emotion can occur only with appraisal, or that appraisal theories of emotion are necessarily true. But she does say that they have heuristic value and that they prompt ways of looking at emotion and questions to ask about emotion that would not otherwise occur.

Frijda

Although Frijda's theory of emotion will be described in a later chapter, for any consideration of the relationship between emotion and cognition it is important to consider the theoretical views he puts forward on appraisal (1993). He bases his discussion firmly on the view that all emotions involve appraisal, of two possible types. Primary appraisal is concerned with judging the emotional meaning of an event, and secondary appraisal is concerned with evaluating the resulting emotion.

Frijda's strong point is that emotional appraisals can be very elementary, so much so that they can be barely said to be cognitive. They are merely concerned with what Frijda terms information uptake and the monitoring of action. Such elementary appraisals are not only germane to simple emotions but may be relevant to complex ones as well. Frijda sees this as occurring only sometimes; for the most part, most emotions are preceded by complex cognitions. This is very much concerned with whatever is the prior learning by which events have acquired their emotional significance. Frijda views appraisals in emotion to be automatic and therefore non-conscious, although some antecedents of emotion may involve conscious deliberation and reasoning.

"... emotion can be seen to result from an automatic, essentially simple basic appraisal process that may subsequently be cognitively elaborated. The basic process is sufficient for emotion arousal, and for instigating elaboration." (1993, p382)

However, Frijda points out that appraisal and emotion usually occur within a far more complex sequence of cognitions. On the antecedent side, whatever brings about the basic appraisal process itself comes from previous and perhaps long-lived cognitive complexities. On the consequent side, processes of elaboration follow emotion, which in turn might lead to new emotions or modify the previous ones. In short, emotions occur over time, in episodic form rather than starting and finishing rapidly.

Frijda takes this further, by arguing that all these previous cognitions and emotional reactions themselves help to produce a cognitive structure that has its effect on the generation of new appraisals. He sees emotion-relevant stimuli and their meanings as having accumulated over time, as resulting from previous aspects of the interaction, as dependent on context, and so forth. Everything is constantly being modified.

Frijda is putting forward an hypothesis about the appraisal involved in emotion, and attempting a theoretical demonstration of how it may be simultaneously simple and highly complex.

Cognition–emotion relationship

Zajonc and Lazarus

Of considerable import to the cognitive understanding of emotion in recent years is the matter of the nature of the links between cognition and emotion. Although many theorists have enjoined this debate, it is Zajonc and Lazarus who sharpened the issues most dramatically.

The central matter of the Zajonc (1980, 1984) – Lazarus (1982, 1984) debate is whether or not it is reasonable to regard the systems of cognition and emotion as independent. Zajonc argues that not only does cognition *not* precede emotion, but that emotion and cognition are independent, with emotion preceding cognition.

Lazarus argues that Zajonc's view stems from seeing people as computer-like information processors, instead of sources of meaning. He believes that personal factors colour the processing of experiences, and that we do not have to have complete information before reacting emotionally to meaning. For Lazarus there are no exceptions to the cognitive appraisal of meaning underlying all emotional states, even though the appraisal process might be very rapid with thoughts and feelings being almost instantaneous.

Part of the problem in this debate is clearly definitional. Push the idea of emotion far enough and it seems to bang up against cognition. Similarly, if cognitive processes are followed far enough they seem to arrive at emotion. If, finally, either one is defined partly in terms of the other, then which precedes the other becomes a trivial question.

Kiesler (1982) suggests that one of the difficulties in the debate is that the empirical areas involved in emotion and cognition overlap, but not exactly. He argues that there is such a large range of emotional reactions that although the simple ones might be without cognitive content or instigation, the more complex ones must involve them. He argues in support of both sides of the debate, suggesting that the data provided by Zajonc fit with the notion of two partly independent systems, but without ruling out the possibility that there is only one. In the end, Lazarus's view seems to be the more compelling. As seems to be the constant message of almost all relatively recent theories of emotion, it is difficult to conceive of emotion without cognition, even though the two systems might be independent as well as interacting.

Leventhal and Scherer (1987)

Leventhal and Scherer offer a penetrating discussion of the cognition–emotion debate but, interestingly, from the viewpoint of once again expressing their own theory of emotion (see Scherer in Chapter 5 for its most recent exposition). They see the debate as dependent on two major issues—the extent to which whatever generates emotion and cognition are separate, and whether or not emotion can occur before cognition.

Like a number of other researchers, they regard the debate as a matter of definition, particularly of what exactly should be termed cognitive. Can cognition be pre-perceptual for example. Their point is that it does not much matter. There is a similar problem when defining emotion. Should, for example, a simple reflex be regarded as emotional? Leventhal and Scherer prefer to see emotion as far more complex than this, as the result of what they term a multicomponent mechanism.

The terms emotion and cognition refer to complex, behavioural compounds whose make-up changes over the organisms's life-span and these behavioural compounds are the product of a changing multi-component processing system. (1987, p7)

Leventhal and Scherer believe that if emotion is seen as the result of a multi-component processing system then the precise definitions of terms such as cognition and emotion become irrelevant. Other matters become more important, such as how particular processing influences particular emotional experiences or emotional behaviour.

In brief, Leventhal and Scherer's (1987) theory comes from Leventhal's (eg 1984) earlier perceptual-motor model of emotion. The brief description which follows should, however, be read in conjunction with Scherer's (1993) more recent exposition of his component process model summarized in Chapter 5. Leventhal's model proposes that emotions are processed by hierarchically arranged components which work at three levels—sensory-motor, schematic and conceptual, the two higher levels of which allow emotional learning to occur and thus permit complex cognitive–emotional interactions.

They argue that this type of model makes it necessary to reconsider the Zajonc–Lazarus debate. They offer five main arguments for this. (1) The early sensory-motor level of processing allows distinctions to be made both between emotional and nonemotional reactions and between emotional and cognitive behaviour. This is in line with Zajonc's suggestion to separate the two types of process.

(2) Even in the earliest perceptual-motor phase of emotional reactions, there is complex cognitive involvement. Through appraisals, emotion and

cognition seem to be linked in whatever process underlies them, as Lazarus suggests.

(3) Various mismatches between the components of an adult emotion lead to distorted emotional reactions. There may be a mismatch for example between perceptual memory and ongoing experience. This suggests to Leventhal and Scherer that emotion and cognition are independent.

(4) They argue that a schema can be aroused by any of its attributes. A stimulus is likely to activate more or less simultaneously the cognitive, perceptual and emotional aspects of the schema, thus denying Zajonc's suggestion that emotion precedes cognition.

(5) Leventhal and Scherer's model suggests that large changes occur over the individual's life span in emotional expression and experience. These changes alter the meaning of perceptual events. So there is a continual interaction of the cognitive and the emotional throughout life.

Leventhal and Scherer fit their multi-component model and analysis of the cognition–emotion links into Scherer's (eg 1993) component process model of emotion, particularly with respect to the analysis of appraisal. Emphasis is placed on the arousal of specific emotions by the series of stimulus evaluation checks (SECs) that are crucial to Scherer's model. SECs are carried out by mechanisms that scan the perceptual field, the analysis of which gives some insight into the appraisal process that usually precedes emotion.

Scherer (eg 1986) proposes that the organism makes five types of check: for novelty, intrinsic pleasantness, relevance to meeting plans, ability to cope with perceived event, and compatibility of the event with self concept and social norms. He believes that organisms need the information that such checks afford in order to choose how to respond. The process of SEC develops in three ways: the checks are used sequentially, they increase in complexity and differentiation up the evolutionary scale, and they increase in complexity over the individual's life.

Leventhal and Scherer argue for a rapprochement between the processing that occurs in the perceptual-motor model and the SEC process. They describe ways in which the five types of SEC can be made at the sensorimotor, schematic and conceptual levels of the perceptual-motor model. To take just one example of the relevance of this view to the Zajonc–Lazarus debate, Leventhal and Scherer would account for emotional evaluation occurring without conscious stimulus recognition as one form of schematic processing.

They argue that the perceptual-motor model implies that there are two types of confusion in the emotion–cognition debate—the question of response elicitation and timing, and that of how the components in a response system are organized. They feel that what precedes what at the micro level is irrelevant to emotion theory, and also that it will be rare indeed to find human emotions separate from perceptions or cognitions. Cognitions and emotions are simply interwoven. Which comes first is irrelevant if one believes, as Leventhal and Scherer believe, that schemas are aroused, because this implies the simultaneous arousal of cognitions and emotions.

Generally, Leventhal and Scherer believe that looking at the emotion–cognition question within the framework of an emotion theory such as theirs, renders it all more complex than is suggested by the Zajonc–Lazarus debate. It is far more than whether or not emotion and cognition are independent and which precedes the other. Finally, they argue that the major value of this debate has been heuristic, in prompting the development of new theory and research.

Lazarus and Smith

In 1988, Lazarus joins the emotion–cognition question once more in an analysis, with Smith, of the relevance of the distinction between knowledge and appraisal. Clearly, these are both types of cognition, but they are not interchangeable, even though appraisal and attribution (a form of knowledge) are often treated as synonymous.

They make the distinction thus: "In a nutshell, *knowledge,* whether concrete and primitive or abstract and symbolic, consists of cognitions about the way things are and how they work. In contrast, *appraisal,* is a form of personal meaning consisting of evaluations of the significance of this knowledge for well-being" (1988, p282). Obviously, there are many forms of knowledge, not all of them relevant to emotion. Some are however; for example we can only appraise the significance of something if we know about how things work in general and in a particular context. But this type of knowledge in itself does not lead to emotion; appraisal must intervene. Knowledge is necessary but not sufficient for emotion; appraisal is both necessary and sufficient, according to this view.

Lazarus and Smith point out that most of the cognitive dimensions considered by emotion researchers are concerned with causal attributions, or about contextual knowledge. They do not involve appraisals. The exception might be Scherer's SEC, novelty, which according to Lazarus works at a very low level of functioning and is similar to the orienting response. This might enable appraisal to then occur rather than being a dimension of appraisal, as Scherer sees it.

According to Lazarus and Smith, the two major dimensions of primary appraisal are motivational relevance and motivational congruence. Respectively, these refer to (1) how significant the event is for personal goals and concerns and (2) how consistent the event is with personal wants. The cognitive components of secondary appraisal are: accountability, problem-focused coping potential, emotion-focused coping potential and future expectancy.

These dimensions of appraisal cannot by themselves determine everything about personal meaning; in other words, there is more to appraisal than is given by them. Lazarus and Smith suggest that more cognitive constructs are needed to finish the job of determining what is of emotional significance between the person and the environment. They term these *core relational themes,* each of which implies a particular type of harm or benefit which comes from the environment. So, for example, sadness has the theme of loss, and happiness that of secure personal gain.

Generally, from the standpoint taken by Lazarus and Smith, appraisal is quite close to emotion, whereas knowledge is at some distance and has less obvious links. By contrast, they regard the links between appraisal and emotion as invariant. In the end, for Lazarus, emotion is always concerned with personal meaning, and appraisal is crucial to that. Perhaps it is reasonable to think of knowledge as forming a background to this. Again, this distinction between knowledge and appraisal puts more flesh on the bones of the relationship between emotion and cognition.

Parrott and Sabini

Parrott and Sabini (1989) look at the emotion–cognition debate in an applied setting and begin with an analysis of Zajonc's case for the primacy of emotion. They review Zajonc's five ways of affirming that emotion is primary over cognition and find them all wanting. Instead, they argue that cognition is an integral part of emotion. However, they also point that emotion can be influenced by noncognitive factors as well. For example, there may be emotional reactions to simple stimulation, a change in brightness for example. Also there may be changes in the state of arousal for noncognitive reasons, which may in turn influence emotion.

They argue further that emotional phenomena result from many cognitive processes. Sometimes, these processes may be "unconscious, automatic and habitual" even though the resulting emotion might become conscious without the person knowing what led to it. Certainly, some consideration should be given with respect to emotion to the distinction between controlled and automatic cognitive processing.

Parrott and Sabini regard the strength of their approach as lying in its implications for therapy. They provide several examples of the way in which these types of distinction between different manners of cognitive processing are reflected in therapy. For example, cognitive therapy for depression does not consider the person's cognitions as though they were conscious beliefs. Cognitive therapists assume that the person probably does not know what led to the feelings of depression even though the experiences of the depression itself are readily available. The therapists also teach people to attempt to break 'bad' cognitive habits and replace them with others, even though they might be seen as automatic and uncontrolled.

Like Leventhal and Scherer, Parrott and Sabini also believe that their analysis suggests that the question of whether emotion or cognition comes first should be abandoned. They argue for a concentration on fine-grained analyses of what types of cognition lead to what types of emotion. In the end, they are drawing attention to the importance of distinguishing between at least these two types of cognition and the role that they play in emotion. We do not need an independent emotion system, either theoretically, or to account for the various types of cognitive therapy. It is enough to say that cognition plays its important role in producing various properties of emotion.

Conclusions

There is a relatively large number of cognitively based theories of emotion. They range from the quite simple, such as those of Bull, Siminov, and even Schachter, to the highly complex such those of Oatley and Johnson-Laird and Lazarus. Some of them, although expressed in broad terms, deal in particular with the nature of appraisal, Arnold and Ellsworth providing the obvious examples. In the extreme, they have led to a continuing debate about the nature of the relationship between emotion and cognition. It is worth noting that although it has been suggested that the specific debate between Zajonc and Lazarus has run its natural course, perhaps wasting away in the arid desert of definition, the general matter of the relationship between emotion and cognition is still very much alive. And it looks likely to be so for some time.

In evaluating the cognitive theories, the comments that follow will be concerned with the best, and as it happens the most recent, of them. These are the more complex theories to have been put forward during the 1980s and 1990s, paralleling the ascendancy of cognitive psychology.

In general terms, the best of the cognitive theories provide good summaries of some of the empirical foundations of emotion. Not surprisingly, they are rather light on the behavioural and physiological sides, although they have some overlap with the phenomenological. This obvious concentration on the cognitive does of course mean that they are well focused. They give good accounts of emotion; in other words, they genuinely purport to *explain* it. Also, they tend to be most stimulating of thought; they have good heuristic value. However, the extent to which they lead to testable predictions is less obvious. They do, but often the type of investigation that will test the prediction needs to be devized with considerable ingenuity.

Moving onto Lazarus's (1991a,b) prescriptions for good theory in emotion, it is not surprising that his own theory meets these most readily. Perhaps to an extent they derive from it. However, not all of the cognitive theories fare so well. For example many of them have little to say about behaviour and physiology or about how emotions develop, or even about the distinction between emotion and nonemotion. Even more surprisingly, they tend to have little to say about the biological or sociocultural provenance of emotion. It is surprising since it might be expected that they would come down on the sociocultural side.

Although most of the cognitive theories are not concerned directly with emotion considered as an independent or a dependent variable, they do deal with this indirectly. However, they do not particularly consider the causes of emotion, other than to suggest that these might lie somewhere in cognitive processes.

Using Oatley's suggestions for emotion theory as a framework, again it will come as no surprise that it is Oatley and Johnson-Laird's theory that meets these most adequately. Putting this theory to one side, the others score reasonably well on the functions of emotion, on the question of basic emotions, on the unconscious causes of emotion on the extent to which emotions are to do with evaluations (this is almost the sine qua non of the cognitive theories), and on the discrete nature of emotions. It is also relatively easy to put the cognitive theories within the context of science versus folk-psychology.

On the other hand, the cognitive theories are not much concerned in general with the interpersonal communication aspects of emotion, nor with the extent to which emotion simulates the plans of others. Certainly, though, in Oatley's characterisation of the Lakatos approach to theory, the cognitive theories can deal with more evidence about emotion, particularly that which is germane to cognitive matters. In the Popperian sense, certainly specific predictions can be derived from the cognitive theories, but they do not always cover all aspects of emotion. Moreover, some of the cognitive theories, such as those of Schachter and Frijda for example, although they might be stimulating, they are not easy to disprove.

Reviewing the cognitive theories of emotion is a little like skimming a recent text in cognitive psychology—many of the same topics are canvassed, from information processing to network theory, from considerations of goals and plans to speculation about the modular nature of the nervous system. However, there are certain themes that run through most of the theories. In particular, cognitive theories of emotion are concerned with the nature and detailed functioning of the process of appraisal. And of course most of them assume not only that appraisal exists but that it is integral to emotion.

Relatively important to the earlier cognitive theories in particular is the two-factor view that emotion is best seen as an interaction between physiology and cognition. Some of the earlier theories also drew attention to possible links between perception and action in their accounts of emotion. More recent theories, as well as increasing the emphasis on appraisal, also added in discussion of meaning. This is an aspect of human functioning that appears more and more frequently in some of the more recent and rather large scale theories of emotion (see Chapter 7) and in some of the theories that come from related disciplines such as Sociology.

In the concluding sections of the preceding chapters, mention has consistently been made of cognition finding its way into many of the theories, no matter what their starting point or orientation might be. This will also be the case in succeeding chapters. However, in the present chapter the cognitive approach plays an obvious central role. This is in two senses, one which gives a central role to cognition in accounts of emotion and the other that almost sees emotion as a kind of cognition in its own right.

Finally, it is important to comment on which of the rather well-worked theories considered in this chapter might be the best. Schachter's rather early theory has had tremendous heuristic value, but it has also received much criticism and does not hold up well as a theory in other regards. Also starting some years ago, Arnold deserves special mention, her theory in some ways being rather before its time. She has done more than anyone to explore the place of appraisal in emotion, a tradition that has been carried on in most interesting ways by Ellsworth.

Bower has been stimulating in his cognitive accounts of mood, and Frijda and Leventhal have made cogent contributions. However, if one applies any of the 'good theory' criteria strictly, then it is the theories of Oatley and Johnson-Laird and Lazarus that stand tallest. They are the most complete, most thoughtful, and the most far-reaching. It is interesting that it is these theorists who have also paid considerable attention to what makes good theory. Final pride of place for cognitive theory, in my view, should go to Lazarus however. His theory covers so much ground that it should really appear later, in what I have termed the ambitious approach. But it is so squarely concerned with cognition and the appraisal process that it rests most comfortably here.

7

Ambitious theories

Ambitious Theories is not the most auspicious title that has ever been devised for a chapter. However, there is no better word than 'ambitious' to describe the theories that will be discussed below. So far, each of the chapters has been concerned with theories of emotion taken (largely) from a single perspective. There will also be more of that in some of the chapters which follow. However, not surprisingly some theorists have attempted to go further. They have attempted to incorporate a number of perspectives or to consider emotion at a number of different levels. In this sense, they are rather more complete theories than most of those which have been summarized so far.

There are two reasons for including them at this point. In general, they follow on from the more individual approaches already dealt with, and in particular, they follow on readily from some of the more recent cognitive theories. Indeed, one of the cognitive theories is also included in this chapter, although discussed in a rather different way. It simply seemed impossible to exclude it from either chapter. There is nothing more to say in introduction other than the theories that follow are, in their various ways, impressive in what they have been aimed at achieving.

Leeper

Leeper's (1948) original concerns were against the then prevailing view that emotions have a disorganising influence on behaviour. However, he has refined and extended this view more recently (eg 1970).

He suggests that emotions act as motives because they are mildly aroused most of the time, controlling our behaviour without our awareness. In this motivational theory of emotion, he argues that emotions give behaviour (and mental activity) its goal-directedness, allowing us to choose between alternatives for example, or to solve problems, or to endure sanctions in order to gain a reward. Leeper believes that, historically, psychologists were wrong to stress the extremes of emotion, the more noticeable parts. Now, though, he believes that the idea that emotions function much of the time, subtly, as motives, is simply coming into much psychological theorizing.

Leeper (1970) extends his view that emotions function as motives into seeing them also functioning as perceptions. This is Leeper's foray into the cognitive world, since by perception he means that emotions function as conveyers of information. They represent long-standing perceptions of situations. He is suggesting that there is a strong link between motivation and perception. He develops his ideas with the assertion that emotional motives depend on similar mechanisms to the more obviously physiologically based motives. He believes that there are 'emotional mechanisms' which function through signals that indicate the favourability of environmental circumstances; such mechanisms act like reflexes.

Leeper's views, although presented in unsophisticated theoretical terms, nevertheless are of significance. They have sprung from an attempt to dispel the view that emotion is disorganising, chaotic and interfering. He regards emotion as an active force, involving motivation and perception, which organizes, sustains and directs behaviour.

The importance of Leeper's views come from his bold assertions about their implications. He argues that humans have passed through two great ages, of physical survival and of scientific, technological and educational advance. Both of these ages, but particularly the latter have emphasized objectivity, with the individual taking a back seat. Emotions have often been seen as obstructing this 'ideal' way of progressing or living.

Leeper is drawing on the old distinction between thinking and emotion, or between being rational and being emotional. One outcome of this is a concentration (in the world at large, and by psychologists) on negative emotions such as shame and guilt, the only attention that is paid to the positive side being quite crude. He sees a possible way out of this as depending on the development of a third age in which attention is given to the fact, for he argues that it is a fact, that people experience situations emotionally. His aim is to have society concentrate on emotional subtleties, particularly on the positive side, and perhaps to start to educate people in better ways to develop their emotional lives.

Leeper's contribution, then, is important in suggesting that emotion exists as a driving force in our lives. Rather than seeing it as something which acts as a hindrance to existence, we should use and develop it.

Tomkins

Tomkins' (1962, 1963) theory of what he prefers to call affect is both ingenious and idiosyncratic. It provided some of the impetus for Izard's theorizing, but other than this does not relate all that obviously to other theories. However, it is interesting enough to merit brief discussion, particularly as it rests on strong links between emotion and motivation.

Tomkins argues that the affect system is innately determined and as a primary system interacts with the secondary or learned drive system. It gives urgency to drive. He also characterizes affect as changeable and insatiable, without constraints in time or intensity. Tomkins regards affects as being mainly reflected in facial responses, feedback from which can be rewarding or punishing, but only if it is self-conscious. Innate patterns of facial response are triggered by subcortical CNS mechanisms. He does not wish to deny that emotion is also reflected in bodily responses, but simply to affirm the greater significance of facial responses.

Tomkins believes, as do a number of the other more broadly based emotion theorists, that there are a number of basic (innate) primary affects. These are: interest/excitement, enjoyment/joy, surprise/startle, distress/anguish, disgust/contempt, anger/rage, shame/humiliation, and fear/terror. He believes that which of these primary emotions is instigated depends on the rate of neural firing in the CNS, such rate changes actually promoting emotion as well as being either rewarding or punishing.

Clearly, Tomkins' theory of affect is very widely based and draws on a number of areas of psychological discourse. He ranges from a conceptual analysis of motivation through possible physiological mechanisms to innate factors. Although it is an interesting theory and certainly forms an important background to Izard's theory, it is highly speculative and does not relate particularly well to other theories.

Pribram

Pribram's view of emotion based on *Plans* overlaps with many others. He begins neurophysiologically, continues via appraisal and motivation, and ends in the area of cognition and information processing.

Originally, Pribram (1970; Miller, Galanter and Pribram, 1960) regarded emotion as Plans, these being "... neural programs which are engaged when the organism is disequilibriated". He states that, normally, motivationally based Plans change because they are carried out, but should their execution be blocked, then emotion results. This emotion might open or close the organism to more input, but either way the Plan is stopped. If the Plan is held up for some time, then regression occurs

In these earlier views, Pribram goes on to argue that emotional expression is more primitive and basic than rational behaviour, even though emotions do not *have* to be expressed. There are emotional Plans as well as motivational Plans, both of which can be altered by experience.

In 1970, Pribram changes his views a little, arguing that the idea of emotions as Plans brought too many problems with it. Instead, he begins to speculate about feelings rather than emotions. He distinguishes between what he terms the objective world of sense data and the subjective world of feelings. He goes on to propose that where we have no evidence which allows us to construct the objective world, then we must rely on the subjective. So, if we have no good evidence that we are faced with something that we can see, hear, smell, taste or touch, then we must be feeling it inside. Pribram describes such feelings as 'Feelings as Monitors', a notion which he believes to have a physiological base and which he also believes to be more useful than his original idea of Plans.

From Pribram's perspective, we do not plan to be happy or sad, we simply feel happy or sad. We also construct Plans and implement them. This may be well done and successful, or poorly done and fail. We appraise the success of our Plans and monitor this appraisal; in other words we feel it. So, continuing Pribram's penchant for capitalization, Feelings as Monitors are regarded as Images not Plans. Plans are merely constructed within the matrix that Images provide. Furthermore, Pribram suggests that there are two sorts of Plan—'go' Plans equal motivations and 'no-go' Plans equal emotions, a suggestion which, it must be said, does not make Pribram's ideas any easier to understand.

To summarize, Pribram's suggestion is that emotions should be distinguished from feelings, with feelings being the better processes on which to concentrate. Feelings are Monitors and Images are appraisals of the degree of success attached to the execution of Plans. If the Plans allow the organism to go ahead, they are motivational. If they are blocked and the organism is thwarted, the result is emotion.

Izard

Izard has made an enormous contribution to our understanding of emotion throughout his career. What follows is a summary of his *Differential Emotions Theory* as it is elegantly expressed in three books (1972, 1977, 1991), as well as a long series of articles.

The theory has broad aims. (1) To account for the great complexity of emotion. (2) To deal with all aspects of emotion, ie, neural activity, glandular, visceral and psychophysiological responses, subjective experience, expressive behaviour and instrumental responses. (3) To provide a framework within which to look at innate and learned aspects of emotion and patterns of emotional–cognitive–motor responses. (4) To accord with a general theory of behaviour.

As its name suggests, differential emotions theory derives from a perspective that there are discrete emotions that function as distinct experiences, which also happen to have motivational characteristics. It rests on five assumptions. (1) There are ten fundamental emotions; these provide the human motivational system. (2) Each of these emotions is unique organizationally, motivationally and experientially. (3) The fundamental emotions lead to distinct inner experiences which have particular effects on both cognition and action. (4) The processes of emotion interact with homeostasis, drive, perception and cognition. (5) Homeostasis, drive, perception and cognition also have influences on emotion.

Izard views emotion as a motivational system, a process of personality which gives meaning to human existence and which determines behaviours that may range from rape to human sacrifice. It is one of six interrelated subsystems of personality, the others being the systems of homeostasis, drive, perception, cognition and motor behaviour. And the ten fundamental emotions, which provide us with our main motivational system, are: interest, enjoyment, surprise, sadness, anger, disgust, contempt, fear, shame and shyness. Although these emotions are fundamental and discrete, they interact, and although Izard believes them to be discrete in neurochemistry, behaviour and subjective experience, in particular they are discrete in the feedback that comes from their facial and bodily expression.

In Izard's view, the emotional elements of personality themselves form an interrelated system, which through innate influences may be organized hierarchically. There are regular relationships between some emotions, extending as far as polarities between some. These complex relationships combine, the result being similar to traits or personality patterns. Moreover, *all* emotions have elements in common. They are non-cyclical, have unlimited generality and flexibility as motivators, and influence drives and other personality subsystems.

Izard defines emotion "... as a complex process with neural, neuromuscular/ expressive, and experiential aspects" (1991, p42). So the meaning of emotion comes from an interplay between neurophysiological activity, facial-postural activity and subjective experience. However, there are two auxiliary systems which are also important to emotion: the reticular arousal system which amplifies and attenuates emotion, and the visceral system which helps both to prepare the ground for emotion and to sustain it.

The general emotion system tends to function in an integrated way with the cognitive and motor systems, personality depending on the balance between the three.

Izard gives discrete significance to three sets of processes as causes of emotion—neurotransmitters and brain mechanisms, sensory-perceptual processes, and thought processes. He lists four types of cause within each of these types of process. Neural and neuromuscular activators include: hormones and neurotransmitters, drugs, expressive behaviour and changes in cerebral blood temperature. Affective (sensory-perceptual) activators include: pain, sex, fatigue and another emotion. Cognitive activators include: appraisal, attribution, memory and anticipation. Izard emphasizes the importance of there being both cognitive and *non-cognitive* activators of emotion, as he sees it.

Once emotion has been instigated, its further phases depend on the site and nature of the original activity. Izard sees no fixed number or order to these phases. He believes that many possible mechanisms and interactions are involved, from perception, through neurophysiological reaction to subjective experience, and emotion–cognition–motor interaction.

Furthermore, Izard suggests that for any emotion there are three levels. (1) Electrochemical or neural activity which for fundamental emotions is innate. (2) Efferent aspects of emotional activity innervate the striate muscles involved in facial-postural patterning, patterning which normally gives cues and information to the individual and to the observer. (3) For cues to be useful there must also be feedback to the association areas of the brain, although an awareness of this process is not inevitable; it can be interfered with in many ways. However, if it is normal, then it generates the subjective experience of emotion, an experience which is itself independent of cognition. Unlike many other current theorists, Izard believes that the emotion process can operate independently of any cognitive process, even though there is usually constant interaction between them. For Izard, cognition is *not* a necessary part of emotion, even though it is very important to it.

Izard discusses as some length the difference between theorists such as himself who believe that there are certain basic emotions and those who do not. He characterizes the latter as usually not distinguishing between emotion/feeling and perception/cognition and as believing that we construct emotions socially and culturally.

By contrast, he lists five criteria that some theorists have used to sort out the so-called fundamental emotions. (1) They have distinct neural substrates. (2) They have distinct facial movements and expression. (3) They have distinct feelings that promote awareness. (4) They come about through evolution. (5) They have adaptive organising and motivational properties. He considers the ten emotions listed previously to meet most of these criteria.

Izard's differential emotions theory is well worked and far-reaching, with enormous heuristic value. It has even led to the production of other, more specific theories of emotion, emotional development for example. (See Chapter 9). The theory has numerous implications which it is instructive to read in Izard's original words. However, it would also be helpful to mention a few of these now. Each level of emotion has particular functions which should be taken into account. If feedback is distorted then so will be awareness. A given emotion is a subsystem of the whole system and so has the same qualities as the whole. The emotional system has changed with evolution and also changes within individual development. Emotion is continually present in consciousness. Once an emotion is activated, the life systems are involved and we eventually become aware of the facial expressions *as* the subjective experience of emotion. Autonomic or visceral arousal can occur without emotion. Emotion can be initiated although facial expression is inhibited and there can be facial expression without emotional experience reaching consciousness. As is obvious from this brief list, Izard's theory of emotion has interesting implications. It is a far-reaching theory with a fine provenance, and it rather stands out from those (many) theories which give cognition a necessary role to play in emotion.

In an erudite extension to the theory, Izard (1993) puts forward an argument that because emotions are clearly significant in evolution and adaptation, there must be more than one way for them to be generated. However, as he rightly points out, and as this book demonstrates, much recent theory has been concerned with the role of cognitive processes, particularly appraisal, in the generation of emotion.

As an alternative, Izard describes four types of information processing, all of which can activate emotion, but only one of which is cognitive.

(1) *Cellular* information processing occurs in enzymes and genes and is clearly not linked to sensory input or to cognitive processes that derive from sensory input. The information that comes from this root is based on natural selection and helps to determine both emotional thresholds and the organism's likelihood of experiencing particular emotions. Izard regards this type of background as an important determinant of mood and individual differences.

(2) *Organismic* information processing is also biologically based and hence genetically coded. It can involve sense data from interoceptors and is based on physiological drives. An example of emotion being activated in this way is the anger that can come from pain.

(3) *Biopsychological* information processing depends on links between biological and learned (cognitive) information processing. This may be referring to interaction between unconscious and conscious information, and certainly between genetically coded material and that which comes from cognitive processes. In Izard's view, this depends very much on the biological information.

(4) *Cognitive* information processing is concerned with the acquired or learned side of matters. For Izard, as his emotion theory makes clear, cognition starts where learning and experience generate mental representations that allow comparisons and discriminations to be made. At this point, according to this view, cognition can begin to play its role in activating emotion.

As well as elucidating evidence for these four types of emotion activating processes, Izard argues that they operate continuously not only to activate emotion but also to maintain background emotionality that is pertinent to personality. Izard's core argument appears consistently throughout his work. It is that although cognition and emotion interact, they are also distinct, and the study of emotion will not progress at its optimum if it is swamped by or subsumed under the study of cognition.

Averill

Averill's (1982) views on emotion will also be dealt with in Chapter 8, in which theories concerning specific emotions are considered. He has developed his theories in unusual ways, not the least of which is via an extended analysis of anger. Moreover, since he takes very much of a social constructionist approach, mention will also be made of his ideas in the final chapter.

Averill regards emotions as social syndromes or transitory rules, as well as short-term dispositions to respond in particular ways and to interpret such responses as emotional. He distinguishes between conflictive emotions, impulsive emotions (inclinations and aversions) and transcendental emotions, which involve a breakdown in the boundaries of the ego.

From his perspective, some emotions can have all three of these characteristics, but complex behaviour usually involves conflicts. Such conflicts lead to emotions that are compromises but which nevertheless help to resolve the conflict. For example, at the biological level, aggression is linked to anger but is not equated with it. Averill believes that there is a biologically based tendency in humans to formulate rules and follow them. Similarly, there is tendency to become angry and upset when the rules are broken. All of which means, that from Averill's viewpoint, emotions are highly symbolic, and although biologically based depend very much on appraisals. To continue with the example of anger, at the psychological level it is to do with the correction of a perceived wrong. Any emotion has its object, part of which is instigation, the other parts being a target and an aim. In the case of anger, the instigation is an appraised wrong.

Any emotion is concerned with the upholding of accepted standards of conduct, even though this might be achieved unwittingly. These are rules which guide behaviour, some of them being to do with appraisal. Other rules relevant to emotion concern its expression, its course, its outcome, and the way in which it might be causally attributed. For example, a fairly self-evident rule of anger in our society is that it should be spontaneous rather than deliberate.

From a broad perspective, Averill argues that any theory of emotion should be unrestricted and should relate to all of the relevant phenomena, however complex, as long as they are part of emotion in everyday language. So, for Averill, emotion is both a phenomenon of everyday life and should be studied as such, and is also particularly human. The aim is to attempt to uncover what Averill terms the prototypic attributes of various emotions and to determine the rules that guide them. Averill views emotion as a social construction based on a mixture of biologically determined aspects and a number of levels of cognition, from perception through appraisal to symbolic rules and standards. On the one hand his views bear close comparison with those of a neurophysiologist such as Panksepp, and on the other with those of a social constructionist such as Harré.

Mandler

In a series of well argued books and papers, Mandler (1976, 1984, 1990, 1992) puts forward his constructivist system of emotion. He regards emotion as resting on arousal, cognitive interpretation and consciousness. Undifferentiated arousal is the perception of activity in the SNS, conditions for its presence depending on cognitive interpretation, particularly with respect to interruption and blocking. It functions to maintain homeostasis and allows the seeking of information.

Mandler sees cognitive interpretations as involving structures which promote innate reactions to events, and also evaluations of perceptions of the self. He argues that expressive movements lead to automatic cognitive reactions which are altered by reinterpretation. An interaction between arousal and cognitive interpretation (appraisal) leads to the experience of emotion and emotional behaviour. Arousal gives emotion its visceral quality and its intensity, whereas cognitive interpretation provides a category for the experience. Importantly, Mandler also argues that emotional experience occurs in consciousness, outputs from which are coded into conventional language. Links between emotion and consciousness will be returned to later.

The general thesis which Mandler offers is that ANS arousal necessarily sets the stage for emotional behaviour and experience and allows for its intensity. The quality of the emotion then comes from the meaning analysis which is engendered by the arousal, the general situation and the cognitive state. Thereafter there are outputs to consciousness and to action.

Mandler· suggests that arousal comes about in two ways: by a preprogrammed release from the ANS and following a mediation by meaning analysis which makes mental stimuli into ANS releasers. He is speaking of a continuum which runs from innate to experiential factors. A perceived input from arousal leads to automatic meaning analysis, which in turn generates a search for structures that can assimilate the input, and its analysis, and the perception of arousal. A successful search leads to the structure being placed into consciousness.

The complex general process which Mandler describes involves continuous feedback. Environmental stimuli lead to cognitive interpretations which lead to perception of arousal which leads to emotional experience which leads to perception and evaluation of the experience, which changes the original cognitive interpretation. And so it goes on.

Central to Mandler's analysis of emotion is *meaning*. He argues that the complexity of inputs in emotion makes emotion very rich, the meaning of this richness being given by the structure of the input and its relation to other inputs and existing mental structures. Meaning analysis tells us where we are and what our surroundings are. If there are discrepancies between available evidence and expectations from existing schemata, the result leads to arousal and some emotional synthesis. Some meaning analyses are automatic and others require deliberate evaluation.

In meaning analysis, Mandler makes two interpretations of the interaction between cognition and arousal. In the *passive* view emotion comes from the total relational network from the two sets of structures. For example, an interaction between the perception of autonomic arousal and the evaluation of a situation as positive and joyful gives the feeling of joy. In the *active* view, which Mandler believes to be more appropriate, the inputs from either system are fed into existing structures based on past experiences and innate factors. Both systems may operate and the same set of events may act as arousal releasers and have to be cognitively evaluated.

In more detail, Mandler suggests that structures give analyses of inputs and initial identification of emotion. These are stored, then meaning analysis provides further interpretation and this is followed by the production of arousal, which, with cognitive appraisal of the situation, leads to a specific emotional reaction. He suggests further that a hierarchy of meaning nodes could give various effects, from repression to almost any emotional experience, all of which depends on past experience. So, whether or not an input leads to emotional experience depends on whether or not an arousal switch is triggered, which in turn depends on a particular meaning analysis of the input.

In much of his writings, Mandler emphasizes the importance of consciousness; he also gives it a prominent role in emotion. He suggests that some emotions may *only* be experienced in consciousness and also that many of the determining functions of emotion may occur in consciousness. He argues, as might be expected from the foregoing, that emotional consciousness develops from basic processes which involve both arousal and cognition.

Mandler emphasizes consciousness for a number of reasons, not least of which is that arousal and consciousness seem to arise from similar mental conditions—the need to select and alter the current stream of action. Emotional states push for priority and occur at significant choice points in our lives and intentions. Mandler goes so far as to describe these as guideposts of human existence. It is not surprising then that they depend on consciousness.

Generally, then, Mandler has what he rightly terms a constructivist view of both emotion and consciousness. "Holistic conscious events are constructed out of activated underlying representation, and represent the best 'sense' that can be made out of currently important concerns" (1992, p103).

Mandler assumes a modest position for his theory, which he terms a discrepancy/evaluation theory, averring that it is only pertinent to some aspects of emotional experience. In summary, and similarly to a number of other theories, Mandler's suggests that emotion is dependent on the underlying processes of ANS arousal and evaluative cognitions. Moreover, it is discrepancies in perception, action and thought which occasion SNS arousal. Interestingly, Mandler maintains a distinction between body (arousal) and mind (evaluation of things social) in emotion. And, quite simply, he assumes that the subjective states of emotion have motivating properties, leading to approach and avoidance.

In 1992, Mandler points out that he does not consider interruptions or discrepancies to be emotions, but rather that these *neutral* events set the scene for emotion to occur. He also points out that interruptions/discrepancies are but one route to emotion, albeit an important one, others coming for example from effort and exercise.

Generally, Mandler's theory of emotion is based on evolutionary considerations, viewing the detection of discrepancies or differences as of fundamental importance to survival. The detection of difference is what in Mandler's view gives emotion its intensity. In addition, evaluative cognitions give emotion its qualitative aspects. He sees these evaluations as biologically based, as are all cognitions, and yet as socially constructed. Mandler argues that this way of looking at emotions sidesteps the matter of whether or not there are basic emotions from which others are derived. In other words, Mandler's is to a considerable extent a constructivist or social constructionist theory of emotion, and as such has much in common with theories that will be discussed in chapters 13 and 14.

Buck

Buck (eg 1985, 1988, 1991) puts forward what he terms a developmental-interactionist theory of emotion in which his aim is to find a place for motivation and cognition. He sees his theory as being grounded in the traditional Schachter and Singer type of interactional theory, but notes four major differences. He believes: (1) Evolution has provided us with innate knowledge systems; (2) That the 'cognitive factors' of other theories should be replaced with processing systems of associative and instrumental learning which change with individual experience; (3) That emphasis should be placed on individual development in attempting to understand the relationship between general and specific processing systems; and (4) That there is a third system of behaviour control—linguistic competence.

Primes are the name given by Buck to a hierarchically arranged set of motivational/emotional systems. In obvious order these are: reflexes, instincts, primary drives, acquired drives, primary affects, effectance motivation, and linguistically based motives and emotions. As the hierarchy is ascended so the newer brain structures and learning become more important.

For present purposes, the primary affects are of most significance, although in Buck's theory they simply form one element. They include happiness, sadness, fear, anger, surprise and disgust, a list which places Buck amongst those who believe that primary emotions exist. He states that "The capacity to experience and express the affects is innate and unlearned, but the circumstances under which they are experienced, and the ways in which they are expressed, are learned" (1991, p103). He associates the affects with the limbic system in the CNS and suggests that they promote general response tendencies rather than specific behaviours.

Although primary affects have an obvious relevance to emotion, and might indeed be termed primary emotions by other theorists, Buck argues that *all* of the primes have motivational, emotional and cognitive aspects. Buck defines motivation as the behaviour potential which is built into a behaviour control system, and emotion as what he terms the 'readout' of motivational potential when prompted by a challenging stimulus. If motivation is biological then it is built into biological primes, with biological emotion taking one of three forms, or one of three types of readout. Emotion 1 is adaptation homeostasis, emotion 2 is social expression and emotion 3 is subjective experience. In general, emotion is motivation's manifestation, and all of what Buck refers to as the classic primary affects have all three types of readout.

Moreover, in general the readouts of the primes interact with general-purpose processing systems which are to do with conditioning and learning. These are structured into experience.

Moving on to cognition, Buck defines this within his theory as 'knowledge' rather than 'knowledge about' something. As such he believes that it subsumes subjective experience, as a kind of knowledge. In other terms these are knowledge-by-acquaintance (direct sensory awareness) and knowledge-by-description (knowledge *about* sense data).

Buck believes that this distinction is important for a consideration of the emotion–cognition, Zajonc–Lazarus debate (see Chapter 6). He characterizes the debate as pivoting on what is viewed as being cognition, in that those on both sides regard some form of sensory information as necessary for emotion to occur. He sees Lazarus as defining cognition as knowledge-by-acquaintance and Zajonc as knowledge-by-description. He argues that developmental-interactionist theory suggests that knowledge-by-acquaintance is in and of itself an affective process, which leads on to and in fact determines, knowledge-by-description. Buck defines the process which accomplishes this transformation as *appraisal*.

Buck's analysis of appraisal rests on the direct perception ideas of Gibson (eg 1979) and a consideration of brain physiology. He argues that appraisals are the result of attention being educated to be more concerned with some aspects of the environment than others because of the affordances they provide. This rapidly occurring concern with picking out the value of an event or stimulus for the organism's well-being, Buck refers to as a *filter*, in his characteristic way of using slightly different terms than other theorists of emotion. He regards these filters as the earliest stage in the organism's picking up of events, ie they occur at subcortical and paleocortical levels.

Without going into the possible CNS mechanisms, Buck's emotional filter system can be summarized as follows. Initial filters exist at subcortical and paleocortical levels and determine what goes into the appraisal process. In its turn, the appraisal is an integration of this initial information (knowledge-by-acquaintance) with any relevant motivations/emotions and memories, leading into knowledge-by-description .

So Buck's analysis of appraisal follows very much from Gibson's ecological theory of perception in which the perceptual system has evolved to pick up affordances from the environment because they are critical for survival. Buck goes further by suggesting that the perceptual systems have also evolved to pick up events in the internal body environment—this is information, and provides the basis for subjective feelings and desires. He includes in this pain and temperature, hunger, thirst and sexual arousal, and all of the primary affects.

Although subjective experience, characterized in this way, is always with us, Buck argues that we often filter it out. For example, sexual arousal or feeling in a depressed mood might be in evidence frequently, but we filter them out in favour of ongoing work. Buck regards these subjective states as always functioning, perhaps weakly, whether or not we are aware of them. By the same token, it is possible to dredge up the feeling of these emotional states, just as we are able to conjure up the feel of sitting in our car, say. Of course, the states tend to strengthen when we become conscious of them.

Interestingly, Buck also has something to say about what he terms emotional education. Although his might be called a 'direct perception' theory of emotion, ie, the brain 'knows' directly the experience of motivational/ emotional states, we also learn things about these states. This is emotional education, which begins in childhood and involves learning to attend to some things in the internal environment rather than others, then to understand the events and finally to respond to them. The result of this in general is the individual's level of emotional competence. Again, this is akin, in Buck's view, to perceptual learning (after Gibson).

The second major facet of Buck's theory is *communication*, much of which is concerned with empirical studies which there is no space to discuss presently. However, theoretically, he distinguishes between spontaneous and symbolic communication. He defines communication in general as what occurs when one organism's behaviour influences another's. Within this, spontaneous communication is biologically (innately) based, has external signs, is not intentional (although it can be inhibited intentionally), and has a non-propositional content (ie it cannot be false). Above all, spontaneous motivational/emotional communication has evolved because it is adaptive.

By contrast, symbolic communication is learned, is dependent on culture, is based on arbitrary symbols, and is intentional and propositional. Buck is saying that there are two forms of motivational/emotional communication which proceed together, one biological and non-voluntary, the other intentional and learned. Although they often, if not usually, occur together, spontaneous communication can happen without symbolic communication, but symbolic cannot occur without spontaneous.

Buck argues within the terms of his theory that spontaneous communication rests on the special-purpose systems, although of course, there is an interaction with the general-purpose systems. Spontaneous communication might have evolved to transmit adaptively important messages, but in humans there is the possibility of learning and the influence of language. Moreover, there is a difference in accessibility between subjective experiences and expressive behaviours, the former not being available to another person. Learning about these internal events is at the core of emotional education for the child.

Buck goes on to draw attention to social biofeedback in the process of emotional education, suggesting that we come to understand our feelings partly by the effect that their expression has on other people. Of course, we learn to control our facial and bodily expressions in this way, but also our own feelings and desires, and it is via spontaneous communication. Through a constant process of this type of feedback so the individual learns to respond differently in social contexts; this may be more or less effectively. This process is made richer and more complex in humans by their use of language.

Emotional competence is defined by Buck as "... the ability to deal with the internal environment of one's feelings and desires." It interacts with social competence in obvious ways. To some extent emotional and social competences are concerned with specific relationships. Furthermore, a change in the social environment provides a difficulty for emotional education. Think of what happens for example during adolescence or if a significant relationship ends.

According to developmental-interactionist theory, coping is a further stage in the process of emotional education. This is reasoning about emotion. If the body changes (as in illness, say) or the social environment changes then coping is an effort to restore social and emotional competence to its previous level. Buck suggests that the three sources of rules which are used in bringing about competences of these sorts are the body, the self, and the external environment. The learning of these rules in childhood also leads to the development of the self-image.

One of Buck's final and most interesting points concerns the problem of other minds. How can we ever know what another person is experiencing? He argues that since spontaneous communication is direct, that is, it is biologically based, it gives a way in which the receiver has direct information about the motivational/emotional state of the sender. Others are simply constructed to send such information and we are simply constructed to receive it. We know its meaning directly, through phylogeny and inheritance.

Buck's developmental-interactionist theory of emotion then reaches far beyond emotion, being also a theory of motivation, to some extent of cognition, and also being describable as a systems theory. It is a two-factor theory which emphasises both the physiological and the cognitive, as a good two-factor theory of emotion should. But it fits emotion into a context of the innate and the learned ranging from simple reflexes through to the sophistication of human language. It has a specific place for two types of communication, spontaneous and symbolic, and extends to consideration of emotional coping and emotional education. Buck finishes his 1991 paper disarmingly: "Everything that is real is emotional; the rational is our subsequently linguistically structured elaboration of that reality" (1991, p136).

Frijda

In recent years, Frijda has written an enormous amount on emotion and has contributed a substantial theory (eg 1986, 1988, 1991, 1992; see also Averill, 1988 for comment). From the outset, it should be said that this is not an easy theory to grasp. It is thoroughly researched, has vast ramifications, and has been constructed in such a way that it has so much flesh that its bones are difficult to discern. However, it repays the effort.

Averill (1988) puts the background to the theory with his usual pithy succinctness. He states that Frijda's theory of emotion rests on three principles—there is a biological basis, this is modified by things social and cognitive, and regulation is an integral aspect of emotion.

Frijda begins by describing what he terms the emotion process which contains a core running from stimulus to response, a regulation line (processes intervening in the core), and a line of other inputs. At the end of course, there are outputs.

The core consists of seven phases. (1) The *analyser* codes the event, which comes from outside or inside. (2) The *comparator* appraises the event, leading to pleasure, pain, wonder, desire, or irrelevance. (3) The *diagnoser* appraises the event in terms of what can be done about it. (4) The *evaluator* determines urgency, difficulty and seriousness and produces a signal for control. (5) The *action proposer* produces a plan of action. (6) The *physiological change generator* generates physiological change. (7) The *actor* determines action.

These phases are all sometimes influenced by or regulated by mechanisms, outcome-control processes or by voluntary self-control. The nature of the stimulus events that initiate the core process is also relevant, as are various cognitive dispositional inputs. Frijda goes into some detail about how the various phases of the core emotion process work, and also points out that matters like mood, state of arousal, previous experiences, other people, social definitions and the like, all have an influence. He sees these as the side processes of emotion, which operate by 'situational meaning structure'.

The emotion process, according to Frijda, does not occur in isolation. There is a continuous monitoring of the environment and a continuous tendency to action and changes in physiological arousal. Moreover, the events of emotion take place over time, a point which applies to each of the subprocesses. Everything is constantly changing as the situational meaning structure is revised, and reviews are made of the future, the possibilities of coping, of how controllable the events are, and so on. There is a constant feedback mechanism in play. All of this requires some sort of central monitoring, a structure which can integrate and constantly update all the information which is flowing in. This is accounted for by Frijda's situational meaning structure.

The final point which follows from the emotion process not occurring in isolation is that it relates to other processes. Mainly, it does this by blocking action control for other goals or other stimuli or it does so by enhancing or energizing action.

Unlike many other emotion theorists, Frijda does not see an easy link between emotion and motivation, largely because he sees motivation referring to several different things at once, including emotion since, hunger, say, suggests feeling and action readiness amongst other things. Instead, Frijda contrasts emotion with *desires plus enjoyment*. He views emotion as concerned with keeping an eye on whether or not events will allow satisfaction and via changes in action readiness it facilitates, impedes, or generally regulates action belonging to other goals or programmes.

The contrast is with desires which Frijda regards as promoting new courses of action and establishing goals. Certainly, they are to do with satisfaction, but more the recognition of objects that are appropriate for satisfaction. And the action readiness of desire does not impinge on other programmes, only its own. Then, enjoyments result from the realization that the objects of desire are within reach.

Frijda also points out that the process although described in a linear fashion does not always ensue in that way. From time to time parts of it may precede in different orders, sometimes it may stop short of the entire process, and sometimes the 'emotional' aspect of the emotion process disappears altogether when any urgency and seriousness go. What Frijda refers to as foresight, rationality and habit can preclude emotion, leading instead to cool, instrumental, goal-directed action. He points out that emotion and goal-directed action have much in common, being concerned with satisfaction for example. The difference between them hinges on the appraisal process (for Frijda is yet another appraisal theorist, albeit of a different order from many) and in the 'control precedence signals' and resulting processes.

Frijda goes into some detail as to how emotional experience fits within his scheme of the emotion process. He characterizes it as outputs from various phases of the process that come into awareness, plus pleasure or pain. There is also an awareness of the control process. However, as well as being an output, emotional experience is essential to the emotion process.

The awareness that Frijda speaks of in the context of emotional experience is partly awareness of being aware, but not solely this. He suggests that when it is simply a matter of awareness or knowing something, or as he calls it, irreflexive awareness, then a better term than experience might be unconscious. For example, the appraisal process that generates situational meaning structure goes on unconsciously. So to the extent that emotional experience is in this form, it may be said to be an unconscious process. "One knows, generally, that one has an emotion; one does not always know why, and what exactly makes one have it; and if one does know, it is a construction, a hypothesis, like those one makes about the emotions of someone else" (1986, p464).

In the context of emotional experience, Frijda naturally speaks of feelings. These are an awareness of the situational meaning structure and of any changes in action readiness. Like Pribram, he sees feelings as monitors, as bringing about analysis and evaluation and planning and regulation. In the end, then, awareness of ones feelings feeds back into the situational meaning structure and so has its influence on the ongoing emotion process.

Frijda's theory

The foregoing is by way of preamble to Frijda's theory of emotion proper. In a more formal sense, there are eight areas that he considers of significance in producing the theory.

(1) Frijda defines emotions as *changes in readiness for action*, which can take the form of changes in activation, in cognitive readiness, in action tendencies, and in desires and enjoyments.

(2) Underlying emotions are what Frijda calls *concerns*. At the human level are surface concerns about things such as other people, particular environments, and particular goals. But these follow from a biological basis that endows us in particular ways that set us with behaviour systems. Moreover, emotions are interrelated with all of our major functions and the way in which

we perform them. Some concerns are linked in fact to the general mode of functioning of the individual. And all of this is to some extent dependent on the individual's level of activation which is variable and in itself is one source of emotions.

(3) Frijda points out that only some *stimuli* elicit emotion. They have to be relevant to concerns in such a way that they indicate a match or a mismatch with them. Even when they satisfy these conditions though stimuli will not necessarily lead to emotion. Inputs have to have the proper format as well, which Frijda sees as dependent on links between imagery, sensory stimulation and action outcomes. His point here is that even though emotion elicitation is mainly cognitive, there are constraints. There has to be a sort of cooperation between the stimuli and the concern, otherwise it is only possible to, say, get rid of an emotion partially, or really find out what is important emotionally at a particular time.

(4) Emotion is elicited after *appraisal* has turned events into situational meaning structure. At the simplest level, the coding principles which Frijda believes to be relevant to appraisal are built-in to the system, they are part of information uptake. Pleasure for example is prewired into matches and mismatches between events. He regards appraisal as being partly conscious, but other parts cannot be penetrated cognitively, to use Frijda's language.

(5) For Frijda the defining feature of emotion is *action readiness change*. Included here are activation tendencies and activation modes, and their absence. Which emotions a person experiences depends in turn on action readiness modes, which depend in turn on the availability of action programmes, behaviour systems and activation/deactivation mechanisms. Basic emotions come from what is provided by biological constitution. But action tendencies can also come whatever general modes of relational change might be available, eg, approach, turning toward, withdrawal, turning away, and so on.

(6) Frijda addresses the matter of the link between situational meaning structures and action readiness change. He views most links as innately prepared, or preestablished by the structure of the organism. For example, "promised and actual goal achievement are innate elicitors of joy, of activation increases" (1986, p470).

(7) *Regulation* is important at all phases of the emotion process and over many levels of control. So there are inhibitions and restraints, enhancing, and even voluntary self-control from on high.

(8) Finally, Frijda suggests that the most obvious aspect of things emotional is *control precedence*. This separates emotional impulses from other types of action. Control precedence gives a sort of urgency to an action mode rather than simply prioritising it. He sees this as implying dual control, two action control processes working in parallel. Furthermore, control precedence comes about through the persistent and insistent signals relevant to pleasure and pain. There are other signals to do with desire and curiosity (interestingness) but these do not pertain to control precedence.

Frijda's concept of emotion

Explication of his theory of emotion allows Frijda finally to say something of the concept of emotion as he sees it. For him, emotion is a 'substantive psychological category'. Emotion *is* a set of mechanisms—for generating pleasure and pain by turning stimuli into rewards and punishments, for generating reward/punishment expectancies, for dictating relevant actions, and for controlling these actions.

• What he terms emotion proper depends on a mechanism that monitors whether or not any events help or hinder concerns which are currently being satisfied, or help or hinder expectancies and actions that are relevant to such concerns. He sees this as a dual control mechanism. This leads Frijda to three definitions of emotion. (1) 'Emotion is action readiness change.' (2) 'Emotion proper is relational action tendency and change in relational action tendency generally (activation)'. (3) Emotion is 'action readiness change in response to emergencies or interruptions.' In defining emotion, Frijda goes further and suggests that *abeyance and flexibility* are essential to it. So, there need to be flexible programmes which can nevertheless be held in abeyance, or inhibited.

Frijda avers that his account of emotion is functionalist. Emotions are seen as serving satisfaction, by monitoring events and promoting relevant action. In a sense, he brooks no argument with this point of view, even in the face of apparently harmful emotions, pointing out that it is simply a given, an assumption which at least has heuristic value.

He makes four points in support of a functionalist account of the apparent nonfunctionalities of emotion. (1) Much apparent nonfunctionality of emotions comes from the nonfunctionality of the concerns which underlie them, but Frijda does not go on to discuss why people espouse nonfunctional concerns. (2) He draws attention to the nonfunctionalities which come from apparent concern with short-term gains over long-term gains. (3) Part of the problem stems from the fact that humans have not been well enough designed to cope with everything that comes their way; nonfunctional emotional reactions can come from the organism reaching the limits of what it can do. (4) Because some emotions enable fast action in difficult circumstances it is not surprising that it can go wrong or be less than optimal on occasion.

In the end, although Frijda is expressing a functionalist view of emotions, this does not mean that all emotions are functional all of the time. Some emotional reactions simply *are*. To allow Frijda his own final word in this context: "The most general statements regarding emotions therefore are: Emotions are the manifestations of the individual's concern satisfaction system; and: Emotions express the individual's concerns and the satisfaction state of these concerns" (1986, p478).

In 1988, Frijda took his analysis of emotion a stage further by proposing that emotions can be described in terms of a set of 12 laws. By laws, Frijda means empirical regularities which have underlying causal mechanisms. As much as anything, he is offering these laws as an heuristic device for the establishment of research programmes, since some of them do not already rest on firm empirical foundations.

(1) *Situational meaning.* This refers to emotions being elicited by particular types of event, in other words they relate to the meaning structure of events. If the meaning changes then so does the emotion. This is an overriding cognitive law which clearly has to do with appraisals. It is worth pointing out that amongst the detail into which Frijda goes concerning this law, he makes the point that for emotions to be experienced people do not necessarily have to be aware of the relevant meaning structures. To use the language of Frijda's theory more directly, 'meaning structures are lawfully connected to forms of action readiness.'

(2) *Concern.* Underlying (almost) every emotion is a concern, in other words something of importance to an individual's goals or motives, or of course, concerns. This gives meaning.

(3) *Apparent reality.* By this law, Frijda suggests that appraisals are particularly concerned with reality. Events have to be appraised as real to lead to emotion, and the extent to which they are determines the intensity of the emotion. Perhaps unusually, Frijda includes vivid imagination within his idea of reality, although it is obvious why he does so.

(4), (5) and (6) *Change, habituation and comparative feeling.* Emotions come about through changes. These might be expected or unexpected and in favourable or unfavourable conditions, with the greater change leading to the stronger emotion. The background to this law comes from two further laws: the habituation of the effects of both pleasures and hardships, and the relationship between an event and whatever might be its comparative frame of reference.

(7) *Hedonic asymmetry.* The positive and negative sides of emotion are not equivalent. Pleasure soon disappears without change, but pain can sometimes persist. Frijda believes that a functional, adaptational view of emotion makes the evolution of this law self-evident.

(8) *Conservation of emotional momentum.* Events will continue to produce emotion unless the process is stopped through habituation or extinction.

(9) *Closure.* Emotional responses are not relative; they have an absolute quality that makes them concerned only with their own ends. They go straight ahead and control the action system.

(10) *Care for consequence.* Against the previous law, each emotional impulse produces a secondary impulse that takes into account its consequences and pushes in the direction of possible modification.

(11), (12) *Lightest load and greatest gain.* There is a tendency through situational meaning to minimize the load of negative emotion. There is a similar tendency to maximize positive emotion, or emotional gain.

With his 12 laws of emotion, Frijda is attempting to say, amongst many other things, that emotions are not only based on natural laws but their study has advanced sufficiently that it is possible to make a stab at such laws. This brings with it a maturity with respect to thinking about emotion, both theoretically and personally. This approach also suggests that the long held distinction between emotion and reason is not so much a distinction as a complex relationship in which the laws of both meet and lead to decisions.

Briefly, it should be pointed out that Smedslund (1992) mounts a case against Frijda's laws of emotion on the grounds that they are non-empirical and tautological. Frijda (1992) disputes Smedslund's conclusions particularly on the grounds of his belief that his laws can be proven wrong, or unproductive, and therefore, untrue. The laws might appear contradictory, but Frijda's point is that humans are contradictory and there must be something underlying contradiction.

Ortony

During the last decade or so, Ortony has made an interesting contribution to our understanding of emotion. Presently, however, it is the intention not to deal specifically with his theory of emotion (Ortony, Clore and Collins (1988)) but instead to consider his analysis of the question of *basic emotions* (Ortony and Clore, 1989; Ortony and Turner, 1990; Turner and Ortony, 1992). In passing, it should be noted however that the debate about basic emotions does establish Ortony as what might be termed a componential emotion theorist. As will become clear, a number of other prominent emotion theorists have enjoined this debate, including for example, Ekman, Izard, and Oatley.

Ortony and Turner (1990) begin their seminal paper by listing the considerable range of emotion theorists who have proposed that there are basic, or fundamental or primary emotions. They point out, however, that the lists of basic emotions vary considerably and that there is little agreement about why they should be basic or what makes them basic.

To list basic emotions is not a surprising endeavour since at the everyday level of discourse they appear to exist. Moreover, some emotions appear to be universal, appear to have recognisable facial expressions, and appear to have obvious adaptive value. The idea of basic emotions perhaps helps to account for these regularities. The notion is used in two major ways: to suggest that they are biologically given, or to suggest that they are psychologically primitive.

Ortony and Turner suggest that our myriad of emotions or emotion states cannot be accounted for in terms of what they describe as a chemical or colour metaphor in which new emotions result from a combination of basic emotions. They argue that a more appropriate account would be in terms of the suggestion that various emotions arise from particular sets of appraisals and the like rather than them stemming from basic emotions. They do, however, allow new emotions to arise from old by the processes of generalization and specialization.

They believe that emotion research should progress the better for the search for whatever processes underlie emotion, particularly the generalization and specialization of its construals, plus the various physiological and behavioural responses evoked.

Ortony and Turner regard the core problem with the idea of basic emotion as being the lack of a set of criteria for deciding what is and what is not basic. However, they argue that there might be a class of appraisals that could be viewed as basic that happen to be associated with particular sets of behaviour. For example, perceived threat might be commonly associated with running or freezing. But they feel that it is a group of such components that might make up an emotion, once again doing away with the idea of something simple and basic. Furthermore, they do not deny that there might be basic elements from which emotions are built; this idea is not precluded by doing away with the basic emotion view. These elements though are likely, from Ortony and Turner's perspective, to be components of cognitions, of feeling states, and even of emotions, rather than to be emotions themselves.

Particular critiques of Ortony and Turner's basic view were made by Ekman (1992), Izard (1992) and Panksepp (1992). The criticisms concerned: the apparent universality and uniqueness of some emotions suggesting that they are basic; physiological differentiation in emotions; emotions being mediated by integrated brain systems; and basic emotions having their specific and unchanging feeling states.

In one sense, Turner and Ortony (1992) regard the ideas of these three researchers and theorists as helping to make their points, because the three of them provide different lists of what they regard as the basic emotions, and there is no obvious way to choose between them. They put this down to Ekman's preference to study the face in emotion, Izard's to study things biosocial, and Panksepp's preference for the brain.

Ortony and Turner concede that the idea of basic emotions has had considerable heuristic value in generating a great deal of pertinent research. However, they maintain that the idea that there are basic emotions does not account for emotional diversity, and does not allow study of emotions which do not have particular facial expressions. Their argument is that the idea of basic emotion simply detracts from our ability to deal with the richness and diversity of emotions.

Taking a very different approach, Johnson-Laird and Oatley (1992) make a firm case for emotion being founded on a small set of emotions, consisting, not surprisingly, of those that form an integral part of their communicative theory of emotions. In their view, each of the basic emotions has an innate, universal mental signal which comes from appraisals, or cognitive evaluations concerning progress towards a goal. Such signals lead to subjective experience, bodily change and action plans, and the communicative signals of facial expression.

Part of their argument rests on the idea if there are not common subjective components to particular emotions, then the folk psychology of emotion must be rejected. This folk psychology is of course very much predicated on the idea that there exists a series of basic emotions. Johnson-Laird and Oatley can see no grounds for rejecting folk psychology and indeed argue that Ortony and Turner's componential theory seems to be no more than a variant of the basic emotion view.

Of course, it is perhaps worth pointing out that Johnson-Laird and Oatley's (1992) argument can be seen as an extension of an ongoing debate between themselves and Ortony. (Johnson-Laird and Oatley, 1989; Ortony and Clore, 1989; Oatley and Johnson-Laird, 1990). This debate concerns a semantic analysis of English language emotion terms which, as might be expected from the foregoing, Johnson-Laird and Oatley regard as providing support for their basic emotions view and Ortony does not. To enjoin this further here would add little to the major points that have been made.

Oatley and Johnson-Laird

Oatley and Johnson-Laird (1987; see also Oatley, 1992) put forward a theory of emotion as communication which has been as far reaching as any in recent times; it has a fine heuristic value. It has prompted a great deal of discussion (see Ortony in this chapter for example). Their *communicative theory* of emotion rests on the view that emotions communicate among the various parts of the cognitive system and among people socially.

They regard the cognitive system as made up of relatively autonomous parts which therefore have limited access to and control of one another. Only what they term the top-most level of the system has a sort of integrating function, receiving relevant messages from below and assessing them within a model of goals and knowledge. Consciousness occurs only at this top level of cognitions, which is also concerned with the construction of a model of the self.

Oatley and Johnson-Laird clearly subscribe to the modularity theory of mind in which the various parts of the cognitive system have their specific functions to perform. They offer two arguments in support of this way of looking at mind or cognition. The first is an appeal to good sense of any such system needing to be elaborated in this way simply in order for any procedures to begin and end. Second, it is clear from everyday experience that often one part (the conscious part) of human cognition does not always know what is going on elsewhere in the system. Such dissociation suggests a modular system.

Some parts of this system are innate or evolutionarily determined, but new procedures are also capable of being learned by the human mind. This means that new things can go wrong constantly as the system constructs new parts of itself. Against this background, emotions are seen as 'inserting problems into consciousness', which allows integration to occur with the rest of the system.

In a way it is reasonable to set Oatley and Johnson-Laird's theory of emotion against the background of Mandler's (see earlier in this chapter). They characterize it as a conflict and evaluation theory that suggests that emotion occurs following the interruption of a psychological process. Emotion is also dependent on a process of appraisal. The problem with conflict and interruption theories of emotion, and perhaps the reason that their history is chequered is their possible difficulty with positive emotions.

The usual way of dealing with the positive emotions within this type of theoretical framework is to suggest that they arise because of the interruptions and delays that are an inevitable part of them. Clearly, though, some positive emotional experiences are not like this, they do not involve interruptions. Oatley and Johnson-Laird embrace this possible difficulty by suggesting that positive emotions occur when a goal is achieved or when subgoals are achieved because a plan is progressing well. In particular, they also consider enjoyment and happiness. Enjoyment follows the achievement of an especially significant goal, or when the mind is full of activities such as listening to music or being creative. So enjoyment happens when we are fully engaged in something, and when there are no interruptive re-evaluations of the situation.

Within Oatley and Johnson-Laird's theory, negative emotions follow problems with which it is difficult to cope, the inability to deal with a new goal, a new conflict, or a threat. Such negative emotions are not necessarily unpleasant or even avoided, but may simply provide some useful information, that one's cognitive structures or habits need to be changed in some way. They believe that there are two types of distinctive conscious consequences of negative emotions. Restrictions prompt old plans and actions to be used, and there is also often an inner debate taking place.

Oatley and Johnson-Laird argue that their theory has it over other cognitive theories in that it concentrates on goals rather than behaviour. Moreover, the evaluation part of the theory posits that the evaluations are of events as they relate to these goals, and thus distinguishes the content of emotional evaluations from other types of evaluation.

To cut to the chase, the central postulate of Oatley and Johnson-Laird's (1987) theory of emotion is:

> "Each goal and plan has a monitoring mechanism that evaluates events relevant to it. When a substantial change of probability occurs of achieving an important goal or subgoal, the monitoring mechanism broadcasts to the whole cognitive system a signal that can set it into readiness to respond to this change. Humans experience these signals and the states of readiness they induce as emotions." (Oatley, 1992, p50, italics his)

In this context, emotions functions as alarms that something needs to be dealt with, without saying what exactly has happened or what exactly to do about it. This is a nonpropositional message and contrasts with the usual sorts of cognitive propositional messages. Oatley (1992) terms these messages *control* (to do with control structure of cognition; they are without meaning) and *semantic* (messages that make reference).

Oatley suggests that semantic messages need interpretation and can invoke cognitive procedures usually in a hierarchical sequence. They allow the control of organized plans. By contrast, nonsemantic control signals allow non-hierarchically arranged cognitive modules to be organized to avoid pathological conflicts. This is a much simpler and older (evolutionarily speaking) part of the system. There is no information involved, merely a warning that turns some modules on and allows a sort of propagation through the system.

Some of these sorts of signal are arranged specifically such that they may promote vigilance, or readiness to attack for example. Although Oatley argues that this system is much more primitive than the semantic communication system, he nevertheless believes that since it has survived throughout evolution it must still be of some value to the organism. He sees them as having two particular advantages. They allow a fast coherent sort of response that overrides whatever else is happening. And they permit a sort of endurance, allowing the system to stay in a mood that resists any other changes.

Oatley and Johnson-Laird suggest that particular control signals are associated with five basic emotions. *Happiness* occurs when subgoals are being achieved, and suggest that the plan is to be continued. *Sadness* follows a plan failing or an active goal being lost and suggests either doing nothing or searching for a new plan. *Fear* follows either threat to a self-preservation goal or goal conflict, and suggests stopping, being vigilant, freezing or escaping. *Anger* occurs when an active plan is frustrated and suggests trying harder or being aggressive. And *disgust* follows the violation of a gustatory goal and suggests rejection or withdrawal. To support the idea that there exist these five basic emotions (rather fewer than other basic emotion theorists list) Oatley draws on three types of evidence: eliciting conditions, physiological specificity, and cross-cultural emotional expression.

Oatley lists five junctures concerned with goal evaluation (in birds and mammals) that correspond to the five basic emotions that are integral to this theory. Three of these junctures are to do with attachment—establishment interruption and loss of a relationship, associated with happiness, fear and sadness. Aggression and anger are part of competition and disgust follows from the rejection of food that might be contaminated. Communicative emotion theory suggests then that the other complexities of emotion can be built up from the basic five. Oatley also quotes evidence to suggest that there are specific autonomic effects that go with the facial expressions of these five emotions and that the emotions are also expressed in a similar way pan-culturally.

Although Oatley and Johnson-Laird suggest that there are five basic emotions, they also acknowledge that the jury is out on exactly how many this number should be. They believe that most researchers believe that happiness, sadness, anger and fear are certainly separable for research purposes, although not all such researchers would believe these four emotions to be *basic*. They also suggest that the relevant evidence is not yet available on the status of surprise, disgust, hatred, contempt and desire/interest, although they themselves are convinced about disgust.

Oatley (1992), unlike Buck, argues that emotions allow transitions to be made between various motivational states, and perhaps enhancing motivations, but that emotions are not in themselves motivations. He regards emotions as mental states which, might amongst other things, allow motivations to be managed.

Within the terms of this theory, usually semantic and control signals combine to lead to an emotion, the semantic part indicating to us the cause of the emotion, and the control part allowing the emotion to spread through the system with its particular tone and mode. However, emotions sometimes occur with no obvious reason. As should be obvious from the theory, this occurs when a control emotion is established without any conscious semantic information which would give a clue to its cause.

In this context, Oatley and Johnson-Laird also give an account of moods, which are maintained states rather than states involving transition. The maintenance is made by control signals and is beyond any external events or immediate memories. Crucial here is the breaking of any links between control emotion signals and semantic information. If this type of dissociation and the resultant mood goes on for a long time, say a week, with little change, then they come to be regarded as psychopathological.

The final broad consideration of Oatley and Johnson-Laird's communicative theory of emotion concerns communication itself. Their theory depends on a detailed analysis of the sort of communication that goes on within the cognitive system, but as Oatley (1992) points out there are interpersonal equivalents of this. Our verbal behaviour, which of course has both semantic and syntactic aspects, affects the cognitions of other people. The equivalent of control comes from nonverbal behaviour such as emotional expression.

Furthermore, emotions are regarded within this theory as communications to oneself about changed evaluations. They allow us to deal with our various goals and plans and they also act communicatively to others. Oatley argues that it is through emotions becoming conscious that we actually come to know some facets of our goals and plans that we might not otherwise know about. In its turn, this allows us to further modify our cognitive structure in appropriate ways.

Finally, Oatley and Johnson-Laird suggest that basic emotions have three types of function in communication. (1) They constrain actions by communicating directly to us, thus continuing some states or helping a change to others. (2) They communicate to other people, producing similar states and changes in those with whom we interact. (3) We talk about emotions to ourselves and others and thus communicate semantically. This has its effects.

Conclusions

It should be apparent now that 'ambitious' was a reasonable descriptor to use in heading this chapter. The theories that have been summarized have been constructed around grand aims. In one sense a number of them are theories not just of emotion but almost of psychology more generally. They are predicted on an attempt to fit emotion into a broad theoretical perspective. Do they succeed?

In the appraisal that follows, it is mainly the more recent large-scale theories that will be considered. Leeper, Pribram and Tomkins have an important place in the recent history of emotion research in that they have stimulated both further ideas and empirical investigation. This comment applies particularly to Tomkins. However, they have been essentially replaced by more recent theories that have been put forward with the advantage of being built on far more data (of all types) than were available a few years ago.

At the broad level of evaluation, the theories considered in this chapter are based on extremely thorough summaries of existing knowledge about emotion. Each of them offers cogent and penetrating explanatory accounts and they are all so extensively explicated that many possible testable predictions can be derived from them. By design, their focus is broad (although Averill's theory may partly be excepted from this; it stems from an analysis of anger but does however have broad implications). Also, all of the theories considered in this chapter score very highly on heuristic value. Even when they are rather obscurely expressed, as with Frijda's, they stimulate further thought and ideas almost effortlessly.

Moving to the more particular, if one evaluates each of these theories through a step be step analysis of Lazarus's (1991a,b) 12 criteria, most of the theories fare well on all of them. Of course, they have their individual strengths and weaknesses, their points of special emphasis. For example, since Buck's theory is of motivation and emotion, it does well on its consideration of motivation. Similarly, since Izard's theory is about differential emotions, it does particularly well on the question of discrete emotions.

Interestingly, most of the theories have a strong cognitive component, indeed, many of them dealing in particular with appraisal. Here again, Izard's theory deserves mention because it is the only one of them that makes a clear distinction between emotion and cognition. To Izard, emotion and cognition might interrelate, but emotion also exists in its own right.

Not surprisingly with such broad-based theories, the ambitious ones usually have a place for both the biological and the sociocultural. Even Averill, who is avowedly social constructionist (again, see Chapter 14), takes the weaker form of social constructionism and gives emotion a biological foundation.

In any event, perhaps it suffices to say that the theories dealt with in this chapter meet most of the criteria suggested by Lazarus. In his more general terms, they explicate the possible causes of emotion and they have a place for emotion both as an independent and a dependent variable.

Moving onto the criteria espoused by Oatley (1992), as was stated in the last chapter, it is not surprisingly the Oatley and Johnson-Laird theory that meets these most readily. However, again most of the recent grand theories of emotion meet most of the criteria. They deal with the functions of emotion, they all consider the question of whether or not there are discrete emotions, and they flirt with the notion of the role of the unconscious. They have a place for physiology and they all have a central role for evaluation or appraisal. Some of them are also concerned with the interpersonal communication side of emotion. Finally, some of them even meet Oatley's last and perhaps most controversial criterion, that emotions enable us to simulate the emotional plans of other people.

Again, more generally, these more ambitious theories are certainly couched in terms that they can easily deal with the addition of more evidence. Moreover, specific predictions can be derived from them, although with some difficulty in a few cases, Frijda providing the obvious example. Frijda's theory is a bit of an oddity in that in some sense it is the most formally expressed of them all, having a statement about 'laws' of emotion. The problem is that, like some other aspects of the theory, the laws are a little difficult to pin down.

Overall, the more ambitious theories of emotion are the best to have been described so far in this text. Because they are so wide-ranging it is a little more difficult than it has been in previous chapters to abstract from them the most important themes. Nevertheless, it is reasonable to say that most of them have a place for both a biological substrate and a sociocultural aspect. They all stress the importance of cognition, particularly appraisal, although Izard does make a clear and in his view important, distinction between it and emotion.

Interestingly, a number of these theories develop almost into systems theories. It is then hardly surprising that they tend to place emphasis on other broad 'systems' that might interact with emotion, motivation being the most pervasive example. They also stress broad concepts such as communication and function in general. Some even have a place for a consideration of the importance of meaning to emotion, Mandler providing the most cogent example of this. This is significant in that it not only provides an important link with phenomenological theories but also squarely engages the difficult matter of consciousness.

In general, then, what have been termed here the ambitious theories of emotion are good value, as theories and as theories of emotion. Which is the best of them? This is hard to say since they all have their relative strengths. However, the erudition and thoroughness of Mandler's theory takes some beating, and, again, the breadth and depth of Oatley and Johnson-Laird's is compelling. However, both Frijda and Ortony have made splendid contributions and Izard has a special place. His theory is characterized by the taking of a definite standpoint and an impressive intellectual honesty. This gives it simultaneously some very practical implications (for emotion measurement, testing and even therapy) and a stimulating heuristic value.

8

Specific emotions theory

The purpose of this chapter is not to present an exhaustive summary of everything that has been written about each of the so-called specific theories of emotion. Rather, it is to take some of the more obvious of these and to describe some of the major theoretical contributions to which they have given rise. The point of so doing is to attempt to abstract any common themes or principles that emerge that might in their turn add to an understanding of emotion more generally.

Whether or not it is useful and/or reasonable to conceive of specific emotions at all is considered elsewhere in this text (see Chapter 7 for example). For the purposes of the present chapter, it is assumed, much as it is in everyday life, that specific emotions exist and that it is perfectly reasonable to distinguish between them. For example, in day-to-day interactions there is no difficulty in distinguishing between anger and joy, or between shame and anxiety. Indeed, it makes communication and therefore life in general easier to do so.

One emotion theorist in particular has been concerned for many years with the development of a theory which relies very much on distinguishing between specific emotions. Consequently, Izard's differential emotions theory (eg 1971, 1977, 1991) will be referred to frequently in this chapter as well as having been considered in Chapter 7.

In a recent summary of his theoretical position, Izard (1993) points out that it rests on five assumptions. (1) Emotion systems are motivational. (2) Each discrete emotion organizes perception, cognition and behaviour for adaptation, coping and creativity. (3) Relations between emotion and behaviour develop early and remain stable, even though repertoires of specific responses develop. (4) Emotional development contributes to personality development. (5) Particular personality traits and dimensions stem from individual differences in thresholds of emotion activation and in the experience of particular emotions.

Generally, Izard views the standpoints that there are discrete emotions and that there are basic dimensions of emotion as complementary. There is considerable overlap in the approaches taken by those who espouse these apparently opposed viewpoints and Izard argues that two issues need to be dealt with concerning specific emotions. Can discrete emotions be shown to have functions that are adaptationally useful? And do specific emotions facilitate development, coping and adaptation? Above all, though, from Izard's perspective, if discrete emotions exist they must be shown to serve motivational functions.

Not all of the specific emotions will be considered in this chapter. If for no other reason, this is because not all of them can be reasonably said to have attracted its own theory or theories. However, the majority will be covered, although not from every theoretical perspective. For example, there are a number of theories of specific emotions such as jealousy and envy that come from the everyday world, or from a fictional background. Even for a fairly eclectic book such as the present, it was thought that this would be stretching things too far. It should also be noted that some of the specific emotions, such as anxiety and depression are discussed in more detail in Chapter 11 which is concerned with emotion theory from a clinical perspective.

Anger

Anger is always included in lists of discrete emotions and it is usually categorized as negative. The likely reason for this is that it is an integral part of aggression, hostility and violence which are so negative for society. However, the experience of anger is not always negative. Izard (1991) places it alongside disgust and contempt, describing the three emotions as often interacting in human experience.

From an evolutionary perspective, Izard sees anger as having the rather obvious function of energising the person for defence. Such defence and feelings of physical empowerment that often attend it, might lead to aggression, either physical or verbal, but not necessarily. In passing, it is also worth mentioning that there are also causes of aggression other than anger, some of them emotional. Interestingly, Izard also points out that both the experience and the expression of anger can be positive. He mentions for example the possibility that the controlled expression of anger that is seen as justified might strengthen the relationship between the two people involved.

A number of psychologists have written about anger, but none so cogently as Averill (1982) with his usual social constructionist view. In his treatise on anger, Averill not only shows that it is possible to undertake a penetrating analysis of a single emotion but also that in so doing it is possible to gain a much improved understanding of emotion in general.

Averill characterizes anger as a conflictive emotion which is biologically related to aggressive systems and to social living, symbolization and self-awareness. Psychologically, it is aimed at the correction of a perceived wrong and socioculturally at upholding accepted standards of conduct.

Averill regards emotions as social syndromes or transitory rules, as well as short-term dispositions to respond in particular ways and to interpret such responses as emotional. He distinguishes between conflictive emotions (of which anger is one), impulsive emotions (inclinations and aversions) and transcendental emotions, which involve a breakdown in the boundaries of the ego.

The theory suggests that although some emotions have all three of these characteristics, complex behaviour usually involves conflicts. These result in emotions which are compromises which help to resolve the conflict. Biologically, aggression is linked to anger but is not equated with it. Furthermore, Averill has it that there is a biological tendency in humans to follow rules as well as to formulate them. There is also a biologically based tendency to become upset if the rules are broken. Against this theoretical background, anger (and other emotions), although biologically based, become highly symbolic and reliant on appraisals in humans. Psychologically, anger then is seen as concerned with the correction of a perceived wrong, so, like other emotions, it will have its object, which is partly its instigation, and its target and an aim.

Socioculturally, Averill suggests that anger is about upholding accepted standards of conduct, perhaps unwittingly. Any emotion is concerned with such standards, rules which guide behaviour. Other rules relevant to emotion concern its expression, its course and outcome and the way in which it is causally attributed. As Averill suggests, a self-evident rule of anger is, for example, that it should be spontaneous rather than deliberate.

From this analysis of anger (to which the present brief discussion does not do justice—the original rewards close study) Averill argues that any theory of emotion should not be restrictive and should relate to all pertinent phenomena, if they are seen as part of emotion in everyday language. The important implication here is that everyday emotion, or folk concepts of emotion, can be scientifically useful. The aim would be to uncover what Averill terms the prototypic attributes of various emotions and to determine the rules that guide them. As mentioned elsewhere, Averill's view of emotion is that although biologically based it is largely socially constructed in humans.

In their analysis of anger and hostility from a developmental viewpoint, Lemerise and Dodge (1993) emphasize the functional significance of anger. More broadly than Izard, they see anger as serving a number of functions, including the organisation and regulation of physiological and psychological processes related to self defence and mastery, plus the regulation of social and interpersonal behaviours. They regard anger as functioning as an energizer, an organizer and as a social signal.

Lemerise and Dodge are particularly concerned with how anger develops and is caused. They make the point that the cognitive ability of young children is important in their developing anger, although the basic, original causes of anger seem to be to do with physical restraints and interference with activity. The development of anger becomes closely entwined with the processes of socialisation, one general rule of which appears to be the encouragement of positive emotion and the control of negative emotion (which includes anger).

Of importance in this context is the manner in which parents respond to angry expressions in their children. There are large scale individual differences here, which are dependent on the child, the parents and the circumstances. However, for present purposes these details do not matter. Of importance is that although anger appears very early in life, as Averill suggests and Lemerise and Dodge endorse, its development is best understood in interpersonal terms.

Anxiety and fear

For an extended discussion of theories of anxiety and fear see Chapter 11, and Strongman (1995). For the present these two closely related emotions should receive brief mention because they always appear in lists of the basic emotions. There has been a proliferation of theories of anxiety and fear, their starting points being very similar to those for general theories of emotion. There have been psychoanalytic, behavioural, physiological, experiential/phenomenological and cognitive perspectives.

What is clear from these theories is that anxiety can only be understood by taking into account some of its cognitive aspects, particularly because a basic aspect of anxiety appears to be uncertainty. Also, it is reasonable to conclude that anxiety can be distinguished from fear in that the object of fear is 'real' or 'external' or 'known' or 'objective'. The origins of anxiety are unclear or uncertain to the person. However, anxiety can be motivating and appears to be an inevitable part of the human condition. Anxiety and fear are definitely negative emotions and can be very distressing. Inasmuch as specific emotions can be said to exist, the constellation of anxiety and fear has a definite place amongst them.

Disgust

Disgust is about rejection, rejection of what might be contaminated, or might be distasteful, either physically or psychologically. At its basic level it seems to occur without cognition, although of course we also learn to be disgusted at many things. From a differential emotions perspective, Izard (1991) discusses disgust as fundamentally related to the expulsion of contaminated food, the experience of which only develops when the cognitions necessary to appreciate/understand it have developed.

Usually associated with disgust is contempt, which as Izard puts it is "associated with feelings of superiority" (1991, p279). He characterizes it as a truly negative emotion, predominating as it does in a range of endeavours from prejudice to murder.

In a cogent analysis, Rozin, Haidt and McCauley (1993) describe disgust as one of a few uniquely human emotions. They argue that assuming that there are basic emotions, then it is clear that disgust should be included amongst their number, seeing it as similar to guilt, shame and embarrassment (see later). They see disgust as satisfying Ekman's (1992) criteria for emotions—it has a universal signal, comparable expression in lower animals, a specific physiology, universal preceding events, a coherent response system, a rapid onset, a brief duration, an automatic appraisal mechanism and an unbidden occurrence.

After discussing various ways of looking at disgust, Rozin et al conclude that its cultural evolution suggests that it is concerned with essential human-ness. Clearly, disgust began (in evolutionary history) as a very useful rejection of bad or contaminated tastes. But it has developed in humans far beyond this to a much more abstract type of rejection of potential foods, with a particular concern with body products. They consider that a fear of animal products and mortality and their associated decay has replaced the original condition of the more simple avoidance of bad taste. As with other human emotions, disgust is bound up with the moral order in that it is an important part of socialization.

Grief

There are obvious links between sadness and grief, grief being what most people experience at some time over the loss of something highly valued, usually of course a loved person. Theoretically, the problem with grief is that although it might be seen as a discrete emotion, it might also be seen as more than an emotion. The predominant emotion in the experience of grief is sadness, but other emotions are also generated by grief, anger for example, and also fear and shame.

As Izard (1991) points in parallel with the predominant emotion in grief being sadness, the most common psychological problem associated with it is depression. From the differential emotions theory perspective depression is a pattern of basic emotions, including sadness, anger, disgust, contempt, fear, guilt and shyness. Here though is not the place to consider theories of depres-sion (see Chapter 11).

Interestingly, as with happiness, Averill (Averill and Nunley, 1988) has made a cogent analysis of grief very much from his social constructionist standpoint. In brief, this rests on the assumptions that: (1) emotions are made up of cognitive appraisals, intervening processes and behavioural expression, (2) all three of these are partly determined by the beliefs and values of the culture, and (3) emotional syndromes reinforce these same beliefs.

Averill and Nunley describe grief as involving shock, protest, despair and reorganization, sometimes seen as stages but with considerable overlap and the possibility of occurring in other orders. Within the terms of a systems approach to emotion, they regard grief as a biological system which is related to attachment. It is as though the purpose of grief is to help maintain the social bonds, so it seems to have to work through its course even though it is so full of anguish, in the case of bereavement for example.

However, from this perspective grief is not simply biological, separation (bereavement) having societal implications as well. So most societies have

developed ritualized mourning practices. As well as having a place in biological and social systems, grief also is involved in the psychological system.
Some symptoms of grief are related to the disruption to behavioural possibilities, cognitions and so on which result from the loss. Moreover, grief has
its own rewards, people often assuming some of its more public aspects for the
effects this might have.

Typically, Averill breaks down emotional roles in the way in which he
would also break down social roles. First, the *privileges* of grief act to allow
some feelings to be displayed publicly and to permit the person not to undertake a wide range of social roles that would normally have to be assumed.
Second, grief puts certain *restrictions* on a person, not to laugh too soon or not
to grieve for too long for example. Third, usually a bereaved person has
obligations, to mourn in particular ways for example. And finally, the manner
in which grief can be expressed varies according to age, sex, and the nature of
the prior relationship with the deceased person. Formally, the emotional role
of grief has certain *entry requirements.*

Averill and Nunley also offer an alternative account of grief, as a disease. In
their turn, diseases can be conceptualized via biological, social and psychological systems, and grief fits all of the criteria to be included as a disease. Why
then, asks Averill, should it be viewed as an emotion? He sees the essential
difference as the emotion of grief being part of the moral order, of whatever
systems (political, religious, etc) that help to define a society, whereas disease
concepts lie within the system of health care. He judges that eventually grief
will come to be treated like other diseases.

In the end, Averill is concerned to ensure that emotions are treated in
relation to social as well as biological and psychological systems of behaviour.
Grief considered either as an emotion or as a disease illustrates this.

Happiness

At the outset it should be said that specific positive emotions have not, in
general, been dealt with as well as specific negative emotions. This is not the
place to offer possible explanations for this other than to say that negative
emotions have to be coped with; the aim is to get rid of them or at least to
reduce their impact. Positive emotions are simply to be enjoyed rather than
endured. It is therefore not surprising that psychologists and others have
spent more time in an attempt to understand the negative than the positive
emotions.

One result of this bias is that although there are some empirical investigations of the positive emotions, and considerable attempts made to theorize
about love (see later), other positive emotions have not received much theoretical attention. For example, it is hard to find clear distinctions between
happiness, joy and elation.

From the viewpoint of differential emotions theory, Izard (1991) concentrates on what he calls enjoyment and joy and distinguishes between the

experience of joy and the experience of satisfaction of sensory pleasure. He characterizes joy as involving a sense of confidence and contentment, and often as including a feeling of either being lovable, or more specifically, loved. Izard sees joy as a state that follows various experiences rather than as a direct result of action. So, we are likely to experience joy after stress or negative emotion has finished, or following creativity for example. From an evolutionary perspective its effect is to help in maintaining us as social beings. Izard believes that joy and other emotions interact and can affect perception and cognition. It can slow down behaviour but can also induce a sort of open creativity.

In one of his typically cogent analyses, Averill (Averill and More, 1993) considers happiness in general, and argues that ideas about it have remained obdurately fuzzy because its scope is so broad. He believes that it does not help to deal with more circumscribed concepts such as joy, this merely substituting the part for the whole. Furthermore, Averill and More argue that happiness defies understanding because of its depths of meaning. For example, if happiness in its own right is considered the greatest good then it may well involve pain and suffering, which might seem anomalous. Anyway, in short happiness is more difficult to conceptualize than many specific emotions because of both its breadth and its depth.

Averill and More distinguish between three approaches to understanding happiness, emphasising respectively, systems of behaviour, enabling mechanisms and personality characteristics. They argue that an understanding of happiness must take into account social/psychological as well as biological systems of behaviour. The psychological systems and those which help the development (or actualisation) of self.

From this perspective there are five matters which Averill and More believe must be considered. (1) Happiness is associated with the optimal functioning of behavioural systems, so although people might seek happiness it is not simply for its own sake. (2) Systems are hierarchically ordered and happiness at one level is informed by higher levels and given substance by lower levels; the levels interact. (3) Happiness is closely linked to systems that are concerned with social order, systems that clearly involve values. So, in this sense, happiness is related to values. (4) Happiness often involves compromise in the sense that one system (say the biological) may have to be sacrificed at the expense of another (the social or psychological). When this occurs, happiness cannot be associated with tranquillity, as is sometimes thought. (5) Happiness is an individual matter, each person having a distinct propensity or capacity for it. It might be capable of relatively objective measurement but it remains a subjective or individual construct.

From Averill's perspective, enabling mechanisms are concerned with the inner workings of happiness, or whatever the emotion might be, rather than its origins and functions. Again, any analysis can be made from a biological, psychological or social viewpoint. An important distinction here is between intrinsic and extrinsic mechanisms. For instance, intrinsic mechanisms might be activated in support of systems behaviour, whereas extrinsic mechanisms operate somewhat independently of this.

There has been recent emphasis on 'gap' theories that derive from extrinsic mechanisms of happiness. Michalos (1985, 1986) describes the gaps as between what one wants and what one has, actual and ideal, actual and expected conditions, actual and best previous conditions, what one has and what others have, and personal and environmental attributes. Although they have an appeal to common-sense, such gap theories are in fact rather weak on explanatory power.

The final account of happiness is via personality mechanisms, or more properly, traits. Here, according to Averill and More the important theoretical questions concern the conditions under which happiness is related to specific personality traits. Their final position is that happiness is dynamic, it is never complete, and is perhaps best seen as the optimal functioning of behavioural systems.

Jealousy and envy

Although jealousy and envy form a reasonably important part of everyday life, they have not often drawn the attention of psychologists. They tend to receive passing attention in discussion of the negative side of loving and liking and there are attempts made to distinguish between them. However, a useful discussion is made by Smith, Kim and Parrott (1988).

Jealousy is the reaction to the threat that we might lose the affections of someone important to us and that these affections be directed towards someone else. Envy is more simply a desire to have what someone else has. So jealousy is based on the possibility of losing an existing relationship and envy is based on the possibility of possessing some *thing* that another person has. Generally, jealousy is more powerful and more intense than envy.

Smith et al draw attention to the fact that although these distinctions are reasonable, in everyday life there is considerable overlap between these two emotions. Their research and theory show that the overlap is due to the ambiguity of the word jealousy, which is used to mean both envy and jealousy, envy meanwhile being more restricted. Moreover, the feelings associated with the two are different. Jealousy is linked to feelings of suspiciousness, rejection, hostility, anger, fear of loss, hurt, and so on. Envy is linked to feelings of inferiority, dissatisfaction, wishfulness, longing, and self-criticism. They argue that envy should be used as a useful label for discontented feelings that stem from social comparisons, whereas jealousy remains ambiguous in its use, sometimes referring to what more properly should be termed envy.

Love

If love is an emotion it is probably the most complex of all. If it is some state of being that includes various emotions, some of them decidedly positive, then it is a very complex state of being.

Love has a distinct place in Izard's (1991) scheme of things, but he does not characterize it as a discreet emotion. He views love as basic to the human condition, as involving strong affectionally based social attachments, to be full of interest and joy but also to "... run the full gamut of emotions". (1991, p407). Like many psychologists who have written about love, Izard distinguishes between various types, love for parents, love for siblings and love in a romantic sense, for example. He views all types of love as having certain elements in common; he lists attachment, loyalty, devotion, protectiveness and nurturance. However, romantic love is special because it involves sexual expression, whereas the other types normally do not.

In recent years, psychologists have turned their attention to love rather than putting it aside as too hard, or regarding it as better left to the poets. Amongst the most interesting of these expositions has been Sternberg's (1986, 1987) who reviews theories of love and then attempts to provide his own. He suggests a triangular model of liking and loving, the three aspects being intimacy, passion and decision-commitment. Various weightings in this triangle allow Sternberg to provide a place for the eight types of love, or more properly, love relationships, that he has distinguished.

These are: nonlove (casual), liking (intimacy only), infatuation (passion only), empty love (decision-commitment only, from only one person), romantic love (intimacy and passion), fatuous love (passion and decision-commitment), companionate love (intimacy and decision-commitment) and consummate love (intimacy, passion and decision-commitment). Of this typology, Lazarus (1991) makes the interesting point that it appears to be treating love as social relationships rather than as an emotion.

More recently, however, in a most stimulating book, Solomon (1994) has produced a genuine theory rather than a model of love, although from a philosophical perspective. His account is simultaneously hard-headed and sympathetic and begins with the view that a theory of love is essentially a theory of self, however it emphasizes a shared self. With this theory he is harking back to the Platonic view of love as a joining of two souls.

This notion began with Aristophanes who suggested that love is an attempt to find the other half of the self. Bringing this to the present in Solomon's terms, love becomes a matter of defining oneself in terms of another person. He makes the point that romantic love is a very modern notion, indicating a set of relationships which have only existed for a relatively short time. It is a notion that is based on the idea of two separate and autonomous persons who are free to make choices.

A further core aspect of this theory is that any of the concepts involved in love only work when they are in tension with their opposite. To make this clear, the seeking for union with someone else in these terms is exciting because it is in tension with the notion of the autonomous self. So, and most importantly, Solomon is here describing love as a process and not a state; it comes from movement.

As already mentioned, Solomon is a philosopher rather than a psychologist, but rests his theory of love not just on both of these disciplines, but also on history, literature and anthropology, and especially on personal experience. A theory of love has to make sense personally as well as within more rarefied academic discourse. All these complexities suggest to Solomon that love is something that should be seen as taking time rather than being instant, and it is something that develops and grows. In the end, he argues with this deceptively simple theory that it is time to "reinvent" love, along the lines that he describes but within the framework of the contemporary world.

Although Solomon's theory of love has been given pride of place in this brief account, it remains to be seen whether or not it generates empirical research. It looks likely to, as well as having obvious heuristic value. It has particular importance in that it deals with the topic of love irrespective of disciplinary boundaries. It is becomingly increasingly evident that to understand emotion in general this should be the approach of first choice. (See Chapter 13 for further discussion of this.)

Sadness

Although at face value sadness would be thought of as a negative emotion and it does have obvious negative aspects, it also has its positive side. A life without sadness would have less colour to it than one in which it is not possible to experience, say, mourning, even though it is painful to do so.

From Izard's (1991) differential emotions theory view, sadness is less tense than many of the other negative emotions. Experientially it is made up of downheartedness, discouragement, loneliness and isolation. Typical causes are the commonplace circumstances of everyday life, but those which usually involve loss. It seems to have the effect of slowing down the system and prompts reflection. Izard argues that sadness is so commonplace that it frequently interacts with other emotions, such as anger and fear and shame.

Stearns (1993) makes an interesting analysis of the psychological approaches to sadness. One of the most promising of these is that of seeing emotions, including sadness, as *enabling* and motivating adaptive responses. Sadness is an emotion that concentrates attention on the self and is an indication that the person (the self) needs help. It can be distinguished from fear and guilt in that they have something anticipatory about them, and in sadness the self is usually not responsible for what has happened. Also, it has been argued that sadness occurs when a situation which is bad for the person is nevertheless reversible.

Stearns also discusses anthropological and historical approaches to sadness. Some anthropological work for example (Lutz, 1988) points to sadness not being regarded as negative in some societies. Also, although psychologists have suggested that a distinction between sadness and anger, say, comes from agency or cause, anthropologists suggest that it is a matter of knowing when, to what audience and in what language it is apposite to feel sadness or anger.

Also, sadness does not always involve turning inwards, Stearns viewing its expression in modern America as turning outwards, for help.

From a theoretical viewpoint, perhaps the most important point to emerge from considerations of sadness, is that it is not always a negative emotion. As ever with complex human emotions, judgements about this are mixed up with the surrounding moral order, or values, views on aggression or individual versus collective responsibility and so on.

Stearns also argues that the anthropological research on sadness calls into question the viability of there being a discrete emotion called sadness. Different societies use different means of dealing with loss. The sadness type of reaction either suggests slow movement, a lowered rate of behaving, or possibly the seeking of help. Other societies use different words and hence different concepts. Generally, sadness seems to be closely related to anger.

Embarrassment, pride, shyness, shame and guilt—the self-conscious emotions

Although the emotions considered in this section have usually been studied separately (when they have been studied at all), Lewis (1993) appropriately gathers them under the heading of the self-conscious emotions. These four emotions all are centrally concerned with the self and our cognitions about the self, and how the self relates to and is seen by, others.

Via differential emotions theory, Izard (eg 1991) deals with three of them, embarrassment only being dealt with in passing in his consideration of shame, and pride having no mention at all. Izard points out that although shyness seems to have trait-like qualities of endurance, it appears not to have a universal pattern of expression. He views it as having the possible adaptive value of protecting the individual from going too far into novel and therefore possibly unsafe environments. In the extreme, perhaps like any specific emotion, it can be maladaptive, although the subjective experience of shyness seems to have both positive and negative aspects.

Izard characterizes shame as starting with a sudden intense awareness of self which thoroughly dominates consciousness. Since it is normally concerned with evaluation by others, it usually occurs in social situations, although it can occur when alone. He views shame as having the adaptive functions of sensitizing us to the opinions of others and as prompting the development of social skills. Although shame has its positive side, it also can have many negative consequences particularly in the area of sex, sexual encounters being so obviously bound up with intimacy and self-disclosure. In this context, embarrassment is almost synonymous with shame, or is seen simply as one aspect of it that occurs particularly in situations of public failure, although it is less intense and does not involve the same amount of disruption of thought and language.

Guilt has a central role to play in differential emotions theory. "In discrete emotions theory guilt is the key emotion in the development of personal and social responsibility and the phenomena of conscience" (1991, p389). Izard suggests that shame and guilt often occur together, a possible difference being that shame involves mainly the evaluations of others, and guilt involves mainly self-evaluation. Clearly, then, from an adaptive viewpoint, guilt adds to shame in prompting social responsibility, although again, in the extreme, it can be very harmful to the person. Psychologically, one of the main aspects of guilt that needs exploration is the manner in which it becomes internalized.

In his analysis, Lewis (1993) places great emphasis on the role of self. The important distinction is between emotions that depend on the apparent opinion of other people and those that do not. A significant question then emerges: if there are basic emotions, do they include the self-conscious emotions, or are these in a separate category? (Ortony, 1987, makes an interesting discussion of whether or not guilt should be included in any list of the basic emotions.)

Lewis discusses reflective cognitive processes that prompt self-attributions that in turn might be associated with the type of emotions under consideration here. Lewis's cognitive-attributional theory gives emotions the same status as cognitions and suggests that specific emotions can be elicited through various attributions. He draws attention to three factors. (1) The theory is not concerned with success or failure. (2) The theory does not indicate particular standards, rules and goals that might prompt particular self-conscious emotions. (3) It is assumed that such emotions come from self-attributions that arise from internal events, whereas standards, rule and goals are learned from others. In short, Lewis's theory suggests that the self-conscious emotions arise, cognitively, from attributions.

There are three relevant sets of activities. Standards, rules and goals are established, the success or failure of one's actions with respect to these standards, rules and goals is evaluated, and attributions are made about the self. Part of such attributions will of course be concerned with the self-conscious emotions. For example, guilt would be seen as stemming from a self-evaluation of failure but one which has dwelt on specific aspects or actions of the self that have led to the failure. It is specific, unlike the negative evaluations involved in shame which tend to be about the global self. Within the terms of this theory, pride, to take a further example, is the result of a successful evaluation of some specific action.

Conclusions

With one exception, the theories included in this chapter are not as ambitious or as far-reaching as most of the others in this book. Their aims are restricted to providing an account of a single emotion, or at best a group of emotions, as with the so-called self-conscious ones. The exception, of course, comes with Averill's treatment of anger, and to an extent his treatment of happiness, which he uses as a vehicle to carry on his social constructionist theory of emotion in general.

So, the theories should be judged within this relatively restricted framework. However, even with this limitation, they do not stand up very well to scrutiny. Mostly, they provide definitions of the particular emotion with which they are concerned. Although this is useful enough it does not go very far. They do provide summaries of the existing knowledge, knowledge which is relatively sparse. However, with the possible exception of Sternberg and Solomon on love, they do not provide good explanations, nor lead to much in the way of readily testable predictions. They do of course have a clear focus, but somehow they lack in heuristic value as well.

Apart from Averill, the general exception to these critical points comes from Izard and his differential emotions theory. More than anyone, Izard has attempted to do what the layperson might expect to be done in writings on emotion, and that is to provide an account of the specific emotions. It follows naturally from his theory that he should do this. Even Izard's accounts though go little further than being definitional and descriptive.

Thinking of Lazarus's (1991a,b) criteria that should be met by theories of emotion, the 'specific' theories score well on definition, and obviously on the matter of the discreet nature of emotions. They also do rather well on consideration of the biological or sociocultural background to emotion. However, they are are somewhat wanting with respect to the remaining criteria. They tend either not to be formally expressed or to be in the form of models. Either way, this means that it is hard to find what they might imply about the causes of emotion, and of emotion considered as an independent or a dependent variable.

From Oatley's (1992) perspective, the specific theories have useful things to say about the functions of emotion and of the emotions as discrete entities. Relatedly, they are also clearly grounded in the folk psychology of emotion. In some cases, they are also clearly concerned with the interpersonal communication aspects of emotion, and by definition with the basic emotions. It is almost entirely the so-called basic emotions that the specific emotion theorists are concerned with. However, they do not fare well with respect to the unconscious causes of emotion, nor with the question of evaluations, and nor with the extent to which a specific emotion might be concerned with simulating the plans of other people.

Some of the theories can deal with more evidence in Oatley's characterisation of the Lakatos approach. And in some cases, but not many, specific predictions can be derived from them in the sense of Oatley's view of the Popperian tradition.

It is perhaps not surprising that there have been relatively few attempts to theorize about specific emotions and that what there are do not add greatly to our knowledge. However, various themes do emerge from a consideration of them, an important one of which is that it seems reasonably straightforward to differentiate the specific emotions from one another, conceptually, even though it might not be so easy physiologically. In this sense, they both derive from and have something to feed back into the folk psychology of emotion.

Interestingly, and consistently with every conclusion drawn in this book so far, the specific emotion theorists frequently draw attention to the importance of cognition in their accounts. However, they go further than this and often forge a link between emotion (or the specific emotion under consideration) and personality. Moreover, in their concern with the biological foundations of the specific emotions plus their possible social construction, the theorists draw on much that is without psychology. In other words, they imply that an interdisciplinary approach to emotion might serve us well. This position is endorsed strongly here, and is explored in some detail in Chapters 13 and 14.

The significance of an interdisciplinary approach to emotion is made clear by a number of the specific emotion theorists who draw attention to the importance of the moral order in their accounts. Much of what they describe is concerned with the nature of rules in human, particularly emotion, conduct. As soon as the idea of social rules comes into play, then other disciplines become of obvious relevance—history, philosophy, sociology and anthropology for example.

With the exception of Izard's differential emotions theory, Averill's social constructionist approach, and Solomon's interesting discourse on love, the theories about specific emotions are somewhat disappointing. The reason for this is not obvious. Clearly, many, if not most emotion theorists believe that specific, discrete, and even basic emotions exist. Why then have they not produced cogent theories of them?

That they have not is particularly surprising given the everyday interest that there would be in such an endeavour. Perhaps this is the reason, everyday interest being a little suspect to good scientists. Or, more charitably, perhaps it is because those who have produced general theories of emotion believe that their theories can simply be used to account for the specific emotions. Or it may be that the individual emotions have proved a little difficult to engage in any depth.

Finally, it should be noted that a definite exception to this theoretical desert surrounding the specific emotions comes with anxiety. Vast amounts have been written on anxiety, embracing both empirical and theoretical work. Also, some of the ideas about anxiety have considerable ramifications for the understanding of emotion more broadly. Indeed, the theories of anxiety to some extent reflect the theories of general emotion. As mentioned previously, discussion of anxiety is reserved for Chapter 11 since it is importantly in the domain of abnormal and clinical psychology.

9

Developmental theory

Theorizing about emotion from a primarily developmental viewpoint brings with it a particular set of considerations. Some of these might obtain in general theories of emotion, but not necessarily. An obvious and basic example, is that emotion has to be dealt with from the viewpoint of change, and preferably change throughout the lifespan. In none of the theories so far summarized in this book has there been attention to whether or not the emotional life of the elderly is similar or different to the emotional life of children. Do our emotional reactions change at all throughout life? If so, is this a process of continuous change or does it occur in discrete stages or jumps?

Developmental psychology is inevitably wrapped up with considerations of the influences of nature versus nurture. From the emotion viewpoint, this means that the developmental theorist is likely to pay particular attention to the issue of emotion being biologically or socially based. Or, rather than see this as an all-or-none matter, might be concerned to explore the possible links between the two.

In spite of the specific theoretical considerations that a developmental approach to emotion might bring, any developmental theory is likely to be relevant to a general understanding of emotion. After all, to deal with emotional development it is surely important to first say what emotion is and how it functions. Then, added to this is the obvious question of how it develops, and added to this even further is the possible changing influences of emotion on other aspects of psychological functioning throughout development. For example, see Strongman (1996) for an analysis of the links between emotion and memory from a developmental perspective.

As will become clear, theories of emotional development fall into two fairly distinct groups. Ultimately, they derive from Watson's (1929) work and then that of Bridges (1932) whose description of the course of emotional development still appears in introductory texts. However, their views are not described in detail here. The two categories of theory are distinguishable by time. The first and the simplest appeared in the 1950s and 1960s and the second are more complex and far-reaching in the 1980s and 1990s. For reasons of their worth and contribution, more space will be devoted to the more recent theories, however it will be obvious that certain matters run throughout all of the theories, not the least of which being the role of cognition in emotional development.

Bousfield and Orbison

In its original form, the biological approach to emotional development pivoted on the view that negative emotion is experienced when a need/drive state is blocked. Bousfield and Orbison (1952) were forerunners of this approach, basing their ideas on two lines of speculation. They assumed that: (1) neonates are functionally decorticate, increasing cortical control being a part of development, and (2) infants are partially lacking in hormones that are an important part of stress reactions.

The relative lack of cortical, that is, inhibitory, control at birth should mean that the emotional responses of infants are somewhat like those of animals. This also suggests that emotions in young children, although quick to be aroused, should dissipate rather than persist. Moreover, emotional states are believed to increase in vigour with age, a vigour which is largely to do with adrenal influence. The development of the adrenals follows an odd course, decreasing weight from birth to the age of two. They then increase in weight until about 20, only getting back to their birth weight by the age of 16 or so.

These ideas find brief mention in the present context for their place in the history of emotional development, and would not benefit from further exploration.

Schneirla

Schneirla (1959) put forward a somewhat idiosyncratic theory of emotional development which is included here more because at the time it stood alone than for its influence, which was not great. He defines emotions as:

"(1) episodes or sequences of overt and incipient somatic adjustment, (2) often loosely patterned and variable, (3) usually with concurrent excitatory sensory effects, perhaps also perceptual attitudes characterisable as desirable or undesirable, pleasant or unpleasant, (4) related to the intensity effects of perceptual meaning of a stimulus, (5) synergic with organic changes of A- or W-types." (1959, p26)

The A- and W-types refer to biphasic mechanisms of receptors, central and auxiliary nervous systems and effects which Schneirla regards as basic to all ontogeny. A-type arousal is caused by weak-intensity stimuli and leads to approach. W-type arousal is caused by strong-intensity stimuli and leads to withdrawal.

Schneirla argues that observations of infants suggests that the reactions of neonates are essentially biphasic. He further suggests that some biphasic states are physiologically prescribed, which, as they mature, lead to the development of emotion and motivation, which are themselves closely related.

Aronfreed

Aronfreed (1968) bases his views of emotional development on the concept of *internalization*. The core assumption is that emotional changes mediated by cognitive evaluations form the basis of self-regulatory behaviour through internalization. This approach to emotional development springs from the notion that anxiety becomes associated with punished behaviour, and in future the anxiety may suppress the behaviour. Then, if children learn to suppress aspects of their behaviour without external intervention, they have internalized behaviour.

So, internalization is self-control through cognitive aspects of emotional change. Either pleasure, or fear/anxiety become attached to everyday acts. These positive or negative emotions then become associated with a child's understanding of a situation. In the end, the child becomes happy or afraid when thinking of doing something, and before it is done.

Extending the argument, Aronfreed suggests that internalization follows the experience of an emotional change connected to some behaviour, perhaps just through observation. He stresses the importance of imitation, which the child does because of the pleasure gained from observing a model. Feeling good becomes associated with perceptions and cognitions of the model. Cognitions are crucial since, in Aronfreed's view, they allow the expansion of emotional self-control. The child ends by acting so as to produce 'good' feelings and avoid producing 'bad' feelings. To this point, Aronfreed's theory is similar to that of many cognitive emotion theorists who combine appraisal or evaluation and affective memory.

There is a social aspect to the theory, since internalization is thought to presuppose an initial attachment to a person. This implies that the threat of withdrawal of love or nurturance from the child is important to emotional change and development. Self-criticism is the internalization of this.

Bowlby

Bowlby (1969, 1973, 1980) is the best-known exponent of *attachment theory,* which, while it is not a theory of emotional development *per se*, is very much concerned with the influence of emotion on developing social relationships and personality.

According to attachment theory, at the earliest opportunity a child is predisposed to attach to the caregiver, many specific behaviours being involved. Caregivers, in their turn, are supposed to be biologically predisposed to respond to this. Emotionally, the attachment is a feeling of security. Four types of pattern of attachment have been distinguished (see Bretherton, 1985). These are termed avoidant, secure, ambivalent, and a mixture of avoidant and ambivalent.

Bowlby argues that infants between the ages of one and two begin to develop working models of world, self and attachment figures. These models help the child to make sense of the relationships.

While attachment theorists do not suggest that discrete emotions are there from birth, they do suggest that particular types of behaviours designed to produce particular types of response from caregivers are built-in. The process is seen very much from an evolutionary-ethological adaptive point of view. Bowlby's discussion of emotions centred round the appraisal process, affective appraisals being consciously experienced (that is, felt) or not. So, for Bowlby, emotions can exist without them being consciously experienced.

Bowlby's view of emotional development makes firm links between expression and feeling, and also sees as very important that we are good at interpreting the emotional states of others. We need to be for his ideas of attachment to have substance. Attachment occurs naturally, and does not require particular socialization processes. Any differences in the quality of attachment are heavily dependent on the mother/child or caregiver/child interaction during the early stages of development. Particularly important are maternal sensitivity, maternal acceptance or rejection, maternal cooperation or interference and maternal accessibility.

While attachment theory is not strictly speaking a theory of emotional development, it is a theory of social development which is based very much on the emotional aspects of interaction between the child and the caregiver. As such, it is highly relevant to an understanding of emotional development.

Sroufe

Sroufe (1979) puts forward a theory of socioemotional development, with differentiation of emotion occurring from original distress/nondistress states (following Bridges, 1932) depending on other significant developmental reorganizations. Cognition is central to emotional development from Sroufe's perspective.

Sroufe believes that specific, discrete emotions do not begin to appear until about two to three months. Before this there must be sufficient cognitive ability to allow consciousness, plus the ability to distinguish the self from others. So, emotional experiences come about through recognition and appraisal and are heavily dependent on cognitive development.

From this viewpoint, the socialization of emotion and individual differences in personality development as they link to this are wrapped up with the course of attachment. So Sroufe sees social adaptation in late childhood to depend on early affective bonds.

Clearly, Sroufe's view of emotional development stems from Bridges (1932) and is in line with that of Lewis and Michalson (1983). It is a cognitivist-cum-social constructionist position and contrasts with the more nativist, discrete emotions type of theory.

Giblin

Giblin's (1981) equilibrium theory of emotional development is based on a distinction between feelings and emotions. The first affective responses are feelings, which are unprocessed responses to sensorial qualities and/or physiological changes. They are diffuse and occur in preverbal children. Being overrun by this type of affective life would lead to loss of equilibrium. This is dealt with by the development of emotions, which for Giblin are overt physiological or behavioural responses directed towards changing the environment. They vary according to the situation and appraisals and represent an attempt to maintain stability.

Giblin believes that there are five stages in the development of emotion. (1) From 0 to 8 months there is disequilibrium from sudden or intense sensory sensations; reflexive adjustments follow. Expressions represent pleasure/displeasure and sleep/tension. (2) From 9 to 12 months there also develops disequilibrium brought about by the presence or absence of other people. Equilibrium is achieved by interaction, and a diffused chaos is replaced by more organized responses. (3) From 2 to 6 years, disequilibrium is caused directly and indirectly by stimuli and equilibrium is regained through representational skills and emotional skills. (4) From 7 to 12 years, disequilibrium comes through immediate perception and social comparisons, and emotional responses involve characteristic behaviour patterns. (5) After 13, disequilibrium comes through internal comparisons and emotions start to contribute to the stable conception of the self, particularly through prevailing moods and attitudes.

Although this is an interesting theory and might be said to have some heuristic value, it is difficult to see how it might be developed further.

Fischer, Shaver and Carnochan

One of the fullest theories of emotional development to appear in recent years is that of Fischer, Shaver and Carnochan (1988, 1990). They start from the perspective that any theory of emotional development must deal with both how emotions develop and with how they influence the course of development. To construct their theory they draw on skill theory (1980) which is an approach to the organization of behaviour. They believe that basic emotions are elicited by very simple appraisals in infancy but later, more complex and more culturally dependent emotions depend on more complex appraisals.

Generally, Fischer et al concur with most emotion theorists that emotions are meaningful, organized and adaptive, and that primary or basic emotions are there in infancy. However, on top of this are various cognitive processes such as appraisal and judgement. They speak, as have many before them, of the difficulty in defining emotions, because they have so many features and can vary so much in detail. They do however have an overall organization and function. Fischer et al consider that it is important to explicate three components in understanding emotion: (1) elicitation through appraisal of functionally organized tendencies to action, (2) family categories of emotion arranged round basic emotions, and (3) the definition of each emotion category through a prototypical action script.

They state that emotions begin with appraisal, of change, then with respect to concerns and coping potential. There follows an action tendency and attempts at self-control which are monitored. Through this it is possible to have an emotion about an emotion. From a developmental viewpoint, there is reorganisation of all these processes at different points.

Fischer et al combine the traditionally opposing views of biological versus social construction, by arguing that emotions are arranged in families with three different levels of categories. The top layer divides into positive and negative, the basic layer includes those emotions that are shared across cultures, and the final layer contains the socially constructed emotions.

They use the word *script* to refer both to the way an event is represented generically and to any plan that might be used to enact the event. Further, they suggest that "the prototype for each basic emotion is a script of behavioural and social events for the best or most typical case of the emotion, the essence of the category" (1990, p92). This way of looking at each emotion provides particular behavioural, expressive, experiential and cognitive components.

To summarize the theory so far, the progression is detection of change, appraisals, action tendencies, specific patterns or scripts, which in turn fall into basic emotion families. All of this is there, roughly, "at an early age", but it all develops as well. Furthermore, particular emotional experiences lead to particular developmental pathways, they help to organize development. This organisation can be widespread, from facial expressions to personality disorders.

Fischer et al provide examples of the shaping effects of emotion on development. For instance, a particular individual might have been shaped by the dominance of the experience of a particular emotion. Or there might be particular, specific influences on attachment relationships in infancy. They also refer to the specific example of the development of multiple personality or emotional splitting that is the result of child-abuse.

Skill

Of central importance to Fisher et al's theory of emotional development is the concept of skill. They argue that in development it is the *organization* of behaviour that changes, and this happens through structured skills which the child comes to construct and control. Emotions influence this process whilst changes in the control of skills influence the development of emotion.

"A skill is defined as the child's ability to control variations in his or her own actions and mental processes in a particular context" (1990, p99). They argue that charting the course of emotional development should therefore begin with the specific domain of emotional skills. It is possible, in the usual sense of skill, to *control* emotions as it is to control riding a bicycle, and the concept also points to the importance of the interaction between the person and the environment.

Their point is that all the complexities of emotional development— appraisals, antecedents, responses, self-control—can be considered through an analysis of the skills involved. They characterize emotional development as involved with successive *tiers* of skills

They describe four tiers associated roughly with age periods, a different type of unit of skill characterizing each of them. These are reflexes, sensorimotor actions, representations and abstractions. The age bands are approximately: up to four months, four months to two years, two years to about ten years, and ten years to adulthood. Within each of these tiers, emotional development progresses through a further four developmental levels, from simple to complex. Much of what Fischer et al describe are techniques for making skill analyses of emotional development in an empirical way, a matter beyond the present scope.

However, Fischer et al do not stop at adulthood; theirs is a life-span development approach. They characterize adults with their considerable abstract skills as being involved in extremely complex and subtle, individual emotion scripts. Emotions in adulthood become extended over time and vastly sustained. Emotional life for the adult can become extraordinarily complex with multiple mixed-emotions all moving at different speeds in different directions.

In summary then, Fischer et al provide a developmental theory of emotion which is heavily dependent on the analysis of skills and which considers not only emotional development per se but also the influence of emotion on development more generally. Although it is an idiosyncratic theory in its emphasis on skills, it is based on a combination of the basic elements which appear in most other recent theories of emotional development and of emotion more generally.

Campos

One of the areas in which theoretical contributions have occurred and which is linked to emotional development is that of *emotional regulation*—this is concerned with the control of emotional experience and expression. For present purposes it is perhaps sufficient to provide an idea of this area by giving an account of the views of Campos (Campos, Campos and Barrett, 1989).

In this analysis, the authors begin by suggesting that the idea that emotion is secondary to cognition misses much. Instead, they use a definition of emotion that takes a different perspective. "... emotions are ... *processes of establishing, maintaining, or disrupting the relations between the person and the internal or external environment, when such relations are significant to the individual*" (p395, italics theirs). In turn, significance comes from goal relevance, emotional communication from important people, and hedonic tone. Cognitions have to fit within this framework to be relevant to emotions.

Moreover, from this perspective, emotions are *relational*, they work between people as well as within the person. Campos et al describe this view as giving equal status to a person's appreciation of an event's significance, a person's feelings, and a person's manner of dealing with the environment. They believe that systems theory, ethology and an organizational approach to emotional development prompt the shift to this relational view.

Campos et al list five major implications of the relational view of emotions. (1) It gives four factors a role to play in emotion generation: motivational processes, emotional signals of another, hedonic stimulation, and things ecological. They stress in particular, that an emphasis on emotion generation shows how the emotional state of the other is regulated by the environment.

(2) Action and action tendencies are stressed, which means less emphasis on feelings and more on what an individual is doing to cope with the environment and to complete goals.

(3) Emotion should be understood against a background in which we interrelate to other people and to physical objects. In other words, emotion and its development is relational.

(4) Part of these relational processes are autonomic responses, because they have social communicative import.

(5) The idea of hedonic stimulation fell into relative disuse some years ago but is somewhat revived by the relational view of emotion, particularly with respect to its role in emotional development. So, for example, pain can be experienced by the neonate without a necessary intervention of anything cognitive.

Campos argues that emotion helps to maintain the continuity of self-development through the life-span, and does so through temperamental dispositions. This view emphasizes individual differences, particularly as they are concerned with irritability and inhibition.

Finally, Campos et al point out that to understand emotion regulation, it is important to look at multiple response systems, but nevertheless with emotion seen as a single relational process. So, they believe that attention should settle on emotion elicitation, the social adaptiveness of emotions, and how emotions lead to personality dispositions. Unlike many other recent theorists, they are taking the emphasis away from cognition and placing it on interactions between the person and the environment. In passing, it might be worth noting that those of a cognitive persuasion might consider that person/environment interactions are mediated through cognition.

Izard and Malatesta (now Malatesta-Magai)

A particularly cogent theory of emotional development is put forward by Izard and Malatesta (1987), although as will be seen later, Malatesta's

(Malatesta-Magai's) views have developed since that time. The 1987 theory is presented as sets of postulates with supporting evidence, all of which is based on the assumption that the emotions form a system which is independent of, but interrelated with, life-support, behavioural and cognitive systems. They view emotions as discrete motivators of human behaviour, each of which is made up of neurochemical, motoric-expressive and mental processes. They also see emotions as prime movers in development.

The first three of Izard and Malatesta's 12 postulates of emotional development are neurophysiological.

(1) Each of the 10 or 11 (according to Izard) basic emotions has its own neural substrates, but shares brain structures with others.

(2) Neurobiological growth processes of canalization and plasticity account for invariance and developmental change in the developing emotional system.

(3) The development and organization of the brain allows the independent functioning of the emotions system. This normally interacts with cognition, but at this stage it is not necessary

Then come three postulates concerning emotional expression.

(4) There are two main developmental changes in expressive behaviour. The kind of events and situations that can elicit emotion change, and there is a shift from reflexive movements to enculturation and learning. This applies at all points in development, including old age.

(5) Expressive behaviour moves from being all-or-none and canalized to a more modulated form.

(6) Instruction in emotional expression begins early in life because its regulation is so important socially. It tends to continue throughout childhood.

The final six postulates are in the domain of emotional experience.

(7) The essential quality of the feeling state of the fundamental emotions is activated when the neuromuscular-expressive pattern is encoded. This is an index of an infant's feelings.

(8) The feeling component of each of the basic emotions has unique adaptive and motivational functions.

(9) Throughout the lifespan, some emotion is always present in consciousness.

(10) The essential quality of an emotion feeling does not vary throughout life.

(11) In late childhood and early adolescence the ability to synthesize emotions is joined with the capacity to deal with them as abstractions. This increases the possibilities for conflict and for the integration of personality.

(12) Emotions retain their motivational and adaptive function even when development is not adaptive or when it is psychopathological.

Izard and Malatesta's is an unusual theory of emotional development in the way in that it is set out so formally. Clearly, it derives from Izard's general theory of emotion and has a good basis in empirical research. Moreover, as already mentioned, Malatesta's (Malatesta-Magai's) views have developed further from this starting point. (See next section.)

Finally, in a further paper (Malatesta, Culver, Tesman and Shepard, 1989) Malatesta suggests that any theories of emotional development should be compared as to their stance on six major dimensions. (1) Discrete emotions present at birth, (2) the experience of emotional feelings, (3) the influence of expression on experience, (4) the concordance between expression and feeling throughout development, (5) the socialization of emotion, and (6) the relationship between emotion and personality. These suggestions will be returned to later.

Malatesta-Magai (Malatesta, Magai)

Following Izard and Malatesta's (1987) general, life-span theory of emotional development, Malatesta-Magai and Izard (1991) consider the more specific problem of infant emotion, again though from the viewpoint of differential emotions theory. Their starting point is the basic one of whether or not infants have feelings, and how we can know this. Given the usual problems of the absence of self-report in infants, they argue that it is a question of asking firstly whether or not infant expressive behaviours occur in the same contexts as adult expressive behaviours. And secondly, whether these expressions seem to be functionally adaptive, or simply random events. They believe that there is continuity between infant and adult emotional expression.

Malatesta-Magai and Izard take it as read that the emotion system is to some extent prewired, a part of an evolved (and presumably evolving) adaptive process, particularly since there appears to be consensus about the conditions which reliably elicit the basic emotions. They move the matter of elicitors onto the question of developmental continuity: do we respond to the same kind of elicitors no matter what our point of development might be? The differential emotions theory position is that expressions in infancy are an index of feeling states. Other theorists suggest that infant expression is more likely to be random or unorganized because, for example, true emotions cannot occur before particular cognitive points have been reached in development or because there seems to be low specificity between elicitors and expressions in infants.

Malatesta and Wilson (1988) [see also Malatesta-Magai and Hunziker, 1993] argue that a discrete emotions analysis can deal with these problems. They point to the adaptive functions of the signals associated with Izard's ten (or eleven) primary emotions; these adaptive functions are relevant to do with both the self and with others. For example, anger eliminates barriers for the self and warns others of possible attack. Moreover, both elicitors and emotions are not discrete events, but are complexes or families, so there is no direct correspondence between discrete events and discrete expressions. Emotions are more like instincts than reflexes.

Malatesta-Magai and Izard (1991) make a number of cogent theoretical points in arguing against the received wisdom about infant emotion. (1) Analysis shows that there is an internal coherence with respect to elicitors, rather than there being randomness and no specificity. (2) They argue that to ask that infants be highly specific in their facial expressions to particular elicitors is asking more of them than of adults. Moreover, there do not need to be sophisticated cognitive processes, that might appear later in development, for emotional reactions to occur, although in fact, infants appear to be capable of relatively sophisticated appraisals in any case. (3) Malatesta and Izard also argue firmly that discrete emotion signals are in evidence in very early infancy. There is what they term a morphological maturity by two and half months.

To summarize, Malatesta-Magai and Izard believe that emotions are well differentiated and connected to internal states very early in life. They believe further that this aspect of development rests on the maturation of a process which is linked to cognition and learning. Their emphasis throughout is on viewing emotions as instinct-like behaviours which are functionally adapted to classes of goals which are themselves related to classes of stimuli.

Magai and Hunziker (1993) take this theory a stage further, bringing it back into the lifespan and bringing in the development of personality. The background is the usual one that has bedevilled developmental theory for so long, namely that of continuity or discontinuity. They argue that moments of crisis and transition help to prompt an individual's particular emotional organization. There are times in each life when previously unexperienced strong emotions overwhelm the individual and precipitate crisis. These are moments at which developmental transformation is possible; they are times of discontinuity.

In fitting emotional development into personality development, Magai and Hunziker bring together psychoanalytic, attachment and discrete emotions theory. This leads to a view of personality development relying on affective relationships, emotional biases, life events, and the meanings that are developed by individuals. The beginning of this though comes from attachment and the quality of the emotional experience that attends attachment.

Behind the individual life course lie emotions; they provide significant motivational forces. They believe that by attempting to understand affective experiences and their sources and motivating properties, so there will come understanding of the developmental transformations that occur during the life-span.

Camras

In an article shared with Malatesta and Izard, Camras (1991) expresses an alternative but overlapping theoretical perspective on emotional development. As she puts it "... affect-related facial expressions are present in early infancy but during the course of development they are both modified and integrated into larger emotional systems such as we conceive of in adults" (1991, p16). She views this as somewhat of a constructivist position, and also takes a systems analysis approach.

Camras espouses the *dynamical systems theory*. She characterizes this in its general form as "an attempt to account for the organized coordination of complex systems involving a nearly infinite number of possible actions or states" (p19). A system such as this requires a control mechanism. Often assumed by those who take this approach is that there are lower-order structures which are coordinated to create a synergy amongst the elements. So if one element is affected by the context of action, so might others be because of their synergistic relationship. This makes the control task or centre or structure simpler than it might have otherwise been.

Emotions may be viewed in this way. Here emotions are seen as self-organising systems that might have a central programme and will have elements that are synergistically related. So what happens in an episode of emotion might depend as much on the task or context as it does on some central command system

Within the dynamical systems approach, a change in a single critical component might lead an organism to shift from one major pattern of coordination to another. This might help to account for changes that occur in emotional reactions when the situation changes, for example from private to public. Camras sees the advantage of this approach being the relative lack of central controlling programmes.

The dynamical systems approach has already been taken up by developmentalists (eg Thelen, 1989). They have argued that various structures, such as cognitive abilities, can be seen as organized coordination patterns. They change when the value of the critical components change. This might involve the mere maturation of some physical structure rather than the emergence of a new central control system. Again, some structures might develop/mature before others and therefore not function as part of a coordinated system.

From the viewpoint of emotional development, this would suggest that simply because emotional expression is there in early infancy does not mean that the entire emotional system is functioning. For example it would not mean that there is subjective experience necessarily behind the expression.

Within this framework, control aspects of a system may change with age. Camras argues that this suggests that any theory of emotional development should not be linked to say, just cognitive development or instrumental development; various aspects of development might be relevant at different times.

Camras suggests that patterns of facial expression attended by states of attention or distress, become linked to the developing emotional system, particularly through labels. There might be central control systems involved, but nevertheless each emotion episode will include particular components depending on the action context. From this perspective there is no priority afforded to, say, facial expression. All emotional responses become recruited as they are apposite to a task rather than simply reflecting a built-in capacity. More radically, dynamical systems theory might also suggest that emotions develop without the benefit of central control at all. All structure and pattern might come from the environment and the requirements of any task and the constraints of any context.

The central differences between the dynamical systems theory approach to emotional development and that of differential emotions theory are: (1) Differential emotions theory suggests that facial expressions are direct 'read-outs' of emotion in infants, and dynamical systems theory does not. (2) Differential emotions theory suggests that various expressions (eg distress-pain, anger, sadness and surprise) reflect the same core of experience in infants as they do in adults, whereas Camras suggests that these expressions may change in their emotional status during development.

Harris

Rather than set out a theory of emotional development, Harris (1993) considers aspects of emotional development that any theorist would do well to consider. They are predicated on two major points. Firstly, that, as is integral to Lewis's theory (see later), beyond infancy, we *know* that we are experiencing an emotion. This awareness can be used in a number of ways—to report, anticipate, hide or change an emotional state. Secondly, we are able both to identify and understand other people's emotions—this is a different sort of awareness. Harris attempts to trace the development of these types of awareness in an attempt to understand children's understanding of emotion. Early on in life, that is in the first year or so, infants start to recognize that emotional states are intentional, that is they are directed. Within the next year or two or three, they start to realize that people choose what to do in terms of their beliefs about their desires. Simultaneously, they begin to make sense of emotion (theirs and others) in the same way. According to Harris, this is a universal belief.

At about age six or seven, moral standards begin to play a part in the child's understanding of emotion. For example, although objects might be desirable, pursuing them in socially unacceptable ways might not bring happiness. However, children of this sort of age still do not readily accept mixed emotions.

Another development that occurs between the ages of about four and six is the child's realization that emotional expression might not correspond to or be an exact reflection of emotional state. Whilst it might be difficult to perceive differences between, say, a deliberately manipulated and a spontaneous expression, a child might realize that there does not have to be coincidence between real and apparent emotion.

Finally, there is the question of emotional change, which can be accomplished either by hiding emotional expression or by changing the state itself. With increasing age during childhood so the former gives way to the latter.

In an analysis of the implications of this development in children's under-standing of emotion, Harris emphasizes *emotion scripts* and *the emotional un-conscious*. He mentions a body of work that indicates the readiness with which children work out the types of situation that elicit various emotions. From this, he regards it as possible that children's understanding of each emotion involves a script which has parts for the eliciting situation, the subjective state, and the physiological, behavioural and expressive aspects.

Harris believes that the idea of a script in children's understanding of emotion is important for three reasons. (1) It fits children's understanding of emotion into their broader understanding. (2) It suggests that to understand emotion a child needs to understand sequential causal connections. (3) It would be useful in looking at the development of the understanding of emo-tion across various cultures.

From Harris's viewpoint, the developmental account of the role of the unconscious in emotion does not stress the traditional significance of repres-sion. Here, a child's lack of awareness is nothing to do with motivation, but rather with cognition. A child may experience an emotion without being able to conceptualize or talk about it. This is a matter of relative cognitive lack rather than anything to do with say the repression of something unpleasant.

Finally, Harris's theorizing is not about emotional development in its own right, but is about the development of *understanding* of emotion. As such it is of course relevant to any general theory of emotional development.

Lewis

Lewis has contributed an enormous amount to our understanding of emo-tional development (eg Lewis, 1992; Lewis, 1993; Lewis and Michalson, 1983; Lewis and Saarni, 1985). Perhaps the most succinct description of his views appear in Lewis (1993) and the present exposition is heavily reliant on that chapter which is part of the *Handbook* of which he is joint editor.

In working towards his own theory of emotional development, he first clears away some conceptual undergrowth. He views emotion as a term which refers to a general class of elicitors, behaviours, states and experiences, be-tween all of which it is necessary to distinguish. Also, in order to produce a theory of emotional development, in Lewis's view it is important to consider the matter of the nature, or more basically, the existence, of emotional states. He argues that even if there are emotional states, they do not accord with any precision to our emotional lives, either in emotional expression or experience. Emotion is constantly changing, so emotional states have to be seen as tran-sient patterns that occur in bodily and neurophysiological activity. When awake, we are always in some or other emotional 'state', although this may not correspond to our emotional expression and we may not be aware of it.

From a developmental perspective, it is necessary to determine the nature and derivation of the various states. As ever from a developmental viewpoint, there are two possibilities: (1) emotional states might have their genesis in development, either through maturation or through a mixture of nature and the environment; or (2) emotional states might be innate, with development having no role to play. The first of these possibilities has led to a model in which emotions gradually become differentiated either from an initial (bipolar) state generalized excitation or from two (positive and negative) states, a view which began with Bridges (1932). Lewis believes that the most probable account is that emotional development comes about through differentiation of emotional states depending on a mixture of maturation, socialization and cognitive development.

The alternative view (espoused most obviously by Izard and Malatesta-Magai) is that some emotional states are prewired, existing at birth although not necessarily appearing until later. The question of some emotions being genetically preprogrammed or all emotions being dependent on some or other developmental process is clearly crucial for an understanding of emotional development.

Lewis also attends to the question of emotional experience from a developmental perspective. He regards emotional experience as depending on the cognitive processes of evaluation and interpretation, processes which in their turn are somewhat dependent on socialization. Looked at within a developmental context, emotional experience requires that the organism have some cognitive abilities, plus a concept of self. He argues that two processes are necessary: (1) the knowledge that the bodily changes are unique and internal, and (2) an evaluation of such changes, particularly with respect to the internal/external, awareness/expression distinction.

In general, to *experience* emotion, it is necessary to attend to oneself, that is, to have an idea of 'agency'. In other words, the organism has not only to be able to evaluate the cause of an action but also to consider who is evaluating it, that is, the self. All of which, to Lewis, does not mean that infants do not have emotional *states* before they have self-awareness, simply that they do not experience them. He believes that the rules that determine how we experience emotional states depend on socialization, which in turn depends on the individual, the family and the culture.

Turning to the development of emotional expression, Lewis points out that the various theories of the development of emotional expression depend on whether or not such expressions are considered to be directly linked to emotional states. This is a question which Lewis believes cannot be answered—there may be innate connections between states and expression or the connections may be made through a developmental process.

In the midst of this undergrowth clearing, is Lewis forming a cognitive path to emotional development or not? In his view, if the focus is on emotional experience then emotion is a cognitive matter, and if it is on emotional states then it is not.

Perhaps with a slight tentativeness, Lewis (1993) presents what he terms a *model* of emotional development in the first three years of life. This is based on the conviction that most of the adult emotions have appeared by then, even though others might emerge later, or the existing ones become elaborated. He argues that although there is not much in the way of language to help the early study of emotion, a mixture of studying the expressions and their context allows reasonable inferences to be made.

Lewis assumes that the child is born with bipolar emotional reactions—distress and pleasure, although he also suggests that a state that intervenes between the two is interest. By three months, joy, sadness and disgust (in primitive, spitting out, form) appear. Anger appears somewhere between two and four months. Lewis regards this as interesting because it requires sufficient cognitive capacity to distinguish between means and ends in order to overcome frustration caused by a blocked goal.

At about seven to eight months children begin to show fearfulness, which requires even more cognitive involvement, certainly the ability to compare an existing stimulus with another, a strange with a familiar face for example. Also in the first six months, surprise, at some change in expected events, begins.

Sometime in the second half year of life, consciousness, or objective self-awareness develops and allows the emergence of a new class of emotions—those that are 'self-conscious'. They are embarrassment, empathy and envy.

At approximately two years a further cognitive ability makes an appearance—the capacity for the child to judge its behaviour against some standard, either external or internal. Following from this is what Lewis terms the 'self-conscious evaluative emotions', pride, shame and guilt for example. For these emotions, a sense of self has to be compared against other standards.

Lewis's model of emotional development then has most of it completed by the age of three. There may be further elaboration thereafter but it is based on what is there at that stage. Clearly, his view is that the major stages in the early development of emotions are dependent on cognitive milestones being passed. For Lewis, emotional development and cognitive development are integrally linked, but as a developmentalist, he also sees cognitive development as integrally linked with socialization.

Cognition in development

Recent theorists of emotional development, like most other emotion theorists, are making increasing references to cognition. It would not seem possible to have a meaningful noncognitive account of emotional development, even though Izard and Malatesta-Magai come closer than anyone. The assumption is that cognition underlies the unfolding of the emotions, through such processes as recognition, causality, intentionality and meaning. These are regarded as cognitive control systems.

At this point, some of Piaget's ideas bear on emotion. They are well described by Cichetti and Hesse (1983). From the Piagetian perspective, certain aspects of emotion do not change in development. His work implies for example that almost all emotions and emotional expressions are present at birth. He also had it that the functions of emotions remain constant in the first two years of life, although the situations in which emotions are expressed become increasingly complex.

Emotional change is prompted by motor and cognitive changes, and the emotions of children gradually approximate the meanings which adults give to them. Generally, Piaget implies that infants display more complex sequences of emotion because they become more complex cognitively.

The problem is how exactly are emotion and cognition related as they develop? Piaget's position is one of parallelism, with emotion and cognition developing in a complementary non-causally related way; the structure comes from cognition and the energy from emotion. Cichetti and Hess argue that interactionism is far more likely than parallelism; apart from any other consideration, there is far more to emotion than mere energy.

Buck (1983) also looks at the relationship between cognition and emotion, but within the context of emotional education. He argues that there should be situations that by their nature prompt attempts at emotional understanding and mastery. For example, the novel feelings a child might experience from neurochemical changes might occur when he or she first feels angry with a parent or first encounters sex.

Buck also suggests that the readiness to comprehend these types of experience will depend on cognitive development, a point which he believes has implications for emotional education. Although emotional education is largely ignored, in our society, except to urge suppression, the general ambience of a culture may well reflect the emotional education of its young. Buck argues that the various types of emotional responding are associated with the different types of social learning. For example instrumental responses should be related to a person's expectations about what is the appropriate behaviour. Expressive behaviour and subjective experience would be related to actual emotional states. Reports of subjective experience should reflect labels and interpretations and physiological responding should reflect the intensity of the prior condition of arousal in similar situations.

Conclusions

It is perhaps of interest that there are quite a few theories of emotional development. In general, the earlier theories do not do a particularly good job as theories. Generally, they were constructed in an attempt to provide an explanation of emotional development, but their focus tends to be rather blurred and it is difficult to derive testable predictions from them. Even their heuristic value is not high.

This concluding section will therefore be concentrated mainly on the more recent and more formally expressed theories. However, it should be said that the earlier theorists did draw attention to some significant themes in emotional development. All of them, for example, make reference to cognition and the concept of appraisal in some form or another. They make mention of the possible biological origins of emotion and then of its later social development, often via the attachment process. They also tend to refer in passing to the evolution of emotion and to possible links between emotion and personality from a developmental viewpoint.

The more recent theories, notably those of Izard and Malatesta-Magai, Fischer et al, Campos, and Lewis, all fare well on the general characteristics of what makes for good theory. They provide cogent summaries of existing data, they provide particularly good explanations of emotional development, they are well focused, their heuristic value is obvious and, in some cases they lead to testable predictions, although this is perhaps less obvious.

The recent developmental theories fare just as well on Lazarus's (1991a,b) criteria for emotion theories. They provide definitions,deal with the matter of discrete emotions and interdependence between emotions. At least Izard and Malatesta-Magai are concerned with behaviour and physiology. They all consider the relationship between biological and social foundations and the links with cognition and motivation. They concern themselves with appraisal and consciousness and obviously deal with the generation and development of emotion. They also deal with the influences of emotion on other aspects of general functioning, although not many find room for a consideration of therapy.

Broadly, then, the developmental theories listed above do well on the causes of emotion and with respect to its function as both an independent and a dependent variable. From Lazarus's perspective then they are worthy theories, one of them even being laid out in quite formal terms.

Moving on to Oatley's (1992) criteria, the recent developmental theories find room to deal with the functions of emotions and to consider discrete and basic emotions, although not often from a folk psychological viewpoint. They certainly centre on the interpersonal communication side of emotion and reflect on possible unconscious causes. They also tend to be concerned with evaluations to do with goals but, like most emotion theories, are not much concerned with the simulation of the plans of others, at least not directly.

From the Lakatos perspective, the developmental theories can certainly assimilate more evidence, the development of the Izard and Malatesta-Magai and the Lewis theories demonstrating this most clearly. Specific predictions can also be derived from them.

In a similar way to Lazarus and Oatley providing specific criteria for 'good' theory in emotion (rather than 'good' theory in general) so Malatesta-Magai et al (1989) provide six criteria that should be met by a 'good' theory of emotional development. Again, her theory and those of Fischer et al, Campos, and Lewis meet these criteria reasonably well. They deal with the matter of discrete emotions being present at birth or not. They deal with feelings and to some extent with the influence of emotional expression on emotional experience. They certainly look at the socialization of emotion and at the links between emotion and personality. By and large though they do not have much to say about the concordance between emotional expression and feeling (the exception being the obvious one of Malatesta-Magai).

Apart from being relatively well-constructed theories, the recent developmental theories tend to have carried on exactly those themes that were there in the earlier theories. They have simply dealt with them in a more cogent, complex and useful manner. Matters such as the importance of attachment, the links between emotional development and other aspects of development, the emergence of consciousness, and the relationship between biological foundations and sociocultural developments loom large and important.

New themes also arise. Fischer et al for example emphasize the development of emotional skills, in tiers, with age, and in so doing divide emotions into families (of skills). Campos, within the framework of a person/environment interaction analysis becomes concerned with emotional regulation in the course of development. Also, the moral order comes into consideration.

One of the more interesting facets of these recent rather good quality theories of emotional development is that, unlike most of the theories so far listed, they divide on the question of cognition. At the outset it should be said that they all mention it. However, both the Izard and Malatesta-Magai and the Campos theories do not give it pride of place. Campos places the emphasis on relational matters and suggests that cognition has to fit around these. Izard and Malatesta-Magai, whose theory evolves from Izard's differential emotions theory, regard emotions as instinct-like prime movers. They might interact with cognition but they are not bound up with it as most theorists would suggest.

By contrast, other recent developmental theorists of emotion, such as Fischer et al, Harris, and Lewis give cognition, particularly appraisal, a central role. This is one of the few areas of emotion in which there is a reasonable choice between the cognitively and the non-cognitively based theories. However, it is worth repeating that even the theorists that de-emphasize cognition, still mention it in interaction with emotion.

It remains to say which is the best of the developmental theories of emotion. The most useful things to do would probably be to amalgamate all of the recent ones and to create a new and all-embracing theory; in some ways it would be hard to give up the good features of any one of them, Harris's emphasis on awareness for example. On the other hand, in the end the choice, if it had to be made, would probably have to come down between Izard and Malatesta-Magai and Lewis. Lewis has a strong role for cognition, is concerned with concepts such as self-awareness, but in a rather pleasingly old-fashioned sense rests his theory on maturation and socialization. Izard and Malatesta-Magai set out their formal postulates, give strong consideration to the life-span, and see emotions as prime movers, that are somewhat independent of cognitions.

Between these two theories, in the end you probably pay your money and make your choice. What is certain is that developmental theories of emotion have recently moved on a very long way from Watson and Bridges.

10

Social theory

Emotion is often conceptualized as a social phenomenon. For the most part the stimuli for emotional reactions come from other people and emotion occurs in the company of others. Even if emotions are generated by memories these are often of other people or of the impact they have had on us. Perhaps because of this, for many years, social psychologists focused on emotional expression and its recognition. This is of course an integral part of emotion and is interesting in its own right. Also, the problems which beset the study of expression and recognition and the attempts to solve them are instructive for more general analyses of emotion. However, there is far more to the social psychology of emotion than comes from a study of its expression and recognition. More recently, social psychologists have turned their attention to other aspects of emotion, and have begun to explore emotion in relationships, in attitudes, in group settings, in social climates, and so on.

Whenever we interact with someone we are experiencing and expressing emotion. Simultaneously, we are monitoring and interpreting the other person's emotional expression. The other is doing the same. It is this complex, subtle, and often unconscious process that gives social interaction some of its depth. Our emotional expressions provide stimuli to other people who respond by observing, judging, classifying and sometimes giving an 'answering' expression. We make our responses not just to the expression but also to what we believe the *meaning* to be behind the expression. It is with how we express ourselves emotionally and how well we identify such expressions in others that social psychologists of emotion have typically been concerned.

Clearly, the matter of emotional expression and recognition is but one of many intertwined complexities in social interaction. Emotion theorists in this area therefore have their work cut out more than most. Their theories are sometimes restricted to questions of social interaction and sometimes range more widely. Frequently, they refer to particular types of construct such as the possibility of underlying dimensions or categories of emotional expression. Most of them have to address issues such as the universality of expression and the matter of the significance of social context. Whatever form the theories take that are discussed in this chapter, such issues will inevitably emerge as common themes.

Davitz—a dictionary

Davitz (1969, 1970) builds his theory of emotion in answer to a question: what does a person mean when he says someone is happy or angry or sad? Davitz believes that this question should be answered descriptively, the descriptive answer that Davitz himself provides leading him into a dimensionality analysis of expression and recognition.

Davitz suggests that the meaning of the various emotions depends on experience, and argues that this should be studied through language. A problem which all psychologists face is that of having to use everyday terms in the more rigorous and restricted context of scientific endeavour. From the precise perspective of scientific method, the everyday connotations of words cause confusion. However, in passing it is worth noting that the recent views of those who have become interested in folk theory (Oatley for example) see the connotation of everyday words as a matter of interest rather than confusion.

In his way of dealing with this issue, Davitz aimed to produce a dictionary of emotional terms, drawn from what he describes as 'commonalities of meaning'—verbal descriptions of emotional states. He suggests that any common ground between the various descriptions might appear in mathematical abstractions.

This is not the place to outline Davitz's technique in detail; it is enough to say that it led to him to a dictionary of emotional meaning, which in turn led him to a tentative theory of emotion. This can be reduced to six main propositions. (1) Emotion is partly concerned with private, experienced events—a phenomenological, subjective viewpoint. (2) Emotion embraces specific states which are labelled, and each label refers to experiences about which there is reasonable common ground within a culture. (3) The language of emotion reflects experiences but is also directly affected by linguistic considerations. People make mistakes in their descriptions of emotion and, in fact, learn to label the emotion from the situation. (4) Definitions of emotional states fall into twelve clusters, which can fit into four dimensions of emotional experience: activation, relatedness, hedonic tone and competence. (5) Labelling emotion depends on experience. Any change in experience will change the label and the state. (6) Emotional states come about from stimuli which are psychologically relevant to the four dimensions of emotional meaning.

Davitz is aware that these propositions fit neither phenomenology, nor a psychoanalytic approach, nor a behavioural orientation. In fact, as a theory it leaves something to be desired, since it is both lacking in formal properties and is not well anchored to empirical fact. However, the theory has led to some interesting research, the ideas are relevant to cognitive analyses of emotion, and the dictionary of emotional meaning in itself is an interesting contribution to the social psychology of emotion.

Eibl-Eibesfeldt—ethology

The ethological approach to emotional expression has its obvious and significant starting point in Darwin. Although described some years ago, Eibl-Eibesfeldt's (eg 1970) analyses still give good insights into this type of approach. From an evolutionary perspective, he argues that expressive behaviour often derives from other behaviour that has been associated with frequent arousal or activity. For instance, in many species, social grooming has become ritualized into expressive movements that usually mean that social contact may proceed. The lemur for example greets other lemurs with its fur-combing movements.

Similarly, Eibl-Eibesfeldt maintains that behaviour which once led to attack has evolved into gestures of threat. An unfortunate aspect of such arguments is that they tend to lead to speculations about similar mechanisms in human beings, speculations which are not very helpful theoretically.

The ethological argument is that ritualization—the modification of behaviour which makes it communicative—is the main process underlying the evolution of expressive movements. The changes it makes to behaviour are important in signalling. Eibl-Eibesfeldt (1970) describes a number of such behavioural changes which accompany ritualisation, and suggests that such changes go along with the development of conspicuous bodily structures. Although, at the descriptive level, there are many apparent examples of ritualization in the animal world, and although the ideas may make good sense from the viewpoint of biological adaptivity, it is hard to see their theoretical force beyond this.

Another aspect of the ethological approach is to classify expressive movements according to their apparent function. Eibl-Eibesfeldt divides expressive movements into intra- and inter-specific releasers. Intraspecifics are signals that: (1) promote group cohesion, regulating interaction and attraction; (2) communicate about the external environment, say, the sounding of a warning note; (3) signify threat, certain bird songs or a gorilla's chest-beating for example. Interspecific expressive releasers are those that involve: (1) contact readiness; (2) threat postures.

One of the main advantages that has come from the ethological theoretical perspective in emotion is that it has led to some emphasis on the 'naturalistic' approach in human investigations. This in turn has led to the interesting type of theoretical exposition made by such people as Fridlund (eg 1992) on the place of Darwin in current analyses. Fridlund points out that Darwin notions on emotional expression have been replaced by analyses of signalling that are based on information. From an evolutionary viewpoint, displays which have social intent, and the capacity to be vigilant for these are believed to have evolved together. Fridlund argues that if his type of behavioural-ecology account is applied to human as well as infrahuman facial expressions, then there can be phylogenetic continuity in the analysis of emotional expression.

Frijda—dimensionality

Any consideration of the theories of emotion which stem from social psychologists must make reference to the idea that underlying the many emotions there are somewhat fewer dimensions that may be used to describe or otherwise account for them. Such ideas have their origin in the difficulty of giving theoretical meaning to the vast range of possible emotional expressions, particularly in the face, as distinct from the less useful approach of simply attempting to describe them.

As a general background, it should be said that there have been three main ways of conceptualising emotional expression and recognition. (1) Categories. Emotions as expressed could be classed into any number of distinct, unrelated events. So there might be primary emotions under the control of some innate subcortical programme which result in distinct facial responses. These are unrelated and unordered. (2) Dimensions. Here, expressed emotions are seen as mixtures of pleasantness, activation etc, each such dimension occupying a theoretical n-dimensional space and being orthogonal to the remainder. This type of analysis copes well with similarities and differences between the various emotional expressions, but becomes somewhat unwieldy if many dimensions are proposed. (3) Hierarchy. This is a combination of categories and dimensions. Thus, in a particular region of n-dimensional emotional space there may be differentiation between emotion in terms of the dimensions especially pertinent to that region. Emotions may be comparable as regards dimensions both within and between categories, although each category may have its own distinguishable qualities.

The dimension analysis has been the most common in this area and from time to time various researchers have suggested varying numbers of dimensions to account for emotional expression. Rather than attempt to rehearse them all, some of Frijda's earlier views (eg 1969) will be used as an example (although see Chapter 7 for a description of Frijda's more recent, and more significant, theory).

Frijda (1969) reduced emotional expression to six main factors (dimensions). (1) Pleasantness/unpleasantness. (2) Activation, which he described as intensity rather than sleep/tension as others had thought of it, its low end being a lack of expression rather than sleep. (3) Interest, which is somewhat like other investigators term attention/rejection. (4) Social evaluation. (5) and (6) were described as lesser dimensions and termed surprise and simple/complicated respectively.

If emotional expressions can be reduced to dimensions, at least two questions need to be addressed. First, do the dimensions delineate the meaning which underlies the emotion or more simply do they reflect the words used to describe emotional expression? Frijda maintains that his first four dimensions, at least, correspond to emotional meaning. Second, how many dimensions are there? Various investigators have suggested various numbers, although not many have gone as high as Frijda's six.

Are ideas such as this sufficient to define emotional expression? The answer must be no. Emotions as they are distinguished in the language cannot be distinguished in the same way from their expressions. People use different labels for the same expression and different emotions can produce very similar expressions. This suggests that there is something more to emotional expression than is given by the idea of dimensions (or categories). Any extra such richness could come from cognitive factors.

de Rivera—social relationships

Joseph de Rivera'a views on emotional climate have already been canvassed in Chapter 3. However, de Rivera and Grinkis (1986) also put forward a broadly based consideration of emotion conceived as social relationships rather than internal states (also see de Rivera, 1977).

The basic idea is that our emotion is always relative to another person. So, to use de Rivera's example anger is not something just of the individual, be it physiological, expressive/behavioural, or experiential. Rather, it is a relationship between whoever is angry and whoever is the perceived cause of the anger. In this framework, the feeling of anger must include an awareness of the entire social situation.

de Rivera argues in his structural theory that there are four interpersonal 'choices' involved in emotion. (1) It–me. Is the emotion directed towards the self or to another? (2) Positive–negative. Is it a matter of attraction or repulsion, either towards another or towards the self? (3) Extension–contraction. Does the emotion involve giving or wanting to get, pushing away or pulling back, even in the case of self-directed emotion? (4) Psychological space. Choices (1), (2), and (3) all involve three dimensions of psychological space. (a) Belongingness between the two people. (b) Social recognition and comparison. (c) A sense of being. de Rivera is here referring to the material, social and spiritual selves.

The three basic dimensions of it–me, positive–negative and extension–contraction are seen as orthogonal, thus allowing, as in all such structures, any emotion to have its place in a conceptual three-dimensional space. de Rivera sees all of the emotions in dynamic relationships to one another. For example, "... love is postulated to transform the relationship between self and other so the value of the other is revealed to the self. Thus, the self extends *toward* the other, wanting to give to him or her. This is quite similar to desire, except that in the latter case the other appears valuable *for* the self who wants the other to belong to him or her" (de Rivera and Grinkis, 1986, p354). Following this, all the other emotions can be seen as dynamically related to love in some way, as they are to one another.

Typically, de Rivera tests his structural theory by subjecting judgements of the similarity between emotions to multidimensional scaling techniques. The factors that emerge from such exercises seem to be clearly to do with matters interpersonal, and thus vary according to the four types of interpersonal choice described already.

As de Rivera points out, the view that emotions are relationships is in accord with cognitive theories of emotion. However, the emotion becomes a transaction between person and situation rather than simply an internal response to something external. The theoretical problem that he sees however, comes from viewing emotion as an interaction between a person and *another person*, not merely a situation. Clearly, there are times when our anger or our fear is directed towards some*thing* rather than some*one*. de Rivera suggests, however, that when this occurs, either an object or situation is being 'personified' or that the emotion is being displaced from a person to a thing. Also, he has a clear place for emotions being self-directed, this being no problem for the theory in that the direction is as though to some *other* self that happens to be occupying the same space. In fact, he goes so far as to suggest that with self-directed emotion there is always also a "corresponding other-directed emotion held by an implicit other" (de Rivera and Grinkis, 1986, p367).

de Rivera sees the strength of this type of structural but interpersonal theory as allowing good distinctions to be made between emotions that are often confused, confidence, security and self-worth for example (although not everyone would agree that these are emotions to begin with). While this may be so, it should also be said that there is a broadness to the theory which makes its precise predictive value a little shaky. However, its heuristic value is indisputable.

Berscheid—more social relationships

Some of the most interesting developments in the social psychology of emotion have moved away from expression and its recognition. As already seen to some extent with de Rivera, the emphasis instead is on the nature of emotion as it occurs in human relationships. A seminal analysis of the role of emotions in relationships was made by Berscheid (1983). She characterizes interactions as involving causal connections between the chains of events that make up the interactants' lives. Also, she follows Mandler (1976, 1984) in suggesting that it is the interruption of event sequences that leads to emotion.

Initially, relationships contain a great deal of interruption, and hence emotion, but gradually as the chains of events that exist between two people becomes more meshed, this settles down. The relationship then becomes more tranquil, or humdrum. If there are awkward, emotion-provoking parts of the relationship which the interactants deal with by severing them, emotional investment decreases and the relationship deadens. Thus there might be separate holidays or separate evenings.

If an emotionally tranquil relationship which is nevertheless based on some emotional investment, is severed, the extent of the unpleasantness or trauma depends on how rapidly a new way to complete the interrupted sequences can be found. Thus those who establish new relationships before divorce might cope more easily.

A difficulty with Berscheid's analysis is to account for positive emotion in relationships, since any interruption of another's sequence would seem likely to produce negative reactions. Mandler though suggests that events which interrupt but which seem controllable can lead to positive emotions. Also, if an event is seen as facilitating rather than interfering with an organized sequence, then it is likely to generate a positive emotion—a sudden windfall for example.

To take one further example of Berschied's analysis, the main cause of the breaking up of relationships is a change in the causal conditions that surround them. There are so many possible alternatives in modern western society that it is relatively easy to disagree with a partner and simply go on to fulfil plans in some other way. Ironically, the most enmeshed relationships are, because of their closeness, the most vulnerable to this type of effect.

The main influential change that can occur outside a relationship comes from the effect of a third person, the breeding ground for jealousy. Berscheid suggests that this occurs under three conditions. (1) X's plans are interrupted by events in Y's chain. (2) A partial cause of this is Z, outside the relationship. (3) The causal source is also perceived to be within the partner, Y. Again, the irony is that close relationships are more vulnerable to such effects than are more distant relationships.

Bradbury and Fincham (1987) offer a model of how emotion and cognition interact in marriage, an issue that is also considered in the broader context of close relationships in general by Fitness and Strongman (1991).

There are six points to Bradbury and Fincham's model. (1) The behaviour of one person of the pair, to which the other has access. (2) Following partner input, the 'spouse' processes this in a primary way. This is mainly unconscious and is positive, negative or neutral. (3) Secondary processing involves further extracting of information, with matters such as the seeking of courses for behaviour and areas of responsibility. The tone of the primary processing may well affect what happens in the secondary processing. (4) Then there is the spouse's behavioural output, some private and some public. This feeds forward to affect immediate (proximal) and more remote (distal) thoughts and feelings. So, (5) proximal context is whatever the spouse was thinking or feeling just before processing partner input. (6) Distal context is made up of more stable factors, such as the usual way in which the spouse processed information, normally seeing it in a positive light for example.

Clearly, this is very much a model rather than a theory but it offers a structure for subsequent study. It is interesting in that it relies on an integration of cognition and emotion in a reciprocal relationship between two people who are in a close relationship.

Scherer

Scherer's theory has been discussed at length in Chapter 7, but his work deserves brief mention in this chapter as well because it has been concerned very much with emotional expression, both in the face and by the voice. For example, he (1992) focuses attention on what he terms the facial expression of emotion related cognitive processes which he builds towards his sequential-cumulative model of expression and his component process model of emotion. With respect to the vocal expression of emotion, Pittam and Scherer (1993) for example, point to the assumption of phylogenetic continuity and universality for the vocal expression of emotional states. They point to the significance of both biological and psychological factors in such expressions and their decoding, and again lead towards the component process model of emotion.

Heise and O'Brien—group expression

Moving to even broader aspects of the social psychological aspects of emotion than are found in close relationships, Heise and O'Brien (1993, see also Chapter 13) make an interesting analysis of emotional expression in groups. Here emotions are looked at almost from a sociological perspective, with the reflection of the culture being of prime importance.

One theoretical approach in this domain comes from social constructionism. (See a much fuller discussion in Chapter 14). In this context, the expression of emotion is seen as a sort of intelligent conduct, which is based on cultural rules, with the aim of achieving particular outcomes interpersonally. So, emotional expression is seen as a rather sophisticated form of discourse.

By contrast, the social determinist view is that emotions are involuntary responses that are nevertheless an authentic part of social interaction. Whatever social structure there is in a situation allows emotions to emerge, and they in turn allow people to sense the structure. Seen in this light emotions are about status and power in relationships.

By contrast again, the social interactionist approach is that emotions are both constructed and determined; they simply erupt during social interaction. Heise's affect control theory suggests that people gain cultural meaning affirmed by whatever impressions they produce in their behaviour, so they construct and understand social action to bring this about. Emotions are then seen as momentary personal states that reflect how events affect people.

This is sufficient to give the flavour of this type of theory. Sociological theory of emotion will be revisited in Chapter 13 in which there is a general consideration of theories of emotion that come from outside psychology.

Ekman—facial expression

A number of investigators have contributed much to the study of the facial expression of emotion, Izard, Camras, and Zajonc for example. But none has contributed more than Paul Ekman, so it is his name that heads this section. Camras, Holland and Patterson (1993) offer a very useful review of ideas in this area and some of what follows owes a debt to their analysis.

Although Ekman and Izard do not always agree and their views on the nature of emotion differ, they both (Izard, 1977; Ekman, 1972) began by assuming that the apparently universal recognition of emotion expression depends on an innate programme for each of the primary emotions. However, more recently, they both (Ekman, 1992; Izard, 1991) suggest that facial expressions do not always go with emotions.

Ekman (eg 1982, 1992) believes that there exist three differentiated but interrelated systems of emotion—cognition, facial expression and ANS activity. He admits the possibility that any aspect of emotion might be mediated by cognition, but emphasizes the significance of facial expression. Simply changing facial expression changes how one feels. Ekman stresses pattern changes in expression and physiology, arguing that language is inadequate to account for the boundaries of emotion. A particular emotion, from this perspective, might be highly differentiated in one language and entirely missing in another.

Ekman sees emotion as having ten major characteristics. (1) There is a distinctive pan-cultural signal for each emotion. (2) There are distinctive universal facial expressions of emotion which can also be traced phylogenetically. (3) Emotional expression involves multiple signals. (4) The duration of emotion is limited. (5) The timing of emotional expression reflects the details of a particular emotional experience. (6) Emotional expressions can be graded in intensity, reflecting variations in the strength of the subjective experience. (7) Emotional expression can be totally inhibited. (8) Emotional expressions can be convincingly simulated. (9) Each emotion has pan-human commonalities in its elicitors. (10) Each emotion has a pan-human pattern of ANS and CNS change.

These characteristics lead Ekman to rest his facial expression theory of emotion on three assumptions. (1) Emotion has evolved to manage the fundamental tasks of life. (2) To be adaptive, there must be a different pattern for each emotion. (3) Finally, there is a general coherence in that within each emotion an interconnected pattern in expression and physiology is linked to appraisal. Ultimately, then, Ekman is emphasizing cognition.

In passing, in this consideration of Ekman's contribution, it is worth making brief mention of his work with Friesen. Ekman and Friesen (eg 1969) make a very influential analysis of what they termed nonverbal leakage in a discussion of the importance of the body to emotional communication. They suggest that nonverbal behaviour escapes the efforts that we make at social deception (hiding our feelings) and in fact allows our real feelings to leak out. We attempt to deceive others about our feelings and we may attempt to deceive ourselves.

Ekman and Friesen characterize the deceptions as having three dimensions. (1) Saliency is the degree to which the deception is of obvious importance to the interactants, a function both of the situation and of personality. (2) The roles adopted by the interactants, for example whether they are both deceiving and detecting, or adopting complementary roles, or whatever. (3) Collaboration of antagonism refers to an implicit pact or lack of it about the discovery and/or the continuation of the deception.

Leaving these interesting conjectures aside, the major theoretical hypotheses in this area deal with lateralization, efference and facial feedback. There are two types of lateralization hypothesis. The first is that positive emotions are mediated by the left cortical hemisphere and negative emotions by the right. And the second is that the emotions that go with approach are mediated by the left hemisphere and those that go with withdrawal by the right.

The efference view has it that the programmes for the discrete emotions produce distinct expressions through efference to the facial musculature. Camras (1991, 1992) looks at this in terms of her dynamic systems model (see Chapter 9).

The facial feedback hypothesis suggests that there might be proprioceptive, cutaneous, or vascular feedback from facial expressions that influence emotional experience. The theory urges that the feedback either creates the experience or merely influences it. All of these hypotheses have their support, although Camras et al (1993) conclude that there is particularly strong support for the facial feedback hypothesis.

In their review of facial efference, Adelman and Zajonc (1989) draw attention to a number of interesting theoretical issues. Their core question concerns *how* facial efference plays a causal role in the experience of emotion. Although there is little theoretical development in this area, Zajonc (1985) himself associates emotional efference to vascular systems, a notion originally put forward by Waynbaum in 1907. This is the vascular theory of emotional efference, and is based on the affect of facial muscles on venous blood flow. Zajonc sees this theory as potentially accounting for a number of apparently disparate matters such as biofeedback, placebo effects, unconscious preferences and aversions, and so on.

Adelman and Zajonc derive various empirically testable hypotheses from the theory. However, they also conclude that there is insufficient evidence to reject any of the theories of the links between facial efference and emotional experience. In particular, they draw attention to views that point to the importance of sensory processes (eg Le Doux, 1987). They also point out that the facial feedback hypothesis does not cope well with why some facial expressions feel 'good' and others feel 'bad'.

In some ways, the most interesting aspect of the vascular theory of emotion that Zajonc and his co-workers espouse (see also, Zajonc, Murphy and Inglehart, 1989) is that it deals with issues that cognitive appraisal theories do not, at least as yet. In particular, the theory has it that facial expressions affect the cavernous sinus, restricting venous blood flow and thereby having an effect on the cooling of the arterial blood supply to the brain. A further ramification is that changes in the cerebral temperature could have an effect on the release or blocking of neurotransmitters that are to do with emotion. In general, this theory and some of the evidence to which it has given rise is suggesting possible mechanisms whereby emotion and cognition could function independently.

Conclusions

The obvious and rather surprising characteristic of the emotion theories that have stemmed from social psychology is that with one or two exceptions they do not stand up to much scrutiny. If one concurs with the view that emotion is primarily a social phenomenon, the relative lack of quality in the social theories is odd.

In general terms, they do not provide adequate summaries of existing knowledge, even when this is restricted to facial expression and recognition. Some of the social theories have explanatory power, by recourse to the idea of dimensions underlying emotion for example. However, once the idea of dimensionality has been assumed, there seems little that can be done with it.

With the exception of the Berscheid type of theory and the facial feedback theories that devolve mainly from Ekman, the theories do not lead to testable predictions all that readily. Nor, oddly enough, do they score highly on heuristic value, although a possible exception here is that of de Rivera. However, the social theories do have a clear focus, or rather, several clear foci ranging from facial expression and recognition to social relationships. A difficulty is that these varying foci do not then allow the theories to be put together with ease.

Moving to Lazarus's (1991a,b) criteria for emotion theory, the social theorists define what they are looking at quite well although they do not often go so far as to define emotion in general. Some of them are also very good at considering the discrete emotions and the interdependence between them. However, they are not impressive at distinguishing between emotion and nonemotion. For example, even in the important area of facial expression, rarely is there discussion of nonemotional facial expression and what this might be expressing or signalling.

Few of the theories, although here again the Ekman type of theory is an exception, deal with the physiological aspects of emotion, or the biological, or indeed with the links between emotion and motivation. However, most of them discuss cognition, and in particular appraisal. Here again though, interestingly, it is some of the facial feedback type of theories that attempt clear distinctions between emotion and cognition, even though they spend some time dealing with cognition.

Of course, as might be expected, where the socially derived theories of emotion score highly is in considering emotion from a sociocultural perspective—this, after all, is what a number of them aim to do. Even here though, as will be seen in Chapter 13, in general they do not so well at this as do the theories that come from anthropology and sociology. The social theories also do not have much to add to our understanding of how emotion is generated or develops, although a slight exception to this comes from the Berscheid and Bradbury and Fincham type of theory. Nor do they say much about the effects of emotion on general functioning or consider its implications for therapy.

More generally, the social theories place the causes of emotion squarely in the social environment. They also deal rather better with emotion as a dependent variable than as an independent variable.

Applying Oatley's (1992) emotion theory criteria, again the social theories do not fare well. Of course, they are splendid about, or at least clearly concerned with, the interpersonal communication aspects of emotion—indeed they see emotion as basically about interpersonal communication. As already noted, they also tend to be involved with the idea of the discrete and the basic emotions, even though they do not take a particularly folk psychological view. They do, however, ground their analyses in everyday life.

The social theories are limited with respect to the functions of emotion in that they rarely go beyond the social, and even then are usually quite restricted within this. They have little to say about unconscious causes although by implication they are concerned with evaluations in the sense of the goals of emotion. Also, by implication they cover the simulation of the plans of other people, emotion being seen as essentially social in nature

In Oatley's summary of the Lakatos approach the social theories *can* deal with more evidence but it is in a fairly restricted domain. And in the Popper sense, only some of them can be used to derive specific predictions (particularly those of Berscheid, Ekman, and of course Scherer, although his theoretical contribution has been evaluated earlier).

In comparison then with the developmental theories of emotion the social theories are not particularly impressive. What do they do for our understanding? For an obvious start, although the idea of dimensions that underly emotion might be said to be nearly played out, it has been of use as a way of conceptualising emotions in general. Certainly, it and the various facial feedback notions have been pertinent to an understanding of the highly significant areas of the facial expression and recognition of emotion. It is also in this area that theories have suggested a phylogenetic continuity. This is of importance in a context in which the obvious presence of emotion of some sort in animals other than humans is ignored by many theorists. Some of course, place emotion within a context of evolutionary history, but they tend not to go into detail.

Others amongst the social theories form a useful bridge, as will be seen later, between psychological theory and emotion theory that comes from some of the other social sciences. In de Rivera's case even going so far as to provide a structural theory. And as has to be expected the social theories give us some conceptual insights into emotions as they function in relationships.

The major way in which the social theories are similar to those already discussed in this book is in their consideration of the importance of cognition in their accounts. Even those that derive from Ekman (who, by the way, also has a place for a biological foundation for emotion) feel it necessary to give considerable space to the role of cognition, even though they also distinguish between it and emotion.

Which of the socially based theories of emotion is the best? The choice is not easy to make. de Rivera's theory is interesting, Bescheid's broke new ground and put emotion into a new social framework. Assuming that Scherer's theory is only marginally social, all that remains of note is Ekman's, which it must be said is clearly the best of them. Ekman has certainly made an enormous contribution to the emotion field, but this has been more from his empirical work than his theory. As will be seen later, the best of the socially based theories of emotion in fact come from outside psychology.

11

Clinical theory

One of the traditional ways of regarding psychopathology is to assume that it is partly a matter of emotional dysfunction. By definition, emotion is implicated in all of the affective disorders. Schizophrenia is described as often involving emotional change. The neuroses are dependent on anxiety. Psychopathy rests on an apparent lack of emotion. General psychiatric disorders and various types of abnormal behaviour are believed to stem from 'emotional problems'. Even the mentally retarded are frequently assumed also to be emotionally retarded.

Emotion then is seen as playing a central role in mental disorder, perhaps because of the long-held view that human beings should aim to be rational and intelligent, the primitive emotions getting in the way of this. If the emotions become so insistent as to be impossible to ignore, or so extreme as to interfere with normal life, then the result is termed abnormal. As part of a scholarly and interdisciplinary, but openly and necessarily biased review of human emotions, Oatley and Jenkins (1992) make a cogent analysis of research which has been concerned with how emotions can dysfunction. They do not assume that emotions are *the* significant psychopathologies or even that they are the most important cause of such psychopathologies, but rather seek to determine how much emotions contribute to psychopathology. They do assume that emotions have a biological basis, that they function to allow us to set goals and in the communication of intentions and interaction, that they are often conscious and that they have an important role to play in our folk theories of ourselves and others. In other words, they assume that emotions rest on the criteria that Oatley suggests should be met by any theory of emotion.

The basis for Oatley and Jenkin's concerns is that the emotions in psychiatric conditions might be *normal* with respect to what brings them about. Against this background, they point to the evidence which shows that emotional traits are stable over time, indeed that temperament may be said to exist. However, changing emotional demands will influence such stability.

The other way of looking at this issue is to begin with psychopathology, in which of course, particular emotions are associated with particular disorders, and search for continuities. The type of evidence that Oatley and Jenkins consider is that conduct disorders continue from childhood to adulthood, as do emotional problems. Moreover, there is firm support for emotional behaviour even carrying through generations, harshly raised children becoming harsh parents and abused children becoming abusers, for example.

Oatley and Jenkins analyse stress, asking whether or not particular emotions are linked to particular pathologies. The evidence points to severe loss or threat (one definition of stress) leading to depression (with or without anxiety) and that internal stress consisting of certain personality traits relates to particular physical diseases.

A further way in which emotion is linked to psychopathology is through the effects of one person on another. For example, children of depressed mothers are at risk of emotional disorders as are children with angry parents and children surrounded by emotional disharmony. Such dysfunctional emotional effects can also be seen from adult to adult as well as from adult to child.

Clearly, these sets of considerations have therapeutic relevance. For example, recognition that emotions in one person can generate what look like emotional abnormalities in another, suggests that whatever the specific form of the problems, family therapy could be useful. Or, to go further, it might be possible to use these effects to employ one member of a family to change the emotional reactions of another. In particular, concentrating on the changing emotional demands in a person's life suggests the usefulness of using behaviour modification techniques or cognitive restructuring to deal with dysfunctions.

In recent years, Watts has made a significant contribution to exploring the implications of emotion theory for matters clinical. In particular, he has been concerned with cognitive theories of emotion and in 1992 explicates his views cogently, in a paper which dwells solely, but not surprisingly, on negative emotions. Watts begins by stating that emotion is made up of subjective experience, cognitive, behavioural and physiological elements by speaking of "appraisal processes, affective experience, thoughts and images, physiological state, action tendencies and behaviour".

Watts first stresses the function of emotion and suggests that therapists put some emphasis on emotion management training. A second matter that Watts regards as crucial is the extent to which an emotional reaction is seen as appropriate (a question of socio-cultural interpretation). An emotion could perfectly well be appropriate, even though dysfunctional, such an emotion usually being viewed as not stemming from objective facts. One person might become angry and aggressive at the merest hint of disagreement and react with emotional and physical violence. As Watts points out, it may be necessary for the therapist to recognize that such a reaction is *appropriate for the client* before anything therapeutic is possible.

Watts argues for the importance of distinguishing between different types of cognition as they are linked to emotion. He draws attention to thoughts, already emotion-filled, inducing emotional states, in contrast to emotions arising because of what people believe about their circumstances. Recognizing this difference, a therapist should then decide whether it would be better to concentrate on restructuring (the current euphemism for changing) thoughts or beliefs. These imply different therapeutic traditions.

In this same context, Watts sets aside the problem of how many emotions there are, one or many, and the distinction between basic emotions and the remainder, or between primary and secondary emotion. Instead, he urges that from a therapeutic viewpoint it is important to be aware that emotions differ in how much they are linked by cognitive elaboration. Some emotions may be cognitively simple and others cognitively complex, also some emotions although dysfunctional may occur in almost pure form, singularly, or may be part of a complex mixture. They need not also be cognitively complex because of this. In any event, all of these issues would have an impact on therapeutic strategy.

Finally, Watts appraises recent views on appraisal, considering in particular the attempts to categorize emotions by linking them with patterns of appraisal (e.g. Smith and Ellsworth, 1985, 1987, or Roseman, 1991). He draws attention to three types of dimension of appraisal, each of which has clinical relevance.

For example, appraisals may be based on agency, say, attraction (hate), or event (fear), or attribution (shame). Or appraisals may be based on the degree to which legitimacy is seen as being involved, or finally, certainty is important to some appraisals. Any of these appraisal dimensions might have therapeutic implications for emotion change.

To allow Watts (1992) to conclude for himself: "General cognitive approaches to emotion can provide clinicians with a richer and more precise conceptual framework for understanding emotional disorder." One might add, ... and for developing therapeutic strategies in the treatment of emotional dysfunction.

The aim in the remainder of this chapter is to illustrate theoretical contributions to the role of emotions in clinical psychology by considering theories of anxiety in some detail. Theories of depression will also be briefly considered as will the matter of emotion and health more generally. However, a brief beginning will be made by looking at two more general theories, the first on abnormal emotion broadly conceived and the second on the neuroses.

Gellhorn and Loufbourrow

Although by now rather dated, Gellhorn and Loufbourrow's (1963) theory remains the only one to address abnormal emotion in general. The core of their theory is the hypothalamus. In neurosis for example, they argue that the two divisions of the hypothalamus become simultaneously activated, a condition which leads to imbalance and thence neurosis. Such effects occur after exposure to severe and unexpected pain, 'emotional excitement', particularly where life is threatened, and strong conflicts. Any behavioural changes follow hypothalamic effects, such changes sometimes persisting for years.

Amongst other things, Gellhorn and Loufbourrow argue that the experience of different moods is the reflection of various states which exist between the extremes of hypothalamic action on the cortex, from emotional excitement (sympathetic–ergotropic) to sleep (parasympathetic–trophotropic). Also involved are positive feedback systems, such that if the skeletal muscles are relaxed then emotional reactivity and possibly neurotic symptoms will be reduced (as in some aspects of behaviour therapy). Further, they suggest that the physiological and pathological states of altered hypothalamic balance are characterized by changes in automatic reactivity and by personality changes. These effects result partially from altered hypothalamic-cortical discharges, a matter made even more complex by links between the hypothalamus and the endocrine system.

Gellhorn and Loufbourrow extend their argument with the suggestion that there is an interrelationship between emotional disturbance, automatic changes and behaviour disorder. At this point their thesis weakens. They maintain for example that the fact that many investigators have emphasized the emotional aspects of neuroses and psychoses also points indirectly to the role of the hypothalamus. They suggest that perception depends on emotion and hence on the links which exists between the hypothalamus and cortex. Anxiety modifies perceptual thresholds and perceptions are distorted by neuroses and psychoses. They argue that psychosis is characterized by two symptoms, which again point to the hypothalamus. (1) The psychotic will often not react to physical pain—the hypothalamus is pain-sensitive. (2) The catatonic schizophrenic state known as waxy flexibility can be produced by bilateral hypothalamic lesions.

This brief description is sufficient only to give the flavour of some of Gellhorn and Loufbourrow's basic arguments. They range very widely, but whatever topic they touch, it is with the same guiding principle: the conviction that the hypothalamus, its interaction with the cortex and the balance between its ergotropic and trophotropic systems are crucial to all aspects of emotion, particularly what they term pathological emotion. At times, the theory is highly speculative but it does form a basis of a sort for understanding abnormal emotion, or emotion in a wide range of clinical settings.

Eysenck

H. Eysenck's (eg 1976) theory is restricted to a consideration of the neuroses (see also later in this chapter under Theories of Anxiety). More strictly it is known as the incubation model of the neuroses and rests on a series of criticisms of the conditioned emotional response analysis of neurosis that began with Watson. The three major criticisms of neuroses as CERs are: (1) the account relies on the famous Watson and Raynor (1926) study which has never been satisfactorily replicated, and, in this context, consideration has never been given to genetic influences; (2) many neuroses do not develop from a single traumatic event, and (3) there is direct evidence for strong fears other than those which develop in the way mentioned by Watson.

Eysenck argues that there are two possible outcomes of the presentation of a conditioning stimulus (CS) alone. The conditioned response (CR) might extinguish or might be enhanced, the latter being an incubation of an anxiety or fear response. He postulates two basic classes of CR which lead to such responses—those with drive properties and those without. Those which do not produce drive extinguish and those which do, lead to enhancement (incubation). Eysenck is not arguing that a CS with drive properties (eg, anxiety) is reinforced without the unconditioned stimulus (US). Rather, he has it that the US produces the anxiety originally, and the CS does not. Pairing the two leads to identical effects: anxiety. Hence a positive feedback cycle develops, the CS-only reinforcing itself and incrementing the CR.

Eysenck adduces much experimental evidence to support these views, evidence which also points to the importance of time and duration of the CS-only presentation in determining whether extinction or enhancement will occur. Important sources of influence are personality (particularly extroversion/ introversion and neuroticism with their genetic basis and implications for conditioning) and the strength of the UR

However, Eysenck also suggest that a final link in the chain comes from Seligman's (1971) idea of preparedness. Whilst certain fears may be innate, phobias are highly likely to be prepared to be learned by humans. If so, they are also likely to be selective (to particular CSs), resistant to extinction, easily learned, and probably non-cognitive.

This model can be most easily represented by listing the conclusions that Eysenck draws from it. (1) Maladaptive, unreasoning fears which can be innate or learned through modelling sensitize a person to certain types of stimuli and facilitate the conditioning of fear to these (preparedness). (2) The main process of such learning is classical conditioning, traumatic or repeated presentations of CS and US. (3) The main US in human conditioning is not pain but frustration. (4) CRs may extinguish with non-reinforcement (CS-only). (5) Sometimes CS-only leads to incubation or the enhancement of the response, more frequently the greater the CR—this is neurosis. (6) Incubation only occurs in CSs which have drive properties, which through positive feedback makes it functionally equivalent to the US. (7) The prime examples of CRs with drives linked to CSs are fear and anxiety (and possibly sex). (8) The most favourable conditions for CS-only leading to incubation are: short presentations of strong USs, high N versus low N scores and introverts versus extroverts. (9) CRs which develop from this process are stronger than the original URs and allow for the slow growth of neurosis. (10) The incubation model of neurosis is not open to the objections which can be made to the other learning models of neurosis.

ANXIETY

The aim of this rather long section is to give a thorough overview of theories of anxiety. It is hoped that this will serve a number of purposes simultaneously. Arguably, of the specific emotions, anxiety is the most re-searched and has most theories put forward about it. It is therefore important to cover it in detail. As will be obvious, an overview of theories of anxiety parallels an overview of theories of emotion in general. Moreover, in a chap-ter concerned with clinically based theories of emotion, it has to have a central place. In fact, as it is weighted here, it will serve to illustrate the best of the thinking in this field. Theories of depression and the like will then only be dealt with more summarily.

"The characteristics of anxiety as an emotion are that it is distressing, and that its sources are indefinite." Thus begins the entry on Anxiety in *The Oxford Companion to the Mind,* and whatever one's theoretical persuasion it is unlikely that one would disagree. Although there is considerable overlap between the various theories of anxiety, they can be categorized to a degree. They fall into groups that can be most simply labelled as: psychoanalytic, learning/behavioural, physiological, phenomenological/existential, cognitive, and finally and perhaps most importantly, those which are based on the idea of uncertainty, a theoretical concept which to some extent cuts across the other categories.

For the most part, the theories canvassed here stem from a consideration of human anxiety. Nevertheless, some of the empirical investigations which sur-round the theories have been based on animal subjects. This tradition has derived from ethology (see for example the excellent work by Blanchard and Blanchard, 1990) and from laboratory experimentation, especially that which is neurophysiologically based (see for example, Le Doux, 1994). (Also, see McNaughton 1996 and Strongman 1996 for a more detailed analysis of theo-ries of anxiety.)

Psychoanalytic theory

Psychoanalytic theories of anxiety began with Freud and have not developed a great deal since his time. However, they remain influential, particularly in applied, clinical settings. Freud had two theories of anxiety (1917, 1926 re-spectively), in both of which he saw anxiety as an everyday phenomenon and as a way of explaining neuroses. Everyday anxiety is realistic anxiety which refers to real objects; this has often been referred to as fear rather than anxiety. Neurotic anxiety can take the form of being free-floating, phobic, or involved in a panic attack.

In the first formulation, Freud regarded anxiety as being a transformed libido, the transformation coming about through repression. So, if a person is prevented or thwarted from carrying out some instinctive (sexually driven) act through repression, then anxiety is the result. The anxiety generated then acts to produce whatever symptoms that, in their turn, will stop more anxiety from developing.

In his second formulation, Freud reversed the anxiety-repression linkage and viewed repression as occurring because of the experience of anxiety. In this theory, anxiety is a signal from the ego about real (ie existing) or potential danger. The unpleasantness of a threat causes anxiety which in turn leads to repression as a way of getting the person out of danger.

In both of these theories, a central role is given to the avoidance of over-stimulation, but in the earlier theory there is greater concern with 'automatic' anxiety which results from the trauma of birth and the infant's experiences immediately after birth. These points are reflected in later theories. With both the earlier and the later Freudian theory however, there seem to be three aspects to anxiety—an unpleasant feeling, some sort of discharge process, and the perception of the phenomena involved with this discharge.

The sort of events that Freud believed to be significant in the development of what he termed primary (ie from birth) anxiety are: the birth trauma, the possible loss of or withdrawal of the 'mother', uncontrollable impulses or threats that might occur at about this time, and fears of castration (presumably only in males, although this might be a moot point). Because of all this the mental apparatus is flooded and overwhelmed, the person is helpless and passive and the emotional experiences of anxiety follow automatically. So, in Freud's conceptualization, anxiety is either inherited or learned at birth, but with later additions being possible. Other types of anxiety, such as fear (this is Freud's way of looking at it) differ from primary anxiety only in what gives rise to them.

In the psychoanalytic context then anxiety is a significant aspect of handling a threatening environment, and is also necessary for the development of neurotic behaviour. Later psychoanalysts such as Sullivan (1953) emphasize the social environment rather than early separation, but otherwise the theory is similar. Sullivan makes anxiety into a social, interpersonal phenomenon rather than an intrapsychic one. However, theorists such as Bowlby (eg 1973) compromise and put the emphasis on the significance of the relationship with the mother, arguing that this is based on the apprehension that the mother *not* be there.

Although Freud's theory of anxiety is clearly in the same psychoanalytic tradition as the remainder of his theoretical work, it can be conceptualized a little differently. For example, Izard (1977) suggests that it can be characterized as based on the adaptive functions of anxiety and as being dependant on the cognitive processes that are a part of individual learning and appraisal. It is perhaps important to view Freud's theory in this light since, as will be seen, in recent times, cognitive theories tempered by neurophysiological research have begun to dominate our understanding of anxiety, and yet it is hard to gainsay the strength of some of Freud's views.

Learning/behavioural theory

Theories of anxiety whose provenance lies in the learning area derive originally from Pavlov and Watson. Whatever form they take, their main function is to explain punishment. Put simply, the argument is that organisms learn to avoid noxious stimuli through some or other mediating mechanism. This mediating mechanism is normally called fear or anxiety.

The typical post-Pavlov, post-Watson analysis has it that a conditioned stimulus which is paired with (contiguous with) an unconditioned stimulus (which happens to be noxious and to cause pain) will, after several pairings, lead to a conditioned response. The conditioned response is fear or anxiety (they are often used synonymously by theorists of this persuasion) and are seen as secondary or acquired drives which have arisen through a process of classical conditioning.

Generally, these types of theory have it that the threat of discomfort, an increase in primary drives or overstimulation (shades of Freudian theory) lead to anxiety only if they have autonomic components. Once established, fear/anxiety can function as a secondary drive and establish *new* behaviour through drive reduction. Moreover, a conditioned emotional response may interfere with ongoing behaviour. Again, there is a similarity here with psychoanalytic theory in that anxiety is seen as incompatible with other behaviour (or thoughts).

The theorists who developed this perspective initially were *Mowrer* (1953) and *Dollard and Miller* (1950). Their view of learning has it that drive reduction follows a response, reinforces it, and hence increases its future probability of occurrence. In this context, fear is a significant learned or secondary drive, as already described. For Mowrer, anxiety is a particular form of fear, when the source of the fear is vague or repressed.

Fear is learned because it can become attached to previously neutral stimuli, and it can motivate and reinforce. Anxiety can become built on this through neurotic conflict, neurotic fear being anxiety, and, by definition, having an obscured, that is, an unconscious source. Again with similarities to psychoanalytic theory, these learning theorists view neurotic conflicts as happening in childhood and thus setting the scene for anxiety to develop later in life, although they do not say how repression occurs. In summary though, from this perspective, anxiety is learned and once learned motivates maladaptive behaviour.

Staats and Eifert (1990) have updated this way of thinking to produce what they refer to as a multi-level behavioural theory of anxiety. Although having the same background of the Mowrer and Dollard and Miller theories, it goes further. It rests on two basic premises—that there is a central emotional response at the basis of anxiety, and that anxiety can be acquired through aversive conditioning or more symbolically through language.

From Staats and Eifert's viewpoint it is not necessary for someone to have a traumatic experience in order to develop a phobia, say. It can come about through negative emotion simply eliciting words that are associated with situations, for example negative thoughts and words might become associated with images of panic. They are describing a sort of self-conditioning. The importance of Staats and Eifert's contribution (which is to emotion theory in general rather than anxiety theory in particular) is that they have made a clear link between conditioning theory and cognitive theory.

The final theorist who should perhaps be considered under the learning/ behavioural heading is *Hans Eysenck*, although his approach is a little different from those already described, (eg 1957). (Also see earlier in this chapter.) His learning theory of anxiety rests on his more fundamental personality theory. As is well known, this depends on two major dimensions, extroversion/introversion and neuroticism. In this context, the neurotic individual is particularly sensitive to anxiety-provoking stimuli, this sensitivity being based on the the autonomic nervous system. So, from this perspective, anxiety-proneness is inherited.

However, anxiety can also be learned. Traumatic events lead to uncondi- tioned fear, but can then become conditioned, resulting in new stimuli pro- ducing the original maladaptive anxiety responses. Here, then, anxiety is viewed as conditioned fear.

There is also another possible stage in the anxiety process according to Eysenck. A person inherits an excitation–inhibition imbalance. If this prompts the person to be at the mercy of the influences of social learning, that is to be introverted, then that person is more prone to anxiety, as well as to other emotions such as guilt.

From Eysenck's perspective then anxiety is partly inherited and partly learned. The learning part depends firstly on conditioned fear and secondly on the state of the nervous system. It is interesting to note that Eysenck's theory also provides the basis for Gray's more physiological theory. Eysenck though believes anxiety to be dependent on the visceral brain, consisting of the hippo- campus, amygdala, cingulum, septum and hypothalamus, whereas Gray cen- tres anxiety in the behavioural inhibition system of the septo-hippocampal region.

Physiological theory

Physiological and neurophysiological theories of anxiety will be dealt with in brief summary. They are based largely on an exposition of what parts of the central nervous system might be involved in emotion in general and fear/ panic/anxiety in particular. It is largely through the empirical research that has derived from this beginning that they have added to our understanding of anxiety.

One of the most interesting physiological expositions of emotion comes from Panksepp (eg 1982, 1991, and see Chapter 5) although he does not stress anxiety in particular. However, as already mentioned, other theorists stress links between learning and physiology in accounting for anxiety (eg Eysenck) and others link cognition and physiology, very much in a Schachterian mould (eg Öhman).

The one substantive theory of anxiety which should be dealt with under the physiological heading is that of Gray (eg 1982, 1987). He makes an extensive conceptualization of fear and appropriately enough includes anxiety within this, his views ultimately deriving from the Eysenckian type of learning theory.

Gray regards the behavioural inhibition system as underpinning anxiety, unlike Panksepp (eg 1982) who places anxiety in the fight/flight system. The contrast between these two views is that of anxiety involving response suppression from the behavioural inhibition system or escape as mediated by hypothalamic circuits.

Gray argues that the behavioural inhibition system suppresses any behaviour that threatens an unwelcome outcome, so it only does this if there is *another* system that is mediating the threat. This is likely to be the fight/flight system, and the outcome is likely to be negative when the system being suppressed is fight/flight.

Gray speaks of a complex septal-hippocampal system as at the basis of anxiety (and other emotions), and in particular as acting as an interface between emotion and cognition. However, other parts of the brain are also involved in anxiety but the septo-hippocampal system is central. He also draws attention to the neocortical projection of the septo-hippocampal system in the frontal lobe, and the monoaminergic afferents arising from the brain stem.

Although the present exposition is concerned with theories of anxiety, it is perhaps worth pointing out that Gray's theory depends in part on his analysis of research involving anti-anxiety drugs, especially with respect to finding that lesions in the septo-hippocampal area have similar effects. It is also worth noting that Gray's theory of anxiety is yet another in which attention is drawn to cognition.

Phenomenological/existential theory

Phenomenological and existential theories of anxiety have their origin in Kirkegaard 150 years ago (1844). Here, anxiety is seen as a naturally occurring state of the person. This way of looking at things pivots on the idea that development and maturity depend on freedom, which in turn depends on being aware of the possibilities that exist in life.

To consider such possibilities means that anxiety must be involved. Growing towards the maturity that freedom brings, means dealing with the anxiety that is an integral part of experiencing possibility. We are presented as a natural part of life with a series of choices, from birth onwards. At every choice point there is anxiety. To become truly actualized we must face this anxiety and deal with it—anxiety is unavoidable.

It is interesting that Kirkegaard made a distinction between fear and anxiety that is very similar to that which is still often made. Fear is of a specific object, whereas anxiety is independent of any object, instead being a necessary condition of choice. Anxiety only develops after the development of self-awareness allows a person also to form a self-hood. A fearful person moves away from a feared object, whereas an anxious person is in conflict and unsure. For the person to develop properly, the anxiety must be faced and dealt with.

Fischer (1970) has done much to bring a phenomenological or experiential approach to understanding anxiety into the twentieth century. He does so by attempting to integrate all previous theories. Although this attempt is somewhat wanting, it nevertheless led to a theory

Fischer brings everything together in terms of *anxious experiencing*. This involves five components. (1) There is an identity, which takes the form of milestones towards a way of living. If any of these milestones are threatened so that they might be lost, then anxiety results. (2) There is a world, which consists of a network of relations and involvements for each milestone. If anything in this world seems insurmountable and the world thus becomes threatened, then again anxiety may result. (3) There is motivation in which the world and the person's identity is perpetuated. (4) There is an action, which is involved in achieving a milestone and which expresses being. (5) Finally, there is ability which is a lived evaluation of uncertain competence.

For Fischer, anxiety is both anxious experiencing and the experiencing of the self or of the other being anxious. As should be obvious from this brief description, Fischer's conceptualization of anxiety is vague, although it is experiential or phenomenological and he does not really succeed in fitting all the other types of formulation into the theory, even though the vagueness helps.

Cognitive theory

Apart from the uncertainty theories which appear in the next and final section, two major cognitive theories will be considered here. As will become clear, they also lay emphasis on other matters in their conceptualisation of anxiety, but are included because they have an obvious and central place for cognition. They are the theories of *Michael Eysenck* (1990) and *Öhman* (1993).

M. Eysenck argues that the cognitive system acts as a gateway to the physiological system, so in understanding anxiety it is important to consider both systems. He also talks of self-schema theories, self-schemas depending on the personal relevance of any particular trait to the individual, and assumes that these self-schemas are part of the cognitive system.

As a background to his theory, M. Eysenck shows that there are differences between people who are high and low in trait anxiety in the information that they have stored in long-term memory. This view is supported by the work on mood-state-dependent retrieval and mood-congruent learning. People who are high or low in anxiety also vary in their mood states and so the content of their memory should also vary. This memory approach to trait anxiety also helps to account for changes in trait anxiety that occur over time and also to deal with the fact that some people are anxious in some stress-producing situations but not in others. M. Eysenck also argues that those who are high or low in trait anxiety may also differ in the process side as well as the structure of their cognitive systems.

The theory proper begins with a consideration of why people differ in their susceptibility to stress. Eysenck demonstrates that those who are high or low in anxiety do in fact differ in the structure (content) and processes of cognition. Their memory differs both in broad schemata and in specific items, such as the type and amount of specific worries that they might have. He offers two reasons why those who are high in trait anxiety worry more than those who are low. First, they have more frequent and more highly organized sets of worries in long-term memory. Secondly, the worries of the highly anxious may be more accessible because their more negative mood states assist mood-state-dependent retrieval.

According to the theory, it follows from this that high and low anxiety people will also differ in cognitive appraisal of ambiguity. Moreover, a person might be more susceptible to stress and anxiety in some stress situations than others. Eysenck points out that the evidence about the role of the cognitive system in accounting for differences in susceptibility to stress is unclear, but there are differences in cognitive functioning.

In the end, what is important about M. Eysenck's theory of (trait) anxiety is that it draws attention to the importance of taking into account the cognitive system as well as the physiological and the behavioural.

Öhman (1993) puts forward what he terms an information processing theory of anxiety, although he argues that the information processing sources lead to biologically based defences that in turn produce the anxiety (see Figure 5).

Öhman's theory/model consists of five major aspects.

(1) Stimulus information goes into *feature detectors* which pass the information onto *significance evaluators*. Some stimulus features may be connected directly to the arousal system, which produces alarm. The feature detectors

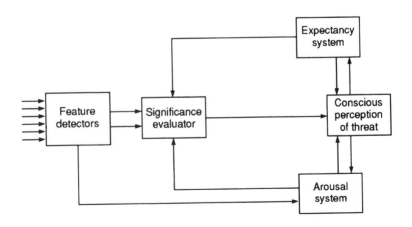

Figure 5.   Öhman's information-processing model of anxiety (adapted from Öhman, 1993)

are set to find threat in biologically significant stimuli. Information will also go on from this level to the conscious perception system.

(2) The *significance evaluators* automatically assess the relevance of stimuli, with expectancies setting the system to look for particular inputs. Meaning is analysed at this point and memory has an important part to play. So cognitive resources are necessary at this stage but there does not have to be any conscious access to what is going on. "The important implication for anxiety is that nonconscious discovery of potential threat through the significance evaluator does not result in activation of the arousal system unless it results in conscious perception of threat" (1993, p528).

(3) The *arousal system* can 'tune up' the significance evaluator and also gives input to the conscious perception system. It is based on emergency reactions of the autonomic nervous system.

(4) The *expectancy system* is based on emotion being organized into memory. This is a standard cognitive system of networks with nodes. It biases the significance evaluators to react to information which matches active memory nodes, which in turn again gives information to the conscious perception system. All of this maintains the bias to find threat in the environment. So the expectancy system biases the incoming information and makes a context for the interpretation of what goes into the conscious perception system

(5) The *conscious perception system* is part of a much larger system—the mind, consciousness, cognitive-interpretative system, or whatever. It integrates input from the arousal system, the significance evaluators and the expectancy systems, and picks out a suitable action to deal with the perceived threat. If avoidance or escape is possible, the result is fear. If not, the result is anxiety. So, again, as with most theories, fear is seen as having a tangible object and outcome, and anxiety as not. "... responses of fear and anxiety originate in an alarm system shaped by evolution to protect creatures from impending danger" (1993, p529).

Öhman sees links between the unconscious aspects of anxiety as suggested by Freud and his own idea of two types of unconscious. Freud had a drive unconscious and a repressed unconscious, which are similar to the unconscious effects of feature detectors and significance evaluators in this model. Öhman even makes the feature detector part of his model equivalent to Jung's collective unconscious, a sort of cumulative human experience (with archetypes viewed as biological preparedness). The significance evaluator is more concerned with individual history and so may set the person to respond more to some threat cues than others.

Öhman argues that his theory suggests that there are two types of anxiety, both of which are distinguishable from fear. In his view, fear is an emotion to do with conscious avoidance and escape. If such responses are blocked then anxiety results. However, a more basic type of anxiety than this comes from unconscious input to the conscious perception system from significance evaluators and the arousal system. The result of this is undirected anxiety, the cause of the anxiety being not available to the person.

In this context, phobias and panic disorders are seen as arising from physiological roots, whereas generalized anxiety comes from a cognitive basis. However, the theory cannot say why some people develop one type of disorder and others develop another.

In summary, Öhman's theory or model is very much in the post-Schachter or causal-evaluative (in Lyons, 1991 terms) framework of emotion conceived as a matter of physiological cues and cognitive interpretations. Öhman takes an intermediate position on the emotion/cognition, (which comes first), debate. He argues that some anxiety effects occur immediately a relevant stimulus impinges, but cognitions from nonconscious biases also have their role to play in the interpretation of threat. The important question is *how* cognition and emotion interact when considering a state of anxiety.

Öhman's model of anxiety is squarely within one of the recent traditions of theorizing in cognitive psychology. It has some reasonable things to say about anxiety, but in the view of the present author it suffers from the same difficulty that is usually suffered by those who engage in what might be called boxology. Because some possible function is named and put in a box in some indeterminate space in the brain does not mean that it actually exists, nor does it in any strong sense provide an explanatory account. In one sense, then, although this theory seems to be quite rich and well worked out it tells us less about the nature of anxiety than the ideas of Kirkegaard expressed so long ago.

Uncertainty

There are three current emotion theorists (all dealt with elsewhere in this text) whose theories of emotion in general, and of anxiety in particular, cut across the more traditional divisions. There is a sense in which all of the theories so far considered see uncertainty as a core part of anxiety, uncertainty at least as being unsure of the future or of what course of actions to take in the face of threat. However, Izard, Lazarus and Mandler refer more directly to the importance of uncertainty in giving their accounts of anxiety. Clearly, uncertainty is a concept which fits most closely within the cognitive domain.

Izard (1977, 1991) suggests that the feeling state common to any type of anxiety is fear, although he argues that anxiety is linked with various other emotions at different times and in different circumstances, eg interest/ excitement, sadness, shame and guilt. Through his Differential Emotions Theory he urges that although anxiety should be treated as a unitary phenomenon, the other discrete emotions that are linked with it from time to time should be taken into account as far as subjective experience is concerned. More importantly, in the present context, he views anxiety as being dependent on uncertainty.

The notion of uncertainty is taken further by *Lazarus* (1991), who brackets anxiety with fright. Fright occurs when there is imminent physical harm, whereas he believes anxiety to be characterized by uncertain, ambiguous, existential threat. His distinction between fright and anxiety is similar to Freud's distinction between objective and neurotic anxiety.

As an appraisal theorist, Lazarus suggests that there are various primary appraisals that might contribute to anxiety. Thus, if there is perceived to be goal relevance, then any emotion might ensue, including anxiety. If there is goal incongruence, then only negative emotions will result, including anxiety. Finally, and most importantly, if the ego-involvement is protection of personal meaning and the protection of ego-identity against existential threat, then anxiety is the only possible emotional reaction.

Uncertainty as the core of anxiety produces a strong drive to objectify it, to make whatever the threat is external and objective in order to reduce the uncertainty. The person's ability to cope is also uncertain. The problem with anxiety, as Lazarus sees it, is that once one objective threat has been coped with, another takes its place since the basic problem is existential.

Finally, *Mandler* (1984) offers the most sophisticated explication of anxiety which is based on uncertainty. He regards previous research on anxiety as being characterized by three main approaches. The causal view has anxiety seen as acquired through learning, distinguishes it from fear and views it as concerned with stimuli that signal threat to the integrity. What Mandler terms the organismic-hypothetical approach sees anxiety as an observed or hypothesized state, sometimes purely theoretical and sometimes a state of the nervous system. The experiential/behavioural approach is concerned, largely via subjective report, with anxiety, defined via expressive behaviour, general activity and a series of behavioural and physiological symptoms, as it affects a wide range of functions.

Mandler synthesizes previous theories, some of which have been discussed presently, as having three common elements. Archetypal anxiety-evoking events exist primitively, innately or congenitally. Responses to these events are transferred to other events that were originally neutral simply through contiguity. This may be externally or through an organism's actions. And events that end or reduce anxiety are related to events that also evoke anxiety, for example, the danger of overstimulation is reduced by reducing the stimulation.

In his own formulation, Mandler argues for a *nontraumatic theory* of the sources of anxiety which he sees as dependent on the cyclical distress of the human neonate. So anxiety is what he terms 'fundamental distress', the main event in which is "... the perception or afferent effect of variable and intense autonomic visceral activity" (1984, p234).

Fundamental distress is a state of unease or anxiety that does not have a specific causative event. Mandler points out that discomfort in the newly born may accompany other states such as hunger, thirst, cold, etc, and to reduce these states does not necessarily reduce the anxiety. The anxiety is reduced by non-nutritive sucking or by the stimuli provided by a 'mother', rocking, nodding, producing regular sounds etc. These two types of event are inhibitors of fundamental distress and hence of anxiety.

Mandler also assumes that these matters are amongst the earliest differentiations that a child makes, as are those which are to do with handling distress.

At such times, the child learns about the *interruptions* of organized sequences of responses or expectations. And, not surprisingly to those who are familiar with Mandler's general theory of emotion, he regards interruptions as possibly leading to anxiety.

The core of Mandler's theory of anxiety then depends on the link between anxiety and interruption. The important question is how does the arousal that stems from interruption turn into anxiety? It happens when there is no response available to the organism which will stop the interruption. This leads to feelings of helplessness and disorganization: these *are* anxiety.

To summarize Mandler's theory, the cyclical distress of the newborn provides the first experience of anxiety. This fundamental distress bears no relationship to antecedent events, although there are specific inhibitors such as sucking and rocking, that bring it under control. The withdrawal of such inhibitors might reinstate the distress. Later on, other organized behaviours might also function to inhibit distress/anxiety.

Furthermore, helplessness turns arousal into anxiety through the unavailability of plans or actions that are relevant to the task or to the situation. The one thing that leads to helplessness is the interruption of plans or behaviour. This may degenerate further into hopelessness if it builds up, goes on for long, or if there are repeated failures. This all becomes related to self-esteem and may lead to depression.

In the end, the imperfections of human beings often lead them into situations in which they are helpless (they are *uncertain* what to do). This results in anxiety and this in turn interferes considerably with effective functioning. Because of this, Mandler argues that it has often been called stress, and so we see the origins of the confusion that exists between anxiety and stress.

Conclusions

The obvious concluding statement to draw from this consideration of theories of anxiety is that the various approaches set off from a very similar set of starting points to those of theories of emotion in general. There have been psychoanalytic, behavioural, physiological, experiential/phenomenological and cognitive roads taken. From this theoretical plurality further conclusions can be drawn, conclusions which represent commonalities that can be extracted from the theories.

Perhaps the first and foremost conclusion is that the weight of opinion makes it clear that anxiety cannot be fully understood without taking some account of its cognitive aspects and influences. This again reflects what has happened to emotion theory in general—it has become highly interrelated with cognitive theory. With respect to anxiety, this is particularly the case since a basic aspect of anxiety appears to be uncertainty, whether it be of what the threat is, how to cope, how to deal with the unconscious, or how to face a multitude of possible futures.

A further conclusion is that there seems to be general agreement amongst most of the theorists that anxiety can be distinguished from fear or fright in that the object of the latter is 'external', 'real', 'known' or 'objective'. Anxiety is characterized by its genesis being, yet again, uncertain, to the individual.

Moreover, although anxiety is clearly a negative, unpleasant emotion, it is motivating, can become associated with a wide range of new stimuli or events, and appears to be an inevitable or even in some views an essential part of the human condition.

To return to the starting point of this analysis, anxiety is indeed distressing and its sources indefinite, but there is clearly more to it than this, a point with which a wide range of theorists, working from multiple perspectives, would agree. Most of the theories make some sense of the existing information, some are more internally consistent than others, some are more general than others, some have predictive power, and all appear to have reasonable heuristic value. For the future, in my view it is probably Mandler's type of theory that will be of most note, a theory of anxiety that is broadly conceived, that clearly has a central role for cognitive factors, and that can embrace the specific issues of behaviour, experience, and in particular neurophysiology that others have deemed important.

Depression

Although anxiety is the main emotion considered in this chapter on emotion theory within a clinical framework, it is also important to have some discussion of depression. Depression is clearly a complex emotional disorder, which, like anxiety, in its milder forms is experienced by most people at some time. It does not usually occur in lists of the major emotions since, much as with love or grief, it is perhaps best regarded as a more general condition that subsumes various emotions. In this case however, the emotions involved are a mixture of sadness and some of the more self-reflective emotions such as blame.

Depression is commonly regarded as involving five sets of characteristics, although it can be exacerbated by many other emotional conditions, such as anxiety. (1) A sad, apathetic mood. (2) A negative self-concept involving self-reproach, self-blame and so on. (3) A desire to avoid other people. (4) A loss of sleep, appetite and sexual desire. (5) A change in activity level, usually in the direction of lethargy, but sometimes in the form of agitation.

Beyond these typical characteristics, a distinction is usually drawn between neurotic and psychotic depression. This is both a matter of degree—psychotic depression is more extreme in all ways than neurotic depression—and kind—psychotic depression is characterized by delusions and neurotic is not. A distinction is also often made between endogenous and exogenous depression, the former being thought to stem from physiological malfunction and the latter from the environment. However, it is often difficult to make this distinction with confidence.

Theories of depression parallel the types of theory that have been described in detail with respect to anxiety, and indeed also run in parallel to the ways in which emotion in general has been viewed.

Psychoanalytic

As might be expected, Freud best exemplifies the psychoanalytic approach to depression. He suggested that if a child's oral needs are over- or under-satisfied then he or she may develop an excessive dependency for self-esteem. Then, if a loved person is lost, the lost person is introjected with full identification. As some of the feelings toward the loved person will have been negative, so now self-hate and self-anger develop. Simultaneously, there develops resentment at the desertion through feeling guilty at the sins committed against the lost person. Then the child mourns in order to separate the self from the lost person. In those who are over-dependent this can lead to self-punishment, self-blame and hence depression. So, Freud saw depression as anger turned against the self.

Many criticisms can be levelled at such a theory. What causes depression in those who have not lost a loved one? Why is love not turned inwards as well as anger? How much is too little or too much gratification at the oral stage? And so on. Psychoanalytic theory is problematic at the best of times.

Learning

The various learning theories of depression see it as a condition mainly characterized by a reduction in activity which follows the withdrawal or loss of a large and accustomed reinforcer. Once the depressed behaviour exists, it might itself be reinforced by attention and sympathy.

The most influential learning based theory of depression is Seligman's (eg 1975) which depends on the central idea of learned helplessness. This suggests that anxiety is the initial response to a stressful situation, and then, if the person comes to believe that the situation is uncontrollable, the anxiety is replaced by depression. Seligman's model came from empirical research with animals, but there seems to be remarkable similarity between this and the relevant human data.

Physiological

There have been two main types of physiological theory of depression. The first is argued on the basis of a disturbance in the electrolyte metabolism of depressed patients. Sodium and potassium chlorides are particularly important in the maintenance of potential and the control of excitability in the nervous system. Normally, there is more sodium outside the neuron and more potassium inside it, but in depressed patients this distribution is disturbed.

The second physiological theory views depression as resulting from an inhibition of neural transmission. This is thought to occur in the sympathetic nervous system and to involve its neural transmitter—norepinephrine. Problematically, these theories make no mention of theoretical links between psychological and physiological factors in depression.

Cognitive

Beck (eg 1967) exemplifies cognitive theories of depression with the starting point that thoughts and beliefs cause emotional states. He argues that people become depressed through making a logical error; they distort events into self-blame. An event which is normally seen as just irritating (say, spilling a drink) is seen as another example of the utter hopelessness of life. So depressed persons draw illogical conclusions about themselves.

Beck refers to such illogicalities as 'schemata'. The depressed person interprets all events from the schema of self-depreciation and self-blame. Four types of logical error are possible here: (1) arbitrary inference when there is no evidence for a conclusion drawn (I am useless because the shop was closed when I went to buy something); (2) selective abstraction in which a conclusion is drawn from only one element of the many possible (it is my fault that the firm that I work for is full of unintelligent people); (3) overgeneralization, or the making of a massive conclusion from a trivial starting point (I am completely thick because I did not understand that one point); (4) magnification and minimization which simply involves errors in judging performance (I told one white lie and completely lost all integrity).

From Beck's viewpoint then, emotional reactions come from cognitions, and the interpretations of the world made by depressed persons do not accord with reality.

Conclusions

This brief overview is sufficient to show that the variety of theories of depression is similar to those of anxiety. It is as apparent in this area as in most other areas of emotion that there has to be a place for cognition.

Psychophysiology, psychosomatics and health

There are possible links between psychophysiological measures, physical symptoms and emotion, pain, and hence psychosomatic disorder. A core question has revolved around the search for physiological response specificity in emotion, a search which has never been highly successful. This, in turn, prompts consideration of links between emotion and illness, a topic which has been nicely dealt with by Pennebaker (see Pennebaker, 1982 and Robinson and Pennebaker, 1991).

If symptoms and emotions are linked, then is there a causal connection? Sensations of symptom-produced arousal may be labelled as a particular emotion, a perceived emotion might precede the sensation, or symptoms and emotion might merely occur together but be independent. Pennebaker suggests that all such linkages are possible.

There is evidence that shows that emotions and symptoms can be linked independently of underlying physiological processes. It may be then that people infer an emotion–symptom link through a linguistic convention that was originally dependent on a physiological basis. Such issues become most problematic in the area of the relationship between emotion and pain. Common links are fear following unexpected, acute pain, an adaptive increase in vigilance and concern to escape. If pain lasts, the emotion appears to be distress, but if the pain is unrelieved the result can be anger and aggression. And there are circumstances in which pain can relieve guilt.

Perhaps most problematic of all is the notion of psychosomatic disorders, which have obvious organic symptoms but an aetiology bound up with psychological variables. Most models of psychosomatic disorder include reference to emotional disturbance (particularly anxiety). however, the extent or form of the emotional involvement is hard to determine and one view is that *all* illness has its psychosomatic components.

There are two major groupings for theories of psychosomatic disorder, biological and psychological. The biological suggests that patterns of autonomic reactivity are inherited (eg Lacey et al 1963). The psychological type of theory suggests for example that anxiety or fear prevents the expression of behaviour and the result is hypertension and the further generation of various physical reactions such as asthma or gastric ulcers.

Lader (eg 1972) argues that two main concepts relate psychophysiology and psychosomatics: arousal and response specificity. He suggests that arousal functions as a construct between physiological measures and any concomitant emotions, with heightened arousal being a necessary condition for the experience of emotion. This will be reflected in any psychophysiological measures but to be meaningful must also be consistent with self-reports and observed changes in behaviour.

The idea of psychophysiological response specificity gives a theoretical base for variation in vulnerability of physiological systems from person to person. The idea is that different somatic processes play different roles in different types of behaviour. This relates to the notion that the particular physiological mechanisms involved in some somatic complaints in some psychiatric patients are especially susceptible to activation by stress.

Lader's model of the psychophysiological basis for psychosomatic disorder suggests that environmental stimulation interacts with individual factors to produce general arousal. Appraisal follows and a specific emotion is experienced. Such interactions may be conscious or unconscious and the emotions may be rational or irrational, in Lader's terms.

Four factors are thought to account for individual response patterns. (1) Emotion is partly dependent on previous experience and physiological patterns vary according to the emotion. (2) Individual differences in responses to emotionally neutral stimuli are variable. (3) There are individual differences in the intensity of physiological responses; bodily systems are differentially involved. (4) The awareness of peripheral changes varies from bodily system to bodily system, hence there is differential feedback.

Finally, severe or chronic environmental events interact with internal factors and produce high arousal and intense emotion. The physiological changes which accompany this may be morbidly severe in one bodily system. Also with high arousal there is a loss of adaptive responses. This complex set of reactions becomes self-perpetuating and if it goes on long enough anatomical changes occur and psychosomatic illness results.

Robinson and Pennebaker (1991) in a more general consideration of emotion and health suggest that for emotion to affect health it must occur for long periods. They regard this as being possible in three ways. (1) If specific emotions affect specific organs systems, there is eventually a wearing effect. (2) It is possible that the particular belief system held by a person affects both emotions experienced and health. This cognitive approach then is suggesting that although emotion and health may be linked they are not causally related. (3) If particular emotions are either expressed or repressed, this may affect health.

Their particular theoretical contribution however is to suggest that any analysis of emotion and health should take into account time, simply because changes in health are to do with long-term changes usually in multiple organ systems. So the idea of personality and its interactions with emotion, and of course, cognitive linkages, remains of theoretical importance.

Leventhal and Patrick-Miller (1993) also make an extended discussion of links between emotion and illness. They draw a number of conclusions. (1) Linkages between emotion and disease can be clarified by regarding emotions as differentiated sets. (2) Emotions should be viewed in their social framework since things interpersonal both regulate emotional reactions and moderate the relationship between stress and health. Emotional distress can be moderated by social factors such that the effects on health are ameliorated. (3) In the health context, emotions should be seen as a multi-level system, including the cognitive, feeling, motor and systemic. (4) Any of these levels of emotions has multiple components which can be affected by neural or by endocrine activity. Again, this is important in considering the emotion–disease links, which in turn can help our understanding of emotion more generally.

Conclusions

There is only one general theory of emotion from a clinical or abnormal perspective, that of Gellhorn and Loufbourrow. Although it was a worthy attempt it cannot be described as a good theory. H. Eysenck's is much better but it is restricted to the neuroses, or in particular neurotic anxiety. Most of the substantive theories in this area are specific to particular types of disorder or clinical issues and it is as such that they should be evaluated. Of course, although concerned with specific issues they might still be relevant to an understanding of emotion in general.

Since the major emphasis in this chapter has been on theories of anxiety, it will be these theories that are particularly attended to in this conclusion. Theories of anxiety range across all of the approaches that have already been seen to emotion in general—psychoanalytic, phenomenological, physiological, behavioural and cognitive. And for the most part they are interesting theories all of which provide reasonable summaries of anxiety and attempt to give explanations of it. They have a clear focus—on anxiety—and certainly suggest new ways of thinking about the topic. However, they do not all lead to readily testable predictions. In this sense the best are those of Gray and Mandler and to some extent Izard, Lazarus and Öhman.

Considering Lazarus's (1991a,b) criteria for emotion theory, the best of the anxiety theories are good on definition and on distinguishing anxiety from other emotions. There is a role for both behaviour and physiology and for the links between anxiety and some of the other emotions. Also, the better anxiety theorists embrace both a biological foundation and sociocultural influences.

The anxiety theories lay an obvious emphasis on cognition in their accounts, particularly appraisal, and they also do well in discussing the generation and the development of anxiety. It almost goes without saying, that anxiety theories are integrally concerned with the effects of anxiety on general functioning and also have comments to make which are relevant to therapy.

Generally, then, the anxiety theories, at least the best amongst them, are concerned with the causes of anxiety, and with its role as both an independent and a dependent variable.

Moving on to Oatley's (1992) criteria, anxiety theories are directly concerned with the function of anxiety, although they tend not to consider it from a folk psychology as well as a science perspective. Some of them, notably the psychoanalytic ones, explore the unconscious causes of anxiety in some depth. They also at least make implications about the way in which anxiety is to do with evaluations. However, only some of them stress its interpersonal aspects and are at all concerned with its effect on simulating the plans of other people. They all see it as a basic emotion.

From the Lakatos perspective, most of the anxiety theories can deal with more evidence, and from the Popper view, as already indicated, the best of them can be used to derive specific predictions.

Theories of depression parallel those of anxiety to some extent, although there are fewer of them and they are not as well developed on the whole. However, Beck's for example certainly fulfils many of the criteria for good theory, whichever particular set one considers. Similarly, the theoretical aspects of the links between emotion and health, more broadly, offer some useful insights. This is particularly so with respect to the problematic area of psychosomatic disorder.

Probably, the most consistent point to emerge from the type of theory summarized in this chapter is the emphasis on cognition. In this, the clinically based theories are little different from most of the others already considered. From the perspective of 'good' theory it is reasonable to say that some of them go too far in the cognitive direction. Öhman's 'boxology' for instance, is not very helpful, even though at first blush it seems to be.

A new concept which emerges, perhaps because of the force of Mandler's theory of anxiety, is that of uncertainty. Clearly a cognitive concept, this has considerable theoretical import. Also, when anxiety in particular and emotion in general is looked at from a clinical perspective then links with personality become obvious.

There are some fairly significant implications of emotion theory for therapy that come to mind when emotion is considered from a clinical standpoint. In a review of the links between emotions and cognitive-behaviour therapy, Strongman (1993) concludes that the links between emotion and cognition have been particularly useful. Recent emotion theory, and nowhere is this more evident than in the better recent theories of anxiety, suggests new therapeutic strategies and reconceptualizations of existing strategies. However, this is not the place to go into these.

It should be clear by now that from the type of analysis which has been made in this chapter, general theories of emotion from a clinical perspective are not very impressive; there are not many to begin with. However, it is worth noting that some of Pennebaker's theoretical concerns about emotion and health are an exception to this. However, theories of anxiety do have some relevance for a general understanding of emotion, although they do not perhaps suggest anything that can be added to what has already been learned elsewhere in this book. It is simply instructive that once again a major emphasis is on cognition, although a number of the theories also centre on both biological and social roots.

It remains to say which of the theories mentioned in this chapter is the best. In some ways, each of them has something to contribute, but there are one or two that stand out as satisfying most of the criteria that have been routinely used herein. Gray's theory is compelling in its emphasis on a mixture of physiology and behaviour, on its background in traditional Eysenckian theory and on its close links with empirical research. M. Eysenck's theory stands out for the clarity of its exposition and its interesting links with memory. Particularly though, Mandler's theory of anxiety has an impressive strength running through it. His idea of uncertainty is powerful and gives a strong conceptual basis to cognitive considerations.

In the end it must be said that the theories embraced by this chapter do not take us very further towards saying what exactly abnormal emotion is. It is certainly possible to think about emotion from a clinical perspective and to do so has interesting implications. But what exactly happens when emotion 'goes wrong' in some way, or even whether it is reasonable to speak of emotion going wrong at all, remain something of a dilemma.

12

Theory from the individual, the environment and the culture

Oatley (1992), in his stimulating book, has a final argument that there should be four bases for understanding emotion. From the perspective of the type of science which sprang from logical positivism, understanding depends on events, measurement and theory. Emotion is no exception. However, Oatley suggests that it would be useful to add in *verstehen*, a sort of empathetic understanding in which one enters into the lives of other people through the imagination. He sees this as being exemplified particularly by fiction. This important idea can be extended further with the suggestion that an understanding of emotion also comes through any of the arts, through our interactions with the natural environment and through our interactions with our own personalities.

This chapter then is concerned with a general search for the meaning that lies behind emotion, at least as it has been represented theoretically in a number of domains. The progression will be from individual factors, through the impact of and interactions with the environment, to the place of emotion in the arts and aesthetics. To do full justice to these topics would require a book in itself, so they are just touched on, particularly insofar as they might add to the theoretical underpinnings of emotion.

The individual

Personality

Pervin (1993) points out that there is no generally accepted theory about the links between emotion and personality from a psychoanalytic or a phenomenological viewpoint, although of course there are both psychoanalytic and phenomenological theories of emotion. However, almost every theory of personality makes some passing reference to affect or emotion.

It is perhaps Mandler (1984) who makes one of the most searching analyses of emotion-personality links. He suggests two relevant approaches to analysing individual differences. The first is to devise personality scales that might characterize individual emotional reactions. The second is to search for particular cognitive systems within a culture that would allow prediction of individual emotional responses.

Personality tests provide one measure of cognitive interpretation. Eysenck for example discusses extroversion/introversion and neuroticism in terms of conditionability and emotionality. Mandler argues that e/i characterizes people according to their tendencies to see events as punishing, threatening or frustrating, and neuroticism (emotionality) is concerned with amount of arousal.

Mandler also takes an entirely different perspective to that of traditional personality theory on the question of individual factors in emotion. He considers the matter of a situation becoming emotionally significant when it is recognized as being personally relevant. An example would come from the reaction we have on seeing an accident. It is graded, depending on the extent of our involvement with the victim. Projection of the self into the situation leads to this effect.

Similarly, Mandler argues that emotion might be related to degree of visual imagery. Generally, visualizers are hypersensitive and verbalizers are calm and equable. Here, he is really beginning to consider cognitive style and emotion.

Bertocci (1988) is one of the few theorists to attempt to describe a close relationship between emotion and personality, although his writing is a little difficult to penetrate. He suggests that the person is a complex unity, which both identifies itself and which, through interaction with the environment, is constantly moving on. The person is laden with hedonic tones, which are important to survival. These are not in themselves wants or emotions but they do influence the expression of wants and emotions. Bertocci argues that emotions should be regarded as part of the meaning of the quality of survival. There, he regards it as important to recognize primary, unlearned, emotions.

For Bertocci, primary emotions are identical with motives. They are emotive-conative predispositions, or unlearned urges, or unconsciously experienced purposive thrusts which do not have behavioural or physiological aspects as necessary conditions.

This theory lays great emphasis on the importance of self-conscious experience in understanding the primary emotions, and suggests that behavioural/physiological accounts are inadequate. Bertocci believes that through conscious experience it is possible to understand the dynamics of unlearned motivation. He employs what he terms *respect-deference* as his main exemplar of primary emotion and uses this to portray emotions as "conative thrusts". Crucial to the experience and modification of these primary emotions are cognitive developments. Moreover, the primary emotions are determined by the meaning evoked in a situation and although the emotion, or motivational disposition, is unlearned, the meaning may be learned.

Bertocci then goes on to describe what is probably the most singular list of primary emotions to have ever been suggested. They include, for example, tenderness-protection, zest-mastery, sympathy-succour, wonder-curiosity, and creativity-enlivenment. This analysis is in terms of the adaptive value of the emotions and is couched very much in terms of what a person can become. In general, there is much wanting about this theory (see Strongman 1989) but at least it makes an attempt to link emotion and personality.

Sex

Sex had to be discussed somewhere in this book, and indeed passing reference was made to it in Chapter 8 on love. However, it is considered in more detail here because it is bound up with so many emotional reactions and for many people affords them what are amongst their most telling emotional experiences as individuals. Two of the more illuminating discussions of sex and emotion have been made by Izard (1991) and Mandler (1984) and it is largely their ideas that will be considered here.

Links between sex and emotion are forged both biologically and psychologically. Izard points out that the sex drive can dominate both cognition and action, an effect enhanced by interest or excitement. The result is urgency. In his view, if interest is combined with joy and particular emotion-cognitive structures, a possible result is love (see Chapter 8).

An emotion such as fear is incompatible with sex, leading to various inhibiting physical effects in both males and females. Such fears appear to be socioculturally determined, either being concerned with the fear of being discovered in clandestine sex or the fear of failure in any sort of sex, clandestine or otherwise. Any such reaction depends on self-doubts which in turn rest on a range of stereotypes.

Although attitudes towards sexual behaviour have changed in Western society during the last few decades, guilt concerning sex remains to some extent. Izard suggests that this may not be a learned relationship. He argues that guilt about sex tends to follow from ideas about commitment and responsibility which are adaptively important. However if sociobiologists are right then males should feel less guilt than females about sexual encounters that society at large might frown upon since they might well be increasing the chances of spreading their genes.

More generally, Izard sees strong links between sex, emotion and cognitive structures. For example, sexual attitudes show variation with age, perhaps due to socialization and parental modelling. Even more generally, societies change from time to time with respect to their acceptance of sexuality.

Mandler (1984) rests his analysis of sex on emotions being determined by an interplay between sympathetic arousal and cognitive interpretation, although with sex parasympathetic arousal also has a role to play. Interestingly, Mandler argues that strongly aroused (sympathetically) love may well inhibit the early stages of sexual arousal.

Mandler also considers possible cognitive structures that might relate appraisals to lust and love. For example, being pushed to love a person rather than to lust after that person may inhibit the sexual response. Whereas, sexual responses may be related to persons with whom such a relationship is not possible. In his view, if different occasions and persons, and hence different cognitions, produce love and lust, whether this be culturally or individually determined, there will be difficulties. Sexual arousal will be problematic and interpersonal relationships impaired.

Clearly, the emotional aspects of sex are a very significant part of life, although they have been under-researched and are not well understood. However, it does seem as though they may be distinct in their arousal and its interpretation, from emotions experienced in other spheres. Whatever theoretical approach is made to an understanding of the emotional aspects of sex it is clear that a major role will have to be given to cognition.

Gender

At the folk psychology level, differences between women and men seem perennially fascinating. They appear to be amongst those facets of individual differences that people rarely tire of discussing. From a scholarly perspective, the simple recounting of possible sex differences in emotion (or indeed anything) is of little account. However, the pervasive stereotype is interesting in its own right. The stereotype has it that in Western society, in comparison with men, women are illogical and emotional, at the whim of their feelings, which they find it difficult to hide.

Shields (1991), in an analysis of recent empirical studies in this area, makes the important methodological or terminological point that a distinction should be drawn between sex differences and gender differences. Sex differences are concerned with the biologically based distinctions (say between primary and secondary sex characteristics) and gender differences refer to matters which are psychologically or culturally determined. She argues cogently for a model which emphasizes gender-in-context rather than sex-differences, and so looks at matters related to social and cognitive influences. This suggests a far more searching theoretical analysis than might be given by a simple rather descriptive account of *sex* differences, that is differences listed by reference to biological markers.

Within this type of context, Brody and Hall (1993) provide a penetrating review of gender differences in emotion, which deals both with everyday beliefs and the results of empirical research. They make the point that the findings are consistent with a perspective that suggests that gender differences in emotion are adaptive for the differing roles played by men and women in Western culture. It seems as if each sex is socialized to adapt to its own gender roles and that these are reflected in dealing with particular emotions in particular ways.

The general stereotype, which seems to hold, is that women are more emotionally expressive than men, and that they also express sadness and fear more than men, who in turn, express anger more readily than women. Such differences are not surprising if emotions are seen from an adaptive perspective. Social goals vary for women and men, depending on age, socialization, socioeconomic status, personal history, culture, and of course, underlying biological predispositions.

In accounting for gender differences in emotion, Brody and Hall draw attention to a number of factors. For example, peer interaction which is differentiated between the sexes leads to a difference in socialization. Such differences are also enhanced by families and for example the amount of encouragement there is to express emotion (for girls) and inhibit its expression (for boys). They argue further that such effects are added to by language differences, girls and boys learning to use language in distinctive ways.

In general then, Brody and Hall regard gender differences in emotion to be based on socialization patterns within the family and peer group. In general, in Western society, women *are* held to account more for their feelings in public, whereas men are encouraged to deny emotions, both in themselves and others. It is interesting to note that differences accounted for in this way, via socialization practices, must be mediated by cognition.

The environment

It is indisputable that the environment, be it natural or artificial, has an emotional impact on the individual. Even though this has been a relatively neglected area of concern, it is clear from shared personal experience that the environment can have profound emotional effects. These can be extremely difficult to describe when they reach the ineffability of the sublime.

There have been two theoretical approaches to this area which have shown promise. The first comes from Mehrabian and Russell (1974) from a background of environmental psychology. Their theoretical basis was generated from the development of measures to assess emotional and approach–avoidance reactions to the natural world.

They consider the emotional aspects of the environment-individual reaction to be intervening variables. They further assume that pleasure, arousal and dominance (as measured by semantic differential scales) are the three basic human emotional reactions. They argue further that approach–avoidance reactions to the environment also come from the emotions a person brings to the situation.

Mehrabian and Russell develop and test various hypotheses concerning approach and avoidance. From this work they argue that the pleasant–unpleasant dimension has traditionally been afforded too much importance, whereas arousal has been relatively neglected. In this context, their major point is that in the modern city environment there has been a rapidly accelerating increase in the rate of information that requires processing. Such environments are massively arousing, a condition which is likely to be so stressful as to be maladaptive. Prolonged information overload leads to fatigue and exhaustion; it is too much to cope with.

This type of analysis is supported by the suggestion that high arousal generated by dwelling in crowded, unpleasant places makes interpersonal relationships suffer to the point of aggression and violence. It is as if the negative feelings generated by the environment are generalized to the people within it.

Coming from a geographical background, Ulrich (eg 1983) offers a different type of analysis of emotional responses to the natural environment. He views emotion as being the basis of conscious experience in any environment.

Ulrich bases his theory on the assumption that emotions are adaptive and moves onto the question: What are the adaptive functions of emotional reactions to the landscape? If people respond to parts of the landscape with feelings of æsthetic pleasantness, is this significant for survival?

There are three elements to the theory. (1) Internal processes which generate emotion. (2) Adaptive functions of emotions in the natural environment. (3) Emotions in this context are related to behaviour. The assumption is also made that thought or cognition, as mediated in the neocortex, and emotion, as mediated in the limbic system, are separate systems.

Ulrich's theory assumes that preferences in the natural environment are for gross configurations, gross depths and general classes of things. The process of emotional appreciation occurs very quickly, even before proper identification has occurred, particularly if water or vegetation are involved. There is a constant interplay between emotion and cognition, however, in Ulrich's view it is only elementary cognition that is involved in most natural environments.

Emotional reactions to the environment act as motivators, arousal changes that lead to behaviour. Strong positive emotions sustain behaviour, adaptively. Or they might lead to physiological restoration through feelings of pleasantness, interest, or through the inhibition of stressful thoughts. All of which may well lead to an increased sense of competence.

To Ulrich, the basic question, perhaps prompted by the work of Izard which has clearly influenced him, is whether or not æsthetic, emotional preferences are culturally determined and hence different between various societies. His studies tend to show similarities across cultures.

Generally, Ulrich's theory is well constructed and could prove to be a useful foundation in this area of research. It is clear that the broad environment has an emotional impact on the individual, something which is an important part of emotion in everyday life.

The culture

In this part of the present chapter, the term 'culture' is being used in a specific way, that is, to refer to what are commonly called cultural pursuits. As has already been mentioned from time to time and as will be even more obvious in Chapter 13, there are some powerful theories of emotion that spring from cultural considerations. But in the case of such theories, the term culture is being used to refer to societal matters.

Links between emotion and cultural pursuits such as literature, music, drama and art are significant. What are commonly called the arts depend on emotional impact. As with emotion and the landscape, emotional responses within the arts are linked with æsthetic preferences. But they are also associated with creativity and with conscious attempts at manipulation by the artist or performer

Literature

That prose and poetry are usually concerned with emotion goes without saying. Frequently, fiction is aimed at portraying, describing and analysing individual emotions. It is also manipulative of a reader's emotions. Whilst the psychologist is usually concerned to characterize the average person, the writer of fiction is often concerned to portray the best possible example of a type of person or event or situation.

Frequently, in fiction, emotion is characterized as precipitated by a startling event. Following this, however, it is usually quite clear that the writer is as aware as the psychologist that emotion involves physiological arousal, and behavioural, particularly facial, expression. Also, it tends to be almost axiomatic that some process of cognitive evaluation precedes the experience of emotion. And following this, fictional characters are then often shown as having to act on their emotions. So even in sophisticated modern times, fictional characters are gripped by passion, and carry on fierce battles between the rational and emotional sides of their make-up. Emotion is also typically seen as an important motivator.

The reader's emotion can be manipulated in a number of ways. It is apparent for example that an absorbing work of fiction prompts much vicarious emotional experience for the reader. Also, the experience of emotion through fiction can allow the satisfaction of a temporary escape from the less pleasant aspects of daily life. This is the sense of escapist fiction. From the crudest romance to the most spellbinding tale of high adventure, the reader is invited to suspend reality and to identify with larger than life characters whose experiences command great pinnacles of emotional satisfaction.

In fact, it is identification that seems crucial for the experience of vicarious emotion. If a reader can find no grounds for identification then a work of fiction seems curiously flat. Such identification is perhaps allied to the projection and empathy which allows us to gain some understanding of the emotional experiences of those around us in the everyday world. In practice the emotional effects of fiction can be powerful, lasting, and even harrowing. Moreover, as Oatley (1992) suggests, it is through fiction that we came to a non-scientific but important understanding of emotion, through *verstehen*.

An issue that remains, and that has been enjoined more by philosophers than psychologists, concerns what exactly it is that we are made emotional about when we are made emotional by fiction. If we know that something is a work of fiction, if we know that what is happening to a fictitious character is by definition itself fictitious, then how is it that we react emotionally?

Neill (1993) makes an interesting analysis of this matter based on the view that our emotional responses are themselves founded on belief. He describes this as representing current philosophical orthodoxy as far as emotions are concerned. In passing it might be noted that if orthodoxy is defined as what is believed by the greatest number, then this view comes close to current psychological orthodoxy as well.

Of course, the problem with respect to the emotional impact of fiction is that since I know that a fictional character does not exist in reality then how can I have beliefs about events in her fictional life so that I pity her, for example? Neill answers this question with the suggestion that our emotional reactions to fictional characters and events are based on beliefs, although they are beliefs about what is fictionally so. It then follows that our emotional reactions to fiction are themselves explicable by a cognitive theory of emotion.

Neill makes a convincing case that pity, as a significant emotion that seems to be frequently generated by fiction, can be seen in this way. And he argues that it is reasonable to generalize from this to other emotions. The emotional reactions we have to fictional characters and events may be slightly different from those that we have to events in real life and to actual people, but we do have them nevertheless. We do pity and envy and fear for fictional characters (although we might not fear them) and such reactions can be accounted for cognitively. Of course, to have beliefs about fiction we do have to first do what the novelist and dramatist frequently wishes us to do, and that is to suspend disbelief.

Music

Much as with literature, it is often assumed that a major way in which music has its effect is through the emotions. To those who listen to music, this effect is indisputable, an integral part of the experience. Moreover, from an observer's perspective, the sight of rows of people with closed eyes rapt in a performance of classical music or of crowds of young people head-banging at a heavy metal concert makes it obvious that the music is having an emotional impact.

The problem comes when the attempt is made to go further than this and to say how music has its effects. There are many *supposed* effects such as fast rhythms, consonant music and rising melodies leading to happiness and dissonant, descending music with drawn out notes leading to sadness. (see Ostwald, 1966). But such statements seem often to be made almost *ex cathedra,* supporting research and theory being sadly lacking.

Although it may seem obvious to anyone who has experienced a shiver down the back during particular sequences of music that emotion is involved, and possibly at a primitive level, demonstrations are lacking. A rather poor literature is based on speculative comments such as music being an abstraction about emotion, a way of reflecting emotion symbolically. This sounds grand but is rather difficult to take any further.

Drama

As with music, the involvement of emotion in drama is obvious to anyone who has ever attended a play. Drama rests on emotional manipulation, but it is a topic which has largely been ignored by psychologists. However, it is dealt with by writers concerned with theatre.

For example, Stanislawski (1929) discusses what he terms the emotion of truth. He regards the actor as a 'living, complex, emotion' who might, on occasion not complete a perfect bodily action or give a proper intonation. This leads to what he terms mannerism or awkwardness, the only way to guard against which is for the actor to develop a strong sense of the truth of what he or she does.

Writing at much the same time, Meyerhold (Braun, 1969) suggests ways in which the actor can build into a part physically and so manipulate his or her emotions and hence those of the audience. "From a sequence of physical positions and situations there arise those 'points of excitation' which are informed with some particular emotion. Throughout this process of rousing the emotions, the actor observes a rigid framework of physical prerequisites."

Brecht addresses the problem of emotion much more directly, seeing the emotions as based on class, an idea noteworthy for its singularity. He suggests that works of art, particularly theatrical works, allow successive generations to share the emotions of those that preceded them.

This is sufficient to give the flavour of the types of analysis made by those who write about the theatre. They are speaking in ways which would make the conventional scientifically based psychologist uneasy. They dive into a sea of speculation and swim strongly in apparent ignorance of the depths beneath them. The usual response by psychologists is dismissive. Although understandable, this is short-sighted. It may be possible to couch the ideas of writers such as Meyerhold in theoretical terms which are more acceptable and workable.

General theory

By far the most searching analysis of the relationship between emotion and the arts is made by Kreitler and Kreitler (1972) Although it is some years since its publication, their book is still a force. Their main thesis rests on the concepts of set and empathy. The experience of art depends on stimuli from the art itself and on responses from the observer/listener/reader. The more responsive the spectator, the more intense the experience and the greater the emotional involvement. Strength of response is thought to depend, amongst other things, on set or expectation, which is of course, a cognitive capacity. Similarly, empathy can also be generated by cognitive set.

Æsthetic meanings are partly shaped by social standards and habits. Sets are shaped from this by developing meanings associated with ideas and from the influence of specific settings in which this might occur. Surroundings make a difference to judgements.

According to Kreitler and Kreitler, emotion is a significant element in the experience of art. Since art is essentially fictional, they argue that the emotional involvement is generated through empathy, which they characterize as a 'feeling into'. This is essentially a reaction people have to others who undergo emotional experiences.

There are two basic theories about how empathy occurs in art. The first involves representation. So, in attempting to understand something, a spectator might dredge up memories relevant to previous emotional experiences. In this sense, empathy depends on cognition and imagining, with the relevant emotional experience being attenuated.

The alternative theory involves the notion of 'feeling into' in which the emphasis is on the actual emotional experience. It is reflected in a tendency to imitate the movements of others, which in turn leads to the imitator enjoying a similar emotional experience to that of the person being imitated.

Although Krietler and Kreitler apply this type of analysis to the experience of many kinds of art, for present purposes it is sufficient to consider literature. In these terms, literature has great power to develop 'feeling into' via the events, situations and characters. It is assumed that the emotion generated in the reader would be weaker than that generated in real life (see Neill, previously discussed). however, in literature there are techniques and devices that enhance empathy. For example, the selective description of expressive movements would make a difference, as might the sounds of the words and the melodies of sentences.

It is also argued that in literature, stimuli to do with emotion evoke kinæsthetic imitation in the reading, which leads to physiological arousal. Emotional experience might follow when such physiological changes are linked with cognitive elaboration. Such elaboration might come from expanding on and enhancing the written material, and from identifying with the author.

The Kreitlers argue that the author depends on a sort of suggestive reporting to bring about a sense of completion in the reader, and that this is similar to the way in which we attempt to understand people in everyday life. In literature this is aided by fantasy. The problem with this type of argument, and there are many of a similar nature, is that it can be distorted to account for almost anything.

A final point which is worth making from the Kreitlers' analysis of emotion and art concerns the stress they place on what might be termed emotional distance. They regard a type of inhibition called 'disinterestedness' as crucial to the experience of art. There are two main aspects to this. An object and its appeal may be separated from the self, at a distance from the practicalities of life. This is a positive condition and seems to help to intensify the subjective experience of the object. A second possibility is the detachment that results when a person concentrates so fully on a work that the result is an experience of richness and complexity. In this instance, there seems to be personal involvement at many levels. The difference between these two possibilities is that the distance involved is either external to the experience or an integral part of it.

Clearly, the experience of art is complex emotionally. It is either enhanced or inhibited by whatever social roles the individual might be playing or by the particular sets being held. Such sources of influence change with culture and with time. Both emotional closeness and emotional distancing appear to be important, the exact nature of which is perhaps dependent on whatever form of empathy is occurring.

Mandler (1982) has been one of the few psychologists who has attempted to deal with the difficult topic of art and emotion as they relate to æsthetics and creativity. He argues that art arouses through its interaction with the experiencing individual. He also places emphasis on set, which he refers to as anticipation. The work of art may or may not be in accord with the anticipation, thus, in Mandler's usual terms, leading to some or other degree of interruption.

The suggestion is that negative emotion results from the confirmation of expectations with low probability. The emotion becomes positive if the expectations are of medium probability and ends up as boredom if they are of high probability. Another viewpoint is that emotional tension depends on competition between incompatible tendencies, and another is that the degree of arousal from a work of art varies with the discrepancies between stimulation and set.

Mandler argues that æsthetically meaningful experience in the emotional sense will depend to an extent on making more and more new interpretations and differentiations. The more complex the object or the work, the more intense the possible emotional experience. A certain amount of artistic knowledge and training is related to any emotional experience of art. A piece of simple, popular music will soon lose its emotional impact, whereas a more complex piece will not.

The essential ingredient in the emotionally positive side of æsthetic appreciation is novelty. This cognitive characteristic can be in the form of new interpretations, new views, or new mental structures, according to Mandler. However, extreme novelty in art can lead to negative emotional reactions. This is because the individual has no mental structures which can accommodate any attempts to analyse the work. With more familiarity and education, more should become assimilated and the reaction become more positive.

In a most interesting passage, Mandler argues that creative persons have to have certain emotional characteristics. For example, they should be able to tolerate the new, emotionally and find such novelty attractive, cognitively. To Mandler, a creative work should involve the destruction of existing structure, a sort of interruption. Also, he believes that creative individuals often have a parent of opposite sex who was frustrated creatively. This is likely to prompt the parent to push the child, constantly interfering with the child's structures and destroying stability. Within a positive relationship, the development of new structures comes to be seen as an emotionally positive achievement. In this way, being creative (through destruction and production) is learned early in life and becomes associated with a positive emotional tone. Of course, society also helps to form cognitive evaluations of feelings and actions. To view the destruction of the old as creative rather than aggressive depends on social values towards creativity and aggression.

Conclusions

In some ways this has been rather a hotch-potch of a chapter, part of the aim being to pick up a few of the theoretical considerations that are not readily embraced by the categorization of theories used throughout this book. However, the chapter is not merely a miscellany. It is concerned with attempts that have been made to look at some of the meanings of emotion in a slightly applied sense. Also, as mentioned in the introduction to this chapter it was hoped to add to the general *verstehen* by doing this.

Some of the theoretical contributions made with respect to emotion and aspects of personality are of considerable use and interest. For example, recent analyses of the methodological and conceptual issues surrounding emotion and gender have been particularly penetrating. Also, the theories of both Izard and Mandler provide reasonable summaries and explanations of the links between emotion and personality. their focus is good and they have a clear heuristic value. They do not however lead to obviously testable predictions

The theoretical accounts of the links between emotion and sex have not progressed far enough to add much to our understanding. Furthermore, the major theory in the area or personality, Bertocci's, although internally consistent and quite an explanatory tour de force, is so at variance with most of the other theories of emotion as to be difficult to compare. It is also couched in terms from which it is almost impossible to derive predictions. At times it is so difficult to penetrate that even its heuristic value which on the face of it should be worthy, is not.

Interestingly, the two major concerns that fall out of the theories to do with personality reflect the biological and the social. The concept of adaptivity arises frequently, as does cognition, of course, but mainly through the possible effects of socialization.

Moving on to ideas about links between emotion and the environment evaluated at the broad level, the theories give reasonable accounts but are relatively restricted. Ulrich's however, certainly has both heuristic value and leads to testable predictions. Again, notions of adaptivity and cognition are given a central role to play, but emotion is also conceived of as integral to conscious experience, and is also viewed as an intervening variable.

It must be said that the theories concerned with the relationship between emotion and culture, although interesting are expressed in such broad terms as to be of limited value. They are focused and do provide explanations of a sort but they are relatively difficult to pin down. Even the Kreitlers' general theory of emotion and art depends on concepts such as set and expectation and empathy which have proved relatively unwieldy in the past. Again, though, it is interesting to note that a central concept to all of this is cognition. Indeed cognitive theory plays an integral part in what is probably the most thought-provoking of the theories in this area, that of Neill concerning the links between belief and emotion in fiction.

In some ways, Lazarus's (1991a,b) prescriptions for emotion theory do not apply readily to the theories summarized in this chapter. They are not concerned with the causes of emotion, nor particularly with emotion as an independent or a dependent variable. They are more to do with emotion as a variable which might intervene between the person and the environment, be this the natural environment or the cultural environment. Or that might even intervene between the person and him or herself.

So these theories meet very few of the criteria, even in some cases eschewing behaviour and physiology altogether for example. However, they do consider the bases of emotion in biological adaptivity and as socially constructed, and they do all have an absolutely central place for cognition. Moreover, some of them become concerned with consciousness and also with the links between emotion and motivation.

Similarly, Oatley's (1992) criteria for emotion theories are less applicable to the theories under consideration here than they have been in previous chapters. Certainly, they tend to be concerned with the functions of emotion and with the evaluative aspect of emotion as it is to do with goals. They also touch on the possible unconscious causes of emotion. The other criteria are irrelevant however. Also, as has already been noted, these theories are difficult to derive specific predictions from, although Ulrich's and Mandler's should perhaps be seen as exceptions to this. Moreover, their capacity to deal with more evidence is indeterminate. Mandler's and Izard's clearly can, but many of the others are expressed in such relatively vague terms that they could either be seen as embracing any other evidence at all, or none.

What then, in general, can be said of the theories that have been covered in this chapter? In Oatley's sense of *verstehen* they do add to our sense of what emotion is, or add to the richness of emotion theoretically. Although they are not the best of the theories that surround emotion, it is interesting that, for the most part, they end by being concerned with the same type of issues. In particular, of course, these include cognition, in one form or another, appraisal, belief, set, empathy, novelty or consciousness.

Of the theories mentioned in this chapter, although Bertocci's is impressive in its aims, the best of them is Mandler's. Mandler makes a genuine attempt to deal with difficult aspects of emotion theory, even going so far as to consider its links with creativity. He has the courage that most theorists lack.

Finally, it should be pointed out that an analysis of the role of emotion in the arts, particularly in fiction, forms a useful bridge between folk psychological approaches and the methodologies of science. There is no doubt that artists of many sorts have great insights into emotion, and that unlike many people in everyday life, they have found a means of expressing them. Those that study emotion from a scientific viewpoint should not set these alternative approaches to one side. It is interesting for example to ponder on the writer's typical approach of providing the best possible example of something rather than the average. This inevitably provides different types of insight.

13

Theory outside psychology

The majority of theories of emotion have come from the discipline of psychology. This is hardly surprising since emotion is traditionally regarded as a matter of individual expression and experience. However, the study of emotion does not *belong* to the psychologist. Perhaps more than many areas of human functioning, it also lies in other domains, and might be better seen as an interdisciplinary affair. Philosophers, historians, sociologists, anthropologists, and, even cutting across these, those who are interested in various aspects of culture (even more broadly conceived than might be by the anthropologist or the sociologist), all have much to add to an understanding of emotion. As well as being an individual matter, emotion is also an historical, sociological and cultural matter.

The aim of this chapter is to place theories of emotion within this broader perspective. Recent theories of emotion from the disciplines which are adjunct to psychology will be described. Although in certain respects they are in accord which recent psychological theorizing about emotion, they also add to the complex richness of the topic.

Philosophy

A glance at the history of Western philosophy shows that there have been philosophical accounts of emotion to some degree since there have been philosophical accounts of anything. Detailed discussion began with Aristotle, although there are hints in Plato. The present purpose, however, is to consider some of the more recent philosophical accounts of emotion. The history as well as contemporary views of the philosophy of emotion are well analysed by Lyons (1992) and Solomon (1988, 1993)

Peters

Peters (eg 1969, 1970) attempts to list what he believes might be 'naturally' called the emotions, a main criterion for inclusion being that the term links emotion and appraisal. Lists of emotions generated in this way also characterize motive.

Although Peters links emotion and motive, he also makes a distinction between them, basing this on a consideration of everyday language. We speak of motives when we are searching for explanations of behaviour—'he ate *because* he was hungry'. On the other hand, we speak of emotions in situations when people are passive, and overcome—'he was blinded by anger', 'she was overcome by desire'. Peters is describing an everyday conceptual connection between motivation and action and between emotion and passivity, or inaction.

Although motivation and emotion are connected in that they both involve appraisal, they are distinct in that emotion is not connected to action. Even when activity is apparently involved, say within the ANS, it is still passive activity in his view. We go white with fear or red with embarrassment, almost uncontrollable responses.

Peters also suggests a *de facto* relationship between emotion and higher mental processes such as memory and perception. An appraisal connected with emotion must alter the general assessment being made at the time. If we appraise something as unpleasant or as bad for us, then this might obscure relevant adaptive behaviour, or might highlight it. Either way, there is distortion; an emotion overcomes us and there is little that we can do.

Finally, Peters describes a connection between emotion and wishing. Motivation is concerned with 'wanting' which leads to action; emotion is concerned with the vaguer 'wishing' which does not lead to action.

Ryle

Ryle's (1948) starting point is that emotions are made up of, or suggest, inclinations (motives), moods, agitations (or commotions) and feelings. Of these, the first three are propensities, not occurrences in the way that feelings are.

A comparison of feelings and inclinations suggests that feelings are what people describe by phrases such as 'a thrill of anticipation' and also names for specific bodily sensations, such as qualms of apprehension. Some feelings are given to specific bodily locations and others are given a general bodily coverage (a flash of anger). Ryle then is suggesting that feelings can be emotions. However, people also characterize emotions as motives. For example, the success of a competent leader is ascribed to certain dispositions, say to be dominant and resourceful, which will sometimes be manifest in behaviour. However, such a person is also expected to feel certain things, although such feelings are not such good indications of qualities of leadership as is behaviour. So, a motive and a feeling are both part of an emotion, but the motive is a disposition and the feeling is an occurrence.

Ryle also compares inclinations (motives) and agitations, mood and feelings, and feeling and pleasure. He suggests that there are three ways in which the idea of emotion is commonly used. In the first two it is used in an attempt to explain behaviour. So it is used in the sense of motives or inclinations on the basis of which more or less intelligent actions are made, or we use it to refer to moods, including agitations or perturbations. The third sense of emotion use according to Ryle is in reference to pangs and twinges. These are feelings and emotions.

Lyons

One of the most thorough and useful philosophical discussions of emotion has been made by Lyons (1980, 1992). He expounds his causal-evaluative theory of emotion via a series of propositions, which will be considered in turn.

(1) Lyons proposes that emotion is an occurrent state rather than a disposition. This is not exceptional; many theories of emotion are concerned with occurrent states. Generally some emotion terms are used in both ways and some are not. For example, fear can be occurrent or dispositional, whereas rage is used only occurrently. Within this framework, an emotional disposition can be reasonably focused (an angry person expresses anger in specific directions) or relatively unfocused (irascibility is a general proneness to react angrily). Lyons believes the occurrent view gives the full case of emotion. Whatever might be latent in an angrily disposed person is also present when anger is occurring, particularly when there is physiological arousal. He suggests a progression which starts with our beliefs about the present situation, which form the basis for an evaluation. This in turn causes wants and desires which cause behaviour, physiological change and subjective feelings.

(2) Causal-evaluative theory derives its name from the suggestion that a state is emotional if and only if it is a physiologically abnormal state caused by a person's evaluation of a situation. Emotion is a psychosomatic state in which both evaluation and physiological change are necessary conditions for emotion, not individually, but together.

To be essential to emotion an attitude must be an evaluation in relation to self, which may be occurrent or dispositional. Also, the physiological change in emotion must be unusual since others are occurring constantly. The abnormality will usually take the form of being in some way more or less than the normal range. Lyons does not expand the nature of the causal link between evaluation and physiological change. If one frequently follows the other closely in time, it is likely to be causal.

(3) Differently from many psychologists, Lyons argues that it is not possible to differentiate between the emotions behaviourally, physiologically or motivationally. He proposes that such differentiation is only possible through cognitive evaluations. In his view, we clearly seek clues to a person's emotional state from behaviour or physiological indicants, but to be sure we need to find the person's view or evaluation of the situation. If we do draw conclusions from behaviour, this is because the behaviour is a typical expression of an evaluative attitude.

(4) Lyons suggests that there is a complex relationship between emotion and desires. Some emotions would not exist unless the person admits to

certain wants or desires. For example, it would make little sense to speak of love without admitting to a desire to be with the loved person. Such emotions (if love is an emotion) need not culminate in behaviour; they do not have to be 'given into'. By contrast, Lyons argues that some emotions have no wants at all attached to them, backward-looking ones such as grief for example. However, it may be that even this might subsume the desire that an event such as the death of another, had not occurred.

(5) In his causal-evaluative theory Lyons also proposes that evaluations lead rationally and causally to specific desires, which then lead to behaviour. He argues that this type of evaluative theory is better than a motivational theory of emotion since it can explain, for example, how various types of behaviour can be part of one emotion. The diversity of fear cannot be explained with action tendencies resulting from motivational theory. Wants/ desires are not tied to particular patterns of behaviour. The evaluative aspect of emotion gives a reason for the emotional behaviour.

(6) Finally, Lyons proposes that if emotions are mainly occurrent, they are tangible, their tangible aspects including bodily change, facial expression, gesture, speech and motivated behaviour. For the psychologist, the problem is that a 'mental' event, an evaluation, is the differentiation between emotions. To Lyons though, evaluations are as tangible as behaviour. He makes the further point that there may be a perfect correlation between the structural/ categorical basis of evaluations and brain states. If this were to be so then an evaluative account of emotion could eventually be reduced to a behavioural/ physiological account—an argument that could apply to any cognitive analysis.

However, evaluations might still provide a way of differentiating between the emotions, even if they are irreducibly mentalist. In Lyons' view, this does not make his theory any more non-objective than one which involves anything equally non-observable, electrons for example. In as much as a physicist claims to be able to see traces of electrons, so the psychologist can reasonably claim to see traces of evaluations in the tangible aspects of emotion occurrences.

Cognitive emotion theory—Griffiths

Lyons theory was dealt with at some length because, in its emphasis on cognition, it typifies current philosophical theories of emotion. Similar theories are offered by Solomon (eg 1976) who argues that emotions are evaluative beliefs, although he also has a role for constructionism, and Marks (1982), who suggests that emotions are a complex of belief and desire with the desire component being particularly strong.

In a very useful analysis, Griffiths (1989), following Stocker (1987), criticizes philosophical cognitive theories of emotion. He characterizes them as dependent on two central claims: (1) "... the occurrence of propositional attitudes is essential to the occurrence of emotions" and (2) "... the identity of a particular emotional state depends upon the propositional attitude that it involves" (1989, p299).

Griffiths goes on to list six problems occasioned by this approach.

(1) Some emotional states, such as anxiety, are regarded as sometimes having no object, and therefore no content.
(2) The judgements thought to underlie emotions appear to be quite different (more rapid, less conscious) from ordinary judgements.
(3) Too many emotions result from equating emotion and evaluative judgements.
(4) Why must someone who feels a particular emotion have particular beliefs?
(5) The typical *philosophical* cognitive theory of emotion leaves out physiological considerations
(6) It can be argued that we can have emotional experiences by imagining things, in this case clearly not having the beliefs/desires of a cognitive analysis.

Griffiths' (1989) general thesis is that even if these types of objection were to be overcome, what he terms the cognitivist programme in philosophy would not answer a number of basic questions about emotion. (It should be noted, however, that this is *not* an argument against the cognitive approach to emotion from a psychological perspective.)

A core difficulty is that the cognitivist cannot give an account of why some (or some groups of) propositional attitudes are emotions and others are not. Griffiths characterizes the theory as being in turn dependent on folk theory to establish its taxonomy of emotions. "The distinctions between one emotion and another are drawn in terms of their content, but content distinctions are taken notice of only when they happen to coincide with distinctions already present in the folk-theory" (p308). So, Griffiths argues that cognitivism can neither explain what an emotion is nor why emotions are classified as they are.

He suggests that the philosophical approach to emotion would better depend on either psychoevolutionary theory or social constructionism

Solomon's questions

Solomon ends his 1993 overview of the philosophy of emotions with what he considers to be the type of questions that it is important for philosophical (and, no doubt, any other) analyses to address. These issues also provide a useful place to end this brief discussion.

(1) What is emotion? What should be considered to be the essence of emotion or essential for it?
(2) Does emotion have to have its subjective aspect? Can there be emotion without feeling? Is feeling sufficient to account for emotion?

(3) Do the neurological patterns in the central nervous system that are clearly associated with the various emotions themselves provide a theory of the emotions?

(4) Should the behavioural, expressive side of emotions be regarded as essential to an account?

(5) All philosophical accounts nowadays, and perhaps since Aristotle onwards, have cognitions as a background, or a necessary aspect or a precondition. Does every emotion have a cognitive base and an object? Moreover, what, in emotion, is the nature of cognition? In more philosophical terms, do emotions have intentionality, that is, are emotions always about something? (See also Griffiths, above)

(6) What are the functions and explanations of emotions? Accounts of some emotions draw attention to someone's beliefs and attitudes about the world, and others to underlying causes that make no mention of objects of the emotion. What is the relationship between accounts made in terms of intentionality and accounts made in terms of causes?

(7) What is the relationship between emotion and rationality? Are emotions irrational? Are emotions arational? Can we compare the rationality of emotions (their reasons, from cognition) with evaluations of deliberate activities? One might also extend this line of question into—what is the distinction between emotional and deliberative activities?

(8) What are the links between emotion and ethics? This abuts the matter of the universality or relativity of emotions, on which (according to Solomon) philosophers take a middle road. Are we overwhelmed by our emotions or do we have some choice?

History

By far the majority of the research on emotion from an historical perspective has been reported by Peter Stearns (eg 1986, 1993), Stearns and Knapp (1993), and Stearns and Stearns (1994), although also see Kemp and Strongman (1995) for a discussion of the history of anger. Much of this research is concerned with an analysis of changes in emotional standards in the past, and of course how these changes are reflected in emotional behaviour and expression. There are obvious links between an historical approach to emotion and approaches that derive from anthropology and sociology, and an equally clear rapprochement with the social constructionist theoretical standpoint. Of particular significance here is the study of change or transition.

What becomes clear from a reading of the work of Stearns and others is that an enormous amount remains to be done with respect to the charting of emotion history. However, it is also obvious that there is a rich history to emotional norms, they have changed rather than remained static. There are also some claims that basic emotions have changed as well. This is not as easy to demonstrate as it is to show that changes in emotional perception and the judgement of the self occur in reaction to shifting social norms.

Theoretically, then, the significant aspect of historical research into emotion is that *change* has to be included as a key theoretical variable. Stearns (eg 1986) argues that historical research also places emotions into an ongoing social process, and furthermore prompts a discussion of particular types of causation in emotional reactions. For example, changes in various economic factors have helped to shape the development of anger. Or a reduction in birth rate has altered the emotional intensity with which individual children are dealt.

Changes in emotional standards can also be analysed in a similar way. For instance, what is expressed, and when, and where, emotionally, has changed over time with changes in social conditions. Again, it is the 'appropriateness' of the expression of anger which provides a good example, the targets of its expression in both the home and the workplace having undergone considerable change in Western society.

Interestingly, Stearns (eg 1986) makes the point that the main findings of historians of emotion apply to cognition. However, this leaves out what might be important biological considerations (see below). His point is that some emotions might be more subject to change, historically, than others, depending on the balance between their cultural and biological determinants.

A further useful theoretical concept that Stearns (eg 1993b) discusses is *emotional culture.* This is "... a complex of interrelated norms, standards, and ideals that govern the endorsement, the expression, and, ultimately, even the acknowledgment of emotions" (p36). He uses this concept to elucidate the more important concept of change. An emotional culture prevails for a time and then seems to give way to another emotional culture, thus leading, to use Stearns' oft-quoted example, to anger being thought much less well of in the middle of the twentieth century than it was at the end of the nineteenth, at least in Western society.

He points out that a significant aspect of emotional culture tends to be gender. Within a prevailing emotional culture there are usually quite different prescriptions for men and women, and these lead to the development of particular roles and identities. Again, anger in Western society provides a good example of this. Even though times are changing, anger is still generally regarded as being an emotion more appropriate for men than women.

This brief section on emotion viewed within the discipline of history has been included in order to point out that this perspective brings with it some extra theoretical variables that might otherwise not be considered by those who seek to understand emotion. To date, work on emotion from an historical standpoint has produced some very interesting descriptions of socio-emotional change, although this is not the context in which to list them. As yet, however, emotional historians have not produced their own theory of emotion, although they have pointed to the significance of concepts such as emotional culture in the analysis of emotion. More particularly, Stearns, amongst others, has shown that emotion does not consist of static phenomena, but that emotion is always in a state of change within society. Theorists of emotion should perhaps take this into account, or at least stay aware of it.

Anthropology

Anthropologists have long been interested in emotion, but it is only in recent years that their interest has been expressed in a form that is accessible to those in related disciplines. White and Lutz have done most to bridge the disciplinary gap between anthropology and psychology (eg Lutz and White, 1986; Lutz and Abu-Lughod, 1990; White, 1993). As might be expected, the anthropological approach to emotion has more in common with emotions conceived as social constructions or as discourse-centred than it has with the biological or physiological.

Theoretically, a basic matter which emerges from recent anthropological writing about emotion is that it is an area which has been almost hijacked, theoretically, by a mixture of folk psychology and psychobiology. As is usual within this tradition, and as much of the present book attests, the typical way of thinking within this tradition is in terms of binary oppositions. White (1993) lists a series of dichotomies that are typical and that work to force emotions (and other phenomena) to be thought of in particular ways. Thus: mind–body, cognition–affect, thinking–feeling, reason–emotion, rational–irrational, conscious–unconscious, intentional–unintentional, controlled–uncontrolled. Simply just to read them is to see how compelling they are.

This tradition of thought has placed emotion *within* the person, as a psychological process or set of processes. This is the approach that has come to be expected of individual psychology. White (1993) points out that one effect of this is "... privileging psychobiological variables in emotion theory to the detriment of social and semiotic factors ..." (p37). Of course, the alternative to this, which can stem from anthropology, is to consider emotional meaning within culture and to study the influences of cognitive, linguistic and socio-cultural processes. This in turn would place greater emphasis on the phenomenological and communicative aspects of emotion. The links between this approach and that which comes from history and the study of culture are obvious.

Lutz and White (1986) describe a number of what they term tensions in the study of emotion, which act to determine *how* emotion is both conceived of and investigated. (1) Materialism versus idealism, with emotions usually seen as material things, although emotions are seen by some as evaluative judgements. (2) Positivism versus interpretavism, the emphasis in the study of emotion being mainly positivistic, concerned with a search for the emotional causes of behaviour. The anthropological view would derive from interpretavism, with emotions seen as central to cultural meaning and a concern with language and the negotiation of emotion. (3) Universalism versus relativism. The search has long obtained in psychology for universal processes in emotion, rather than for cross-cultural differences. (4) Individual versus social. The main tradition is for emotion to be viewed as a matter of individual psychology, rather than social processes. Emotion is seen as *in* the individual. (5) Romanticism versus rationalism. Rather than distinguishing between psychological and anthropological ways of thinking, this distinction represents two ways of thinking within anthropology. Emotion might be evaluated positively as part of natural humanity or equated, negatively, with irrationality. The argument sustained by White and Lutz is that each of these alternatives prompts a particular stance towards the study of emotion. So, for example, emotion might be seen as an entity which is explained by some other variables, or it might be seen as something which in its turn can explain cultural institutions, or even be an integral part of cultural meaning.

In general then, anthropological approaches to emotion take emotion out of the person and instead see it as constructed within cognition, and language and interaction. Anthropologists suggest that any theory of emotion should at least have a place for culture, communication and social interaction, rather than simply seeing these somehow as *effects* of emotion, or as things that follow on from emotion. Human emotion has cultural meaning and it is to this that the anthropologist draws attention.

Sociology

Although the sociology of emotion has a long history, it is Kemper (eg 1991, 1993) who has done most in recent times to bring it to a wider, interdisciplinary audience. Kemper's fundamental starting point is that the sociology of emotion, or presumably the sociology of anything, is not reducible to anything else such as psychology. "... for the most part psychologists study emotions as a property of generic human beings, while sociologists study emotions as a property of socially specific people, alive in a particular time, living in a particular culture in particular circumstances" (1991, p301). In this context, any theory of emotion must deal not only with individual, internal matters such as cognitions and physiological change, but also external matters such as social processes.

Kemper makes a searching analysis of the various sociological models of emotion, only some of which will be summarized here, in order to give an idea of the theoretical considerations to which they prompt us.

The first type of model (see Kemper, 1978) is based on social relations and sees emotions as dependent on *power and status*. The social relations involved in emotion are not only *real*, but may also involve anticipation, imagination or recollection. The theory suggests that large numbers of human emotions can be understood as reactions to the meaning that underlies power and status. In this context, Kemper makes an analysis of security, anxiety, guilt, happiness, shame, embarrassment, depression, liking, optimism and pessimism, and even love.

To consider one detail of the theory, Kemper suggests that guilt, shame, anxiety and depression come about through a socialization process that depends on the type of punishment used (power or status: physical or psychological), the proportionality of the punishment to the punished act, and whether or not the person doing the punishing is a source of affection. This leads to 2 × 2 × 2 outcome model of how the major negative emotions are socialized.

In a second model, emotions are seen as the forces that lie behind group cohesion (see for example, Durkheim, 1954 and Goffman, 1967). Collins (eg 1990) and Kemper and Collins (1990) extend this view into a theory which depends on the concept of *emotional energy*. This is the feeling that follows ritual interactions in groups which turn out successfully. It depends on focused attention in the group, a common emotion, and a feeling of solidarity. Again, underlying emotional energy are power and status, interactions based on these having their emotional effects. Ultimately, from this perspective, emotional resources come from power and status. In some ways, the significance of Collins' theory of emotional energy is that it makes sense of many of the emotional experiences of everyday life.

The third type of model that Kemper describes comes from the ideas of Scheff (1990) in which concern centres on the emotions that are at the basis of social control. Scheff suggests that we are always experiencing either pride or shame, depending on how we are dealing with the strictures of the world around us. This is an interesting theory, and quite unlike any that are found in the psychological literature, because it gives pride of place to one emotion, shame. It leads to social order, or disorder, if it is ignored.

The fourth type of sociological theory depends more on *culture* than on social structure, (eg Hochschild, 1990; Thoits, 1990) and is concerned with emotion management. For example, Hochschild suggests that how we feel depends on appraisals which in turn depend on variables such as social class, gender, race, etc. On top of this, there are culturally determined rules about the appropriateness of what is felt and what is expressed. So, in general, emotion serves a signalling function which prompts us into *managing* emotional lives, something which is achieved by various types of acting.

Kemper (1993) describes a fifth type of sociological theory of emotion which depends on the view that the self is a social creation which comes about through *role taking*. Because such role taking occurs mainly through language, this type of theory has come to be known as *symbolic interaction*, or *reflexivity* (eg Rosenberg, 1990).

Rosenberg is concerned in particular with how emotions are labelled, believing that this is fundamental to emotional expression and experience, all of which comes from role taking or reflexivity. He suggests that we make three types of check on our feelings. We learn what is meaningful in our culture (I'm happy because I've been promoted), we recognize social consensus (I'm happy because everyone else is happy) and there are what he terms 'cultural scenarios' (I've got a new car, I must be happy).

A further distinction is made by Schott (1979) in this context, between reflexive and empathic role-taking emotions. The reflexive type can only be achieved by putting oneself in the place of another and seeing oneself from that perspective. Thus we have guilt, shame and embarrassment. Whereas the empathic role-taking emotions bring about altruism, because we put ourselves in the place of another who might be suffering.

Heise and O'Brien (1993, see also Chapter 10) describe *affect control theory* in some detail, which Kemper believes to be amongst the most significant sociologically based emotion models. It is based on the view that "... people construct and understand social action so as to have important cultural meanings affirmed by the impression generated in manifest behaviour" (1993, p493). Also relevant to this model is the semantic differential, the three dimensions of affective meaning of which (evaluation, activity and potency) Heise and O'Brien suggest can be used for measuring the sentiments that are part of the identities that people create for themselves during their social encounters.

Within affect control theory, people are affected by events, and emotions are transient states that reflect this. "The emotion depends on the current impression of the person, and on how that impression compares to the sentiment attached to the person's identity." (p 493). Affect control theory links with emotion management in that if an emotion is socially undesirable it can be changed. It can be replaced with a new emotion or a past event is reinterpreted such that it generates a new emotion.

Towards the end of his 1991 paper, Kemper argues for a rapprochement between psychologists and sociologists through a socio-psychophysiological theory of emotion. He is urging an exploration of the links between the biology and the sociology of emotion, the body and society. He is suggesting that any model or theory of emotion should keep in mind the various limits imposed by both the body and society.

Of course, there are theoretical links between psychologists and sociologists of emotion, particularly through cognition. Even here though, they tend to take slightly different approaches. The psychologists attempt to spell out what exactly the cognitive processes in emotion might be, whereas the sociologists only specify any cultural cognitive processes in the broadest social interactionist terms. Kemper also stresses the importance of affect control theory within a psychological framework, and naturally enough also draws attention to the more structural models of Collins and himself. Clearly, any theorist of emotion would do well not to omit what are usually conceived of as sociological variables from consideration.

Within a sociological framework, a final theory to mention must be that of Rosenberg (1990). Although he believes that emotions are basically organismic, his contribution is an explication of reflexivity which he suggests is an integral part of emotion.

"Reflexivity refers to the process of an entity acting back upon itself" (1990, p 3).

Rosenberg refers to two types of reflexivity. The first is cognitive, in which all a person's cognitive processes can be used to consider or deal with, the self.

The second concerns agency, in which we can act or do things to ourselves, either as a whole or in part. The parts can be external (public) or internal (including things such as cognitions and emotions). Rosenberg is arguing that through reflexivity people can affect their own internal processes, including emotion, and in particular its physiological aspects. "The central message ... is that reflexivity works a fundamental change in the nature of human emotions. Once the internal state of arousal comes to be 'worked over' by these reflexive processes, they acquire a totally different character" (1990, p3).

Rosenberg suggests that there are three ways in which reflexivity affects emotion. (1) Through identification, that is in interpretative processes. (2) Through emotional display, that is in behaviour which is intended to affect other people. (3) Through emotional experiences, that is in internal states of arousal which are intentionally, rather than unintentionally, created. Importantly, Rosenberg also distinguishes between emotional display and emotional expression, the former being intentional and the latter unintentional. Perhaps even more importantly, he also distinguishes reflexive and nonreflexive emotional experiences, again the difference between what is intentional and what is spontaneous. His particular interest is in the reflexive processes because they stem from social interaction.

Rosenberg takes some care to explicate the details of reflexivity in the identification, display and experience of emotion. For example, he suggests that since people cannot control their emotional experiences directly, instead they attempt to control their causes. So from this perspective, we try to control our emotions by controlling our thoughts, either by only attending to some things rather than others or intentionally shifting our viewpoint. Alternatively, we try to control our emotions by controlling our bodies, for example by physical exercise or drugs.

In the present context, it is not the details of Rosenberg's analysis of reflexivity in emotion which is important but rather his general view. Through social interaction human beings are able to be both subject and object and to take themselves as objects of processes that are to do with cognition or agency. In particular they are able to reflect on physiological states which are to do with their own emotions and in so doing change, or at least affect, these emotions.

Culture

It may seem odd that this chapter includes a specific section on culture when it already contains sections on history, anthropology and sociology. There are obvious areas of overlap between any approaches to emotion that might be made under any of these heads. Clearly, for example, cultural meanings are of concern to some historians, to anthropologists and to sociologists of a particular persuasion. However, there have been recent developments in the culture of emotions *per se* that make it appropriate to consider them under their own head. It is almost as if there is developing what might be called a cultural psychology of the emotions.

Shweder (1993) suggests that cultural psychology is aimed at elucidating the meanings that underlie psychological processes, to explore how these meanings are distributed throughout the world and ethnic groups and to study how they are acquired. Within this type of framework, culture is seen as an amalgam of meanings, conceptions and schemes that are activated through normative social institutions and practices. Importantly, such practices include language.

According to Shweder, acts of meaning such as conceptualisation can take place either very rapidly or automatically. Examples in the emotion sphere are given by shame and embarrassment. In fact, within the area of emotions, there are four significant questions in cultural psychology. (1) What in terms of meaning allows an experience to be defined as emotional rather than something else? (2) What particular emotional meanings exist in particular parts of the world (geographically or ethnically)? (3) States can be experienced in various ways. To what extent in different parts of the world are particular states experienced through emotion rather than in some other (somatized) way? (4) How are meanings, particularly emotional meanings, acquired, especially with respect to everyday discourse and social interpretations?

The broad aim of cultural psychology is to decompose emotional states into narrative slots in order to try to determine the meaning of other people's mental states without necessarily being dependent on the researcher's own language.

A significant way into what might be termed the cultural psychology of emotion is through linguistics. An excellent start has been made in this direction by Wierzbicka (eg, 1992). The main thrust of her argument is that the emotions that we think of as basic, in either folk psychological terms or in the terms of academic theories of emotion, are 'cultural artefacts' of our language. It is likely that all languages have provided such prompts. She is therefore assigning to language a core role in how emotions are conceptualized and suggesting that any analyst of emotion should attempt to deal with the way in which language obstructs direct access to the emotions.

Her argument is not that there might not be universal emotions, nor is it that it is impossible to penetrate the emotions of those whose culture is different from the investigators. Rather, she is urging that the study of emotion be conducted from a perspective that is truly universal, that is, independent of language and culture. Thus, even if there are universal facial expressions that can be matched with particular emotions, such emotions are not necessarily characterized properly by the terms of say the English language, such as happiness or sadness.

Wierzbicka believes that our understanding of emotion would progress better if it were based on what she terms universal semantic primitives. Her point is that much of the analysis of emotions conducted by psychologists has been in culture-dependent terms. Emotion words such as anger for example tend to be explicated in terms which are themselves dependent on our culture. (One might take this argument further and question just how much the *many* cultures which happen to share a form of the English language actually have in common, emotionally, or in any other way.) Instead, Wierzbicka argues that emotion analyses should depend on explication by very simple concepts, which at least come closer both to being universal and to being semantic primitives.

One example of the type of language-based explication of emotion that Wierzbicka makes will help suffice.

"*angry*
X feels something
sometimes people think something like this (of someone)
   this person did something bad
   I don't want this
   because of this, I want to do something
   I would want to do something bad to this person
because of this, they feel something bad
X thinks something like this
because of this, X feels something like this" (1992, p303)

It should be clear from this example that Wierzbicka is attempting to use the most simple and basic (and therefore, it is to be hoped, universal) terms in her descriptions. It should be noted in passing that in speaking of anger she also gives examples of cultures in which explications of anger, although similar, are also different. So, in this sense, anger is not universal.

To make one final point about Wierzbicka's important suggestions, she takes Johnson-Laird and Oatley (1980) to task for speaking of happiness, sadness, anger, fear and disgust as universal and as categories of direct experience. To do this she believes that they would have to demonstrate how these categories can be discriminated, and not simply in terms of the cultural artefacts of the English language. In short, we cannot simply use the emotion terms of our particular language merely because it is convenient to do so.

In an analysis that is as penetrating as Wierzbicka's, Russell (1991) comes to a similar conclusion. Although based on cultural comparisons it does not rest as squarely on language as Wierzbicka's. He reviews research in three areas—emotional lexicons, emotions as they are inferred from facial expressions, and the dimensions which appear to be implicit in judgements of emotion made across different languages and cultures.

Russell goes on to review five hypotheses that have been addressed with respect to similarities and differences in emotion words across cultures and the integration of categories and dimensions. (1) There are universal basic categories of emotion, although lesser categories might be specific to cultures. He makes the point that even if there might be universal basic emotions in expression, these might or might not be related to universal categories for understanding emotion. Moreover, even if there are universal basic emotions they might not be best denoted by English emotion words.

(2) There are universal basic categories of emotion, although the cognitive models developed for emotion may differ widely between cultures. Languages might differ in their cultural boundaries but there could be universal focal points.

(3) The categories of emotion derive, in the historical development of language from a single unpleasant state of physiological arousal.

(4) Wierzbicka's idea of near-universal semantic near-primitives, already discussed, provides a framework to consider cross-language comparisons.

(5) The final hypothesis is that a category of emotion is a script, this being a "... knowledge structure for a type of event whereby the event is thought of as a sequence of subevents" (1991, p442). This will have both universal and culture-specific aspects.

Russell's conclusions are that the emotions are categorized differently by those in different cultures and speaking distinct languages. Because categorization of emotion is culture specific it does not follow that emotion itself is not universal. However, the important point here is one that Russell shares with Wierzbicka, and that is since English language categories for emotion are not universal they might not be labels for universal experiences. As Russell neatly puts it, "... they are hypotheses formed by our linguistic ancestors" (p444).

Russell also concludes that emotion categories are in fact extremely similar across cultures and languages. All emotion words and categories are an integral part of a folk theory of mind. It might follow from this both that *any* theory of emotion ultimately derives from a folk theory and that this should be recognized and folk theories be explicitly taken into account when constructing other types of theory, even when such types are based on the formalities of science.

Conclusions

It can be seen from this chapter that some researchers in disciplines related to psychology have made important contributions to emotion theory. However, although important, and interesting, to what extent can these contributions be regarded as good theory? This is the first of several questions that should be asked of the material summarized in this chapter. In answer it is perhaps best to work through each of the disciplines in turn.

Recent philosophical theories of emotion certainly provide good accounts or explanations of emotion, even though they do not necessarily provide good summaries of existing knowledge or data. They focus well on emotion and on possible distinctions between emotion and nonemotion. They have good heuristic value but for the most part they do not lead to easily testable predictions

By and large, the recent philosophical theories of emotion are epitomized by Lyons' causal-evaluative theory, which has much in common with Schachter's psychological theory, or indeed any psychological theory that emphasizes a mixture of cognitive appraisal and physiological arousal. In terms of the

Lazarus (1991a,b) prescriptions for emotion theory then, these theories do well on the cognitive/appraisal side of things. They also tend to have room for motivational considerations and to be expressed more in terms of social variables than biological. Attempts are made to distinguish between emotion and non-emotion and to discuss discrete emotions. However, they fall down on the remainder of Lazarus's criteria.

In more general terms, the philosophical theories are concerned with the causes of emotion and with emotion as an independent variable. They are not, however, much concerned with emotion as a dependent variable.

Moving to Oatley's (1992) prescriptions, the philosophical theories fare reasonably well. They do tend to be concerned with the functions of emotion, with discrete emotion, both from a folk psychology and scientific psychology approach, with unconscious causes, with interpersonal communication, with evaluations and with basic emotions. They have little to say though about the simulation of the plans of other people. More generally, they tend to be so broadly expressed as to be able to embrace any amount of new evidence, although whether or not they can do so well is another matter. Also, as already noted they are typically not couched in terms from which specific predictions can be easily derived.

In this context of theory evaluation it is worth bearing in mind the problem that Griffiths' (1993) sees with recent philosophical theories of emotion. He regards them as not good at distinguishing emotion and non-emotion, as not having much of a place for the contentless emotions, such as anxiety, as not dealing well with either physiology or imagination, and as being too dependent on folk theory. These are all debatable points, the force of the last one being particularly difficult to appreciate.

The theoretical considerations about emotion that have derived in recent times from history and anthropology are not currently in the form of theories, either formally or informally expressed. However, they both draw attention to the importance of cultural variables in any understanding of emotion. They draw attention to emotion not being static, but to some extent dependent on change, in both time and space. Furthermore, although they are both (as are members of all of the disciplines canvassed in this chapter) concerned with meaning that might underlie emotion, they tend to place emotion *outside* the individual. For psychologists of course its natural resting place is within the individual.

There is a long history of emotion theory in sociology. Taken as a whole, the sociological theories can be evaluated in similar terms to the philosophical theories. They provide reasonable summaries of some existing knowledge and definitely are expressed in terms of ready explanation. They are well focused and have a useful heuristic value; they clearly promote new thoughts. However, again, they do not lead to readily testable predictions. Of course, though, like the philosophical theories, they are not aimed at having predictive power.

In Lazarus's terms, once more the sociological theories are good on the causes of emotion and on emotion considered as as an independent variable.

They have little to say, however, about emotion as a dependent variable. As might be expected they tend to stress the social rather than the biological and they have a core role for cognition. They also bring other conceptual matters into consideration. These will be discussed a little later.

Differently from the philosophical theories, the sociological theories do not fare so well within the framework that Oatley suggests. They are concerned with the function of emotions and of course with emotions as to do with interpersonal communication. They are also concerned with the discrete emotions and have some of their origins in folk theory although this is not often made evident. They can deal with any amount of new evidence but they cannot be used to derive specific predictions with much ease.

Finally, what have been categorized here as cultural theories of emotion actually do well in terms of what makes for good theory. They are focused, of great heuristic value, give ready explanations and can be used to develop testable predictions. In Lazarus's terms however they do not cover much theoretical territory. Since they are restricted to cultural meanings and the significance of language, they give no room to biological matters, or behaviour or physiology (except through language of course). They are however concerned with how emotion is generated and develops. As with the other contributions summarized in this chapter, the cultural ones bring new theoretical matters into consideration. These will be mentioned later.

In Oatley's terms perhaps the main strength of the cultural theories of emotion is that they are based squarely in folk theory as well as in science. However, they are also concerned with the causes of emotion, with emotion as interpersonal communication, with the basic emotions, with emotions as to do with evaluations and even with the simulation of the plans of others. They can deal with more evidence and they can be used to derive specific predictions. They fare well.

Generally, then, theories of emotion from outside psychology are a mixed bag, some of them being very good on most measures of good theory, and some not. What use are they to our understanding of emotion? What do they tell us? The important answer to this question is that they tell us or point us in the direction of different things than do the typical psychological theories. Of course, many of them emphasize cognition, and motivation, and so on. But they also bring important new theoretical concepts into account. For example, there is stress on the importance of change, of the cultural meanings that might underlie emotion, of social variables such as power and status and role, and very basic concepts such as reflexivity.

Penetrating a little more deeply, theories in the areas dealt with here begin to come to grips with the way in which people might be regarded simultaneously as both subject and object when dealing with emotion. Or with the possible significance of symbolic interaction. Or with entirely new concepts such as Wierzbicka's universal semantic primitives, which she puts forward in the context of emotion being considered as a cultural artefact of language. It is also through these approaches that folk theory begins to be built into conceptions of emotion even more firmly than it is placed there by psychologists such as Oatley and Haviland.

From the viewpoint of generating an understanding of emotion, the theoretical issues dealt with in this chapter should at least be kept in mind by anyone who might attempt to devise yet another theory of emotion. Perhaps the case should be made more strongly however. These issues *should* be built into any new theory of emotion, even if it is from a psychological basis. This does not mean that such theories should do away with some of the psychological concepts that have arisen so frequently throughout the history of emotion theory, but rather that once matters such as change over time and place, or the issue of the extent to which emotion is an artefact of language have been thought of, it is impossible to leave them out. As Kemper suggests it should be perfectly possible to have a sociopsychophysiological theory of emotion. But perhaps historicocultural should also be added to this in some way.

14

Emotion themes

This final chapter has a number of aims. The first is the identification of themes within the psychology of emotion that are both current and significant and that have been considered in the recent literature. These are necessarily themes that have to be thought about if we are to develop an understanding of emotion. A second aim is to draw whatever conclusions it is possible to draw from the overview of theories of emotion that has been attempted throughout this book. Finally, it is hoped that it will be possible to say a little about what any theory of emotion should include and to discuss some recent directions of theoretical development and to speculate a little about the future.

Summary of theoretical perspectives

Perhaps the best place to begin is with a very broad overview of the theoretical perspectives which have been discussed in this book. This should allow attention to centre on major themes, on issues which it is necessary for any theoretical analysis of emotion to embrace, and on which theories appear to be the most cogent. It should also be relevant to the recognition of pointers to future developments.

Chapter by chapter, and it is to be hoped, systematically, the many theories of emotion have been broadly appraised as to their worth according to various prescription for what a 'good' theory and particularly a 'good' theory of emotion should include. Irrespective of what sounds like a moral imperative, it is important to say what most (but not all, of course) of the theories considered here *have* included.

The 'better' theories deal with what emotion is, its nature, origins and development and the distinction between emotion and non-emotion. They make room for experience, for behaviour and for physiology, and in so doing consider the biological (functional, adaptive) and the social (learned, constructed) foundations of emotion. Above all, they deal with the relationship between emotion and cognition, even if this is simply (in some few cases) to make a distinction between the two.

Moving to a slightly more detailed overview, the phenomenological theories tend to be narrow and restricted to the nature of emotional experience and consciousness. They add to the richness of our understanding of emotion but do not stand out as theories. They do however give a central role to cognition.

Behavioural theories of emotion are simpler than the phenomenological but just as narrow. Oddly, they also bring cognition into the picture. By contrast, the physiologically based theories are relatively broad and, at least in their more recent form, can be called 'good' theories. Again, they give a crucial role to cognition.

What have been termed in this text the ambitious theories of emotion, the large scale ones are also 'good' theories, in general, almost being theories of psychology rather than just emotion. Turning though to those theories which are centred on particular emotions rather than on emotion in general, the focus becomes restricted again. Even within the narrower focus however, these theories do not go very far, although they do begin to point to the importance of an interdisciplinary approach to emotion.

Recent theories which start from a developmental perspective are quite impressive. As well as stressing cognition, they bring new themes such as attachment into consideration. They also do rather well on considering both the biological and the social foundations of emotion. By contrast, and perhaps surprisingly the social theories, with one or two exceptions, are not so good, being rather restricted. However, they do put cognition into a central role.

The broadly based clinical theories are not very impressive, although some of the more specific theories of anxiety are excellent. Again, cognition is regarded as a core matter. As it is also in more applied types of theory that stem from considerations of the individual, the environment and the culture.

Finally, theories of emotion from related disciplines such as philosophy, history, sociology and anthropology make a very interesting contribution. They add enormous breadth to our understanding of emotion, bring new theoretical concepts into consideration, nad once again give a prominent role to cognition.

Within the context of this very broad overview there are some theories that stand out above the remainder. In particular, the theories of Ekman, Izard, Kemper, Lazarus, Mandler, Oatley and Johnson-Laird, Panksepp, and Plutchik stand out, although other people have made extremely important contributions as well. The issue of the best theory of emotion will be revisited.

Biological foundations

One of the major themes that must be discussed at this point is that of the biological foundations of emotion. Even those theorists who do not address this matter directly seem to have the matter there almost as a hidden agenda. A good starting point is with Plutchik's theory. As is well known, he has long taken an evolutionary perspective on emotion, constructing his very practically based theory on functional grounds. A similar perspective has also frequently been taken by those who have been primarily concerned with the biological bases or physiological substrates of emotion, Panksepp for example. However, the evolutionary approach in general is very usefully discussed by Nesse (1989), who bases his analysis on the belief that emotions will only be understood via a functional approach and hence a consideration of the influence of natural selection. "... emotions are coordinated systems of response that were shaped by natural selection because they increased fitness in certain situations" (1989, p264). In more detail, "The emotions are specialized modes of operation shaped by natural selection to adjust the physiological, psychological and behavioral parameters of the organism in ways that increase its capacity and tendency to respond adaptively to the threats and opportunities characteristic of specific kinds of situations" (p268).

Nesse bases his analysis on a prescription for making evolutionary explanations first put forward by Tinbergen (1963). Four aspects have to be covered. (1) Proximate explanations of physiological and psychological mechanisms, (2) the ontogeny of such mechanisms, (3) an evolutionary account of how an emotion, or an emotional capacity, came to be that way through natural selection, and (4) the phylogeny of the emotion. And to make any such analysis, there must be the belief that emotions *can* be explained in evolutionary terms, that is, they are directly shaped by natural selection.

This evolutionary viewpoint rests on the idea that for each of the so-called basic emotions (and Nesse is prepared to agree to such a list) there should be a set of conditions which bring about fitness, in a biological sense. He illustrates this by considering a number of emotions. For present purposes it is enough to discuss just one of the emotional areas with which he deals—what he terms the social emotions.

Nesse bases his analysis of the social emotions on reciprocity theory. This has two aspects. The first is the selfish gene which helps to account for behaving altruistically towards kin. Relationships with non-kin are accounted for by the idea that cooperation allows many tasks to be accomplished more efficiently than competition, although competition might well benefit the individual if the individual wins. These ideas allow the possibility of a number of emotions. For example, if cooperation is repeated, emotions based on positive feelings such as come from trust and liking will develop. Opportunities also develop for experiencing pride (that one has done one's duty, or given more than one has received, and so on) or humiliation and obligation (if one has received more than one has given). Such feelings promote a push towards balance in relationships. Of course, if one is treated unfairly then anger might be the result. Nesse's adaptive view of anger is interesting. He suggests that it is of evolutionary value because it both protects a person against being exploited, and points to the value of continued cooperative, balanced relationships. Similarly, an emotion such as guilt helps to bring back a relationship after some transgression or defection from it.

Nesse sees the apparent universality of some emotions and yet the culture-bound form of their particular characteristics and cues as being consistent with an evolutionary approach. He regards natural selection as the mechanism that brought about both the consistencies and the particular patterns.

This type of analysis is also applied to emotional problems or disorders. Nesse argues that the evolutionary view suggests that there are three types of emotional problem. (1) Where there is something wrong with the mechanisms. (2) Where the emotion itself is maladaptive. (3) Where the emotion is painful. Moreover, from this perspective, he believes that a particular class of disorder has been underplayed; those in which what might be described as a *normal* experience of a painful emotion (say, guilt or anxiety) is lacking.

As is often the case with accounts of psychological functions that are based on evolutionary considerations, there is a pleasing neatness and consistency to Nesse's analysis. The problem as he sees it is to find the best ways of explicating the details of an adaptive explanation. From this perspective, any theory of emotion should take into account the notion that emotions give adaptive advantages in particular situations, the forces of natural selection applying to emotions as well as to nonemotional functions.

Nesse argues that the more significant implications of this view are within the clinical area. For example, he suggests that clinicians have to realize that we "have bad feelings for good reasons". As he puts it more formally "Fear, anger, sadness, and loneliness are not abnormal, they are defenses that help us to deal with situations that increase fitness" (1990 p284).

A different but equally compelling discussion of emotion viewed from a biological perspective is made by emotion historians Stearns and Stearns (1994). Their particular concern is to explore the links between biology and culture, their way of saying nature and nurture, as far as emotion is concerned. In summarizing their viewpoint links will be made with some of the discussions that occur later in the present chapter.

The Stearns describe two types of evolutionarily based approach to emotion. The first emphasizes emotion having been there at least throughout human evolution, functioning to improve the chances of survival. The second emphasizes the pre-speech communicative function of emotion. They point out that the three major lines of 'evidence' considered relevant to this are concerned with physiological response patterning, infant emotional expression and the possibility of cultural universality in facial expression.

On the other side of the coin, the Stearns characterize the social constructionist view (see extended discussion later in this chapter) as suggesting that context and function make emotional life what it is. Typically, they stress the importance of cognitive appraisal (rather than a basic emotions approach), and demonstrate enormous emotional variety from culture to culture, and even from time to time within a culture.

They argue that areas such as emotion would benefit from a rapprochement between the biological and the constructionist viewpoints. However, this has not yet happened, the two camps usually dealing with each other only critically. Stearns and Stearns believe that the lack of common effort is the result of three matters.

(1) The biological/psychological approaches to emotion were established long before the constructionist.

(2) The Stearns do not use the term 'binary', but they use similar terms to characterize the typical either/or thinking that characterizes many researchers. Nature versus nurture would be a typical example. The constructionists are also prone to oversimplified thinking, but in their case it is more in terms of absolutes or extremes.

(3) The third issue is the most trenchant, and goes to the question of the *type* of science that is acceptable. The basic emotions approach stems from a background of laboratory science, replicability, and so on. The constructionist approach moves onto wider ground and includes the much broader study of culture, even embracing disciplines such as literary theory. Mostly, such an approach does not permit such bastions of traditional science as replicability.

Stearns and Stearns conclude, amongst other things, that a way forward from these difficulties (and they are difficulties which ramify into the politics of research) much hinge on theory linking the gap between science and cultural analysis. These issues will be returned to later in this chapter.

In a treatise on the links between biology and emotion in which he specifically does not attempt to offer yet another theory of emotion, McNaughton (1989) nevertheless puts the biological/evolutionary approach to emotion in a balanced perspective. His basic point is that while what he terms teleonomic arguments do not provide final accounts of emotion, they do generate the appropriate types of question for psychologists to ask about emotion. It allows questions to be asked in such a way that they can be tested empirically. Moreover, as McNaughton sees it, even when such questions cannot be asked, the biological approach puts emotion on a firm enough foundation that unwarranted assumptions are not made. It might be noted here that the social constructionist approach does not automatically lead to unwarranted assumptions either.

McNaughton does not make huge claims for the biological approach to emotion. He sidesteps the detailed discussion of emotion theory and even suggests that it is still premature to offer a definition of emotion. However, he sees the biological approach as a way of integrating emotion data and as a basis for exploring mechanisms that might underlie such data. From this perspective it does not matter whether or not a researcher is correct in his definition of emotion. It is enough that researchers outline their area of study as emotional and then try to say what its specifications or part of its specifications are on the basis of a teleonomic argument. This is certainly one approach.

Gender

This book is not the place to attempt to expand on feminist theory. However, it is important to point out that it is beginning to have an impact on emotion

theory (and research). It is important therefore to consider some of its implications in this context. From a psychological perspective, there have been
far more men than women who have studied emotion, (although my impression is that there are more women who work in this area than might be found
in perception, say). This might be seen as a strange state of affairs since in folk
theoretical terms, emotion is regarded as more in women's domain than
men's. Of course, the history of psychology though reflects the development
of science, and, traditionally, science is men's work. Women who do it must
do it in the same way; science is, after all, science.

Or is it? One of the many things to emerge from feminist scholarship,
(although this is not its only genesis) is that science can take forms other than
that which stemmed from logical positivism. In an extremely stimulating
book, *Emotion and Gender,* Crawford, Kippax, Onyx, Gault and Benton
(1992) demonstrate this and in so doing provide insights into emotion which
fall somewhere between those that come from traditional science and those
that come from folk psychology.

The major contribution made in by Crawford et al rests on the methods
they used in their research. These centred on memory work which involves a
group of researchers who explore and interpret and re-explore and re-
interpret their memories in a particular area (anger, for example) in strictly
determined ways. The interpretations are not guided by an experimenter, all
of the researchers/memory workers playing equal and reiterative parts.

This is a technique in which there is no distinction between experimenter/
researcher and subject. A group is formed and memories are recorded under
precise instructions, but with no attempts at interpretation at this stage. Then
all the memories are read and analysed by the group as a whole, again under
strict guidelines such as looking for similarities and differences. Then it is back
to more memories. Over some months or years, the memories are theorized
about and the theories themselves compared and discussed. In all, it is a sort
of collective recursion, both of memory and theory.

Crawford et al end their book by discussing how emotion is gendered; they
make their theoretical as well as their methodological contribution. For example, it is clear that one of the most basic aspects of women's emotion is
social responsibility. They grow up to be emotionally self-reliant but highly
responsible for the emotional well-being of others, both men and women.
There also appears to be a huge difference for men and women that depends
on where their emotional experiences occur. For the women, inside the house/
home is linked with the positive aspects of emotion, such as warmth and
happiness, whereas the outside is cold and hostile. For men it is quite different, their interesting emotional challenges being mainly outside. As
Crawford et al point out, these differences are interesting because much of the
violence that is perpetrated on women occurs in the home and is done by men.

They also argue that women and men are placed differently with respect to
the ethical systems of justice and responsibility, so they construct their emotions differently. "Men expect and take for granted that they will be looked

after and cared for; it is expected of them that they will make the world a just place to live in. Women expect and take for granted that the world is a just place; in turn they are expected to be responsible for the well-being of others. Women have little control over issues of equity and justice, and are forced to rely on others; hence their concern when these expectations are not met" (1992, p192).

From the perspective reached by Crawford et al, not only is morality important in the construction of emotions but so also is power. From the viewpoint of women's emotions the predominant matter is powerlessness and the pain that this causes. Then the socialization of women's emotion is characterized by an increasing sense of power as self-reliance develops. The most significant power of all comes from changing the agenda, changing the way in which emotions are thought about and studied for example. Crawford et al have gone a long way towards doing this.

To take just one other and somewhat applied perspective in this area, Shibbles (1991) argues that rational-emotive therapy (as a particular form of cognitive-behaviour therapy) is particularly suited to feminist therapy. He characterizes RET (and the cognitive philosophical theory of emotion) as resting on seven main points. (1) Emotions are more than feelings. (2) They are cognitions which lead to feelings. (3) Our emotions stem from out own assessments. (4) The environment does not just cause emotions passively. (5) Faulty thinking leads to negative emotions. (6) If we change our assessments then our emotions will change. (7) Emotions only change through a change in assessment, they cannot simply be released.

Within this framework, an emotion such as anger is seen as being non-adaptive. It is harmful and irrational. By contrast, Shibbles characterizes some feminist thinking as being concerned with having women 'get in touch with their anger' and express it as though this were useful. Shibbles suggests that this is counter-productive in that it simply generates more anger, and is not based on an appropriate theory of emotion. Shibbles analyses blame and humour in a similar way.

The general message here is that Shibbles believes that RET and the philosophical cognitive theory of emotion are very similar and contrast with feminist notions about emotions such as anger. The vaguely therapeutically based goals of feminists, and others, might be better realized with a cognitive theory of emotion than with a hydraulic type of theory which is based on an emotion such as anger being something which builds up and has to be released. In passing, it might be noted that this is a curiously 'male' theory.

To conclude this brief discussion of emotion and gender it might be interesting to consider some of the points made by Shields (1991) in a research review of the topic. She states "... that the greatest effect of gender lies less in what each sex knows about emotion than in what each sex is likely to do with that knowledge, particularly in contexts in which gender is salient" (1991, p238). She argues strongly that beliefs about gender should play a part in emotion research. The matter of particular note concerns links between emotionality and the constructs that underlie expressiveness. For example, there is an expectation that men and women express different kinds of emotion. Is this based on differences in facial expression or not? In general, to study emotion from a gendered viewpoint demonstrates that one of the most significant influences on emotion is sex.

Social construction of emotions

In the previous section, gender was considered at some length because it is a sort of bridge between the biological and the social approach to the understanding of emotion. Now it is time to move onto the latter. In recent years much has been written about emotions as socially constructed. The discussion that follows relies particularly on Averill (1982), Harré (1986), Kemper (1987), Fisher and Chon (1989), Ratner (1989), Greenwood (1992) and Oatley (1993). Also, some of what follows will extend the discussion of the links between biology and culture (Stearns and Stearns, 1994) already canvassed in this chapter.

Theory deriving from social constructionism (or social constructivism—the terms are used interchangeably) has it that emotions (or at least adult human emotions) come from the culture or social concepts. For human adults there are internal and external stimuli that are interpreted, this interpretation mediating between the stimuli and any emotional response that might ensue. This means that any culture has its distinctive patterns of emotions that come from social practices. From this perspective, then, emotion is relative and changeable. It is usually contrasted with emotion in animals or human neonates where emotions are immediate and biologically determined reactions, in which the catchwords are universality and continuity. It is almost impossible to consider ideas of emotion being socially constructed without immediately comparing them with what Ratner (1989) terms naturalistic theories.

Social constructionists usually distinguish between two types of emotion, those which have 'natural' analogues (that is, they occur in animals and human neonates) and those which do not. Examples of the former are joy, sadness and fear and of the latter anger, shame and love. Such emotions are entirely socially constituted.

Oatley (1993) points out that the social constructionist view of emotion, although based to some extent on the inferences of cognitive analyses, also has the extra components that come from folk theories of emotion. He describes two forms of social constructionism. The strong form is that *all* human emotions are socially constructed, that is they are based on beliefs and shaped by language, and ultimately stem from culture. So, they are not modifications of natural states but derive solely from culture. The weaker view is preferred by most of those who are in this camp. It is that some emotions are socially constructed and some are more socially constructed than others. Interest then centres on how any social construction occurs.

Oatley goes on to make some interesting comparisons between various types of theory. For example, as has been seen throughout the present book, some theorists believe that the only biological constraint on emotion is that of arousal. Others, such as Oatley himself (eg Oatley and Johnson-Laird, 1987, in their basic theory of emotions) believe that constraints come from the brain adopting a particular mode of functioning when recognising stimuli relevant to a goal.

The usual way of determining the extent of the social construction of emotions is to make comparisons between cultures. As has already been seen (Chapter 13), this can be done either historically or anthropologically. Typical types of comparison might be between the prescriptive aspects of emotion in various cultures, determining how appropriate it is for particular emotions to be expressed in particular circumstances. Or cross-cultural comparisons are often made between the various socialization practices that obtain in different societies.

Typically, as Oatley points out, the social constructionist approach to emotion also involves attempts to describe *how* emotions are socially constructed in adults and what emotions accomplish in terms of social roles and obligations. Hochschild's (1983) analysis of emotions in particular settings is a good example of the former, and Averill's (1982) searching analysis of anger is a good example of the latter.

Oatley concludes that, rather than a theory of emotion *per se*, social constructionism offers an approach to understanding emotion. It does embrace certain theories, Averill's or Harré's for example. Its particular strength is that it gives a way of considering the extent to which emotions are apposite to their circumstances. In other words, it begins to suggest what the purposes of emotion might be. Its other strength, at this point, is perhaps that it has obvious links with the various cognitive approaches that have come to predominate almost all theories of emotion.

Ratner (1989) develops his analysis by making a strong critique of naturalistic theories of emotion from a constructionist standpoint. He begins by giving a very useful 11-point summary of the naturalistic approach, taken largely from Zajonc, Izard, Ekman and Plutchik, which will be further summarized here. It should be noted that this could be regarded as the strong rather than the weak naturalistic position. (1) Emotions and cognition are independent. (2) Emotions determine cognition and cognition serves emotion. (3) There is continuity between animal emotion and the emotions of human infants and adults. (4) In comparison with cognitions, emotions are spontaneous and communicable. (5) There are a few basic emotions. (6) There is a physiological mechanism underlying each basic emotion. (7) Emotions are dealt with by the right side of the brain and by the subcortex, and cognitions by the left side of the brain and the neocortex. (8) Some facial expressions are (near) universal. (9) Emotions can be conditioned without awareness. (10) We can hold emotional impressions of people without appraisal. (11) Emotions are global and cognitions 'piecemeal'.

Ratner goes through these points in turn and rebuts them vigorously, particularly and not surprisingly emphasizing the significance of cognitive appraisal in emotion, at least as it is given a central position by so many theorists. He goes on to consider more moderate naturalistic approaches, which he terms interactionistic. Here, although there might be biological bases to the emotions, much is provided by social factors. The natural part is still seen as basic and universal, whereas the social is seen as derived from this and as variable. Overall, Ratner argues "Rather than cling to the gutted ship of biological reductionism, it is necessary to abandon it altogether and find other moorings for psychological theory" (1989, p226).

An alternative conceptualization is to see biology as forming a substrate that gives emotion its potential but which does not determine it. Various emotions, such as joy, sadness and fear, might well occur spontaneously and hence naturally in young children, but by the time these children are adults these emotions have had their character changed by sociocultural influences. Thus, while there may be prototypical facial responses, the actual facial expressions displayed by adults are many and varied and depend on both the individual and the culture.

In the end, as Ratner sees it, the interactionist approach suggests that biology gives emotion its potential and culture produces actual concrete emotions. However, Ratner would prefer to do away with the biological altogether, seeing it as too deterministic. He believes that a full theory can come from assigning culture the complete power to constitute emotions. "Actually, the social constructionist theory leads to far greater emotional freedom (than naturalistic theory) by recognizing the social psychological basis of emotions and emphasizing the possibility of changing it" (1989, p228).

Greenwood (1992) offers a characteristically stimulating analysis of what he terms the social *constitution* of emotion, rather than its social construction. He is concerned with the manner in which emotions may be said to be social in nature instead of socially constructed. He begins by illustrating what is wrong with some aspects of these approaches by pointing out that the ideas that stem from Schachter and Singer's (1962) influential work and from Nisbett and Ross (1980) do not provide social theories of emotion. At best, they offer theories about the development of emotion labels.

Continuing in critical vein, Greenwood points out that the social constructionist argues that we do not have emotional states, so again does not provide a social theory of emotion. Social constructionist approaches, according to Greenwood, are about emotion discourse. In his view, it can only become a social theory if it is assumed that emotions are constituted by socially learned labels. Greenwood believes in the usefulness of a realist perspective in which conceptual meaning depends on a theoretical model. He regards "emotion avowals" as falling within the purview of "The meaning of our psychological ascriptions to self and others is not specified by any form of operational definition that relates these ascriptions to empirical laws" (1992, p9).

Within this type of framework, Greenwood believes that we constitute our emotions through the ways in which we represent reality, ways which are dependent on social learning. "... emotions are evaluative representations that are constituted as particular emotions by socially learned intensional contents that are directed upon (usually) socially appropriate intentional objects. This account may be classified as an account of the *social constitution* of emotion" (1992, p11).

Greenwood suggests that if emotions are socially constituted in this way, then ideas of self-knowledge of emotion have to be considered. In his view, it is wrong to assume that there is something inside us that is emotion with certain characteristics that we can come to know by various self-referential processes. From Greenwood's perspective, such internal entities do not exist. All I can know of my emotion is to do with the social objects to or at which it is directed. I also know something of how I represent any actions associated with it. What we know about are the intensional contents and intentional objects of our emotion. For example, I know what I feel about my children— the feelings and their object is all there is.

Scherer (1992) in reply to Greenwood, argues that his theory does not convince because it neglects to account for an entire emotion episode, and because it does not deal with the dynamic nature of emotion. Scherer also feels that Greenwood does not satisfactorily deal with experience, self-knowledge and verbalization. Greenwood argues back, but this is probably not the place to explicate this further. For now it is enough to say that Greenwood has provided an interesting view of emotions as socially *constituted* rather than socially constructed.

Another interesting, although relatively mild attack on the strong social constructionist view of emotion is made by Kemper (1987) in a stimulating review of Harré's *The social construction of emotions* (1986). He challenges the book on five grounds.

To begin with, Kemper argues that Harré and his co-writers are too strongly against physiological approaches to emotion, feeling that since emotion, like other aspects of human functioning, has a physiological aspect, it should be taken into account in a complete theory.

He argues that the social constructionists take the view that emotions are prescribed too far. We cannot, in his view, be successfully commanded to feel an emotion, because emotions are not simply under cortical control. Somewhat like Greenwood, Kemper believes that the social constructionists tend to miss out the social relational aspects of emotional development.

Kemper criticizes social constructionists for not dealing with specific moral contexts and emotions that might be linked to them, whilst they nevertheless maintain that emotions occur in a moral context of rights, obligations and duties. Perhaps more trenchantly, he also points out that the social constructionist position seems simultaneously to suggest that we are determined creatures and that we are free agents.

Finally, Kemper makes the assumption that "... human interaction preceded the ability to talk about it ..." (1987, p364). So, if emotions are the result of social practices, they also must precede talk. However, the social constructionists, post-Wittgenstein give pre-eminence to language in their accounts of emotion. Kemper is not of course arguing that social practices should not be taken into consideration in any account of emotion, but merely that language is only one aspect of social practice.

Post-modernism themes in emotion

Post-modernism is not easy, but it is here and should be engaged with. It is the aim of this section to look at emotion through post-modern eyes, and to describe some of existing emotion theory that can easily placed within a post-modern context. To do so, it is first necessary to say a little of the form a post-modern social science would take. Much of what follows is taken from Strongman, Strongman and Harré (1996).

Post-modern social science celebrates the emotional feelings, nonemotional feelings, intuitions, individuality, and the introspective. In this respect post-modernism can be seen as the attempt not only to fuse science and literature (as Clifford and Marcus, and Pratt point out in 1986), but to locate affective states and displays firmly within the prevailing discourse, as themselves discursive acts. Beyond this, affective tone in discourse may be analysed in the search for the meaning of emotions and a post-modern substitute for the modernist's causality. The study of emotions based on the thesis that they are the product of biological and environmental factors reflects modernist ways of conceiving social science and the dichotomous, dual-process categorization of thought into substances and qualities, subjective and objective, nature and nurture approach of Western psychological thinking. For the most part, this of course is the approach that has been characterized in the present book.

Within post-modern thought, intertextuality becomes a substitute for causality in that instead of positing a system of independent verification it emphasizes the interconnectedness of events, concepts, happenstances, and discourses. For example, it makes no sense to say that a wind or an idea 'starts', for its origin is already located in the influence of every other wind or idea. Intertextuality is concerned with the interrelatedness of things and is multifarious and pluralistic, whereas the causality of modernist science stresses the linear and binary structure of cause and effect.

Exploration of recent avenues of approach in the psychological study of emotion points to the plethora of possible contributions enabled by the narrative, discursive, and linguistic approach of post-modernism. Post-modernists are in sympathy with those approaches of the social constructionists who stress the function of the 'self' within emotion discourse, and with anthropologists who have adopted discursive approaches to the study of emotions (eg Lutz and Abu-Lughud, 1990) (although post-modernists depart from them in the constructionists' emphasis on analytic methodology).

To locate our emotions in discourse involves the detection of points of affective stability and instability within the intertextual symbolic expression of discourse. While it would make no sense to locate a modernist's emotion 'source' in discourse because no such definition will be found, emotional meaning may be derived in a post-modern interpretation from the affective response that is incited by the aporiae within our linguistic construction of emotion words. (As will by now be obvious, the language of post-modernism is a little different from that of modernist science.)

When we are looking for emotion in language we are, despite the analytic intentions of modernists, looking for something that is neither 'here' nor 'there' but rather is located or experienced at the point of intertextual symbolic interruption in the text, a textual aporia to which we assign a label to our affective response.

Thus, the meaning of the word 'anger' for example is not derived from the word itself (nor is emotional tone necessarily located in the word) however used, because it can be used in ignorance (say, by an Eskimo who had another word for it). We cannot conceive of 'anger' without naming it. However, the word 'anger' can never convey the exact quality of the bodily feeling in which it is expressed in various cultures. Our use of the word 'anger' always falls short of conveying the exact quality of that particular cluster of emotions, although it does at least consistently announce something similar from one time to the next. The word 'anger' masks the aporiae of the intertextual symbolic expression of the affective state which is constructed in language to denote something always beyond the text (affect).

Emotion words like 'anger' are located always at the point of *differance* or departure from the text, the point of instability, they are neither 'here' in our reading of the text, nor 'there' in what is written. Rather, they are located in the aporiae between, which, in the terms of post-modern irony, defines them, for each person, exactly. For example, although a person is acquainted with how it feels to be, say, jealous, the word 'jealousy', however precisely used, cannot convey the immediate quality of the experience.

The locating of emotion displays and feelings within discourse, as discursive acts, in many ways parallels the aim of post-modern social science, in its attempts to provide knowledge systems based on competing discursive alternatives. We construct our emotions through language and these emotions are constantly updated and modified by language. The language is never stable so no 'definition' will be found. Only upon deconstruction there appears the space in which the emotion can be situated, albeit amorphously.

For example, the private experience that occurs when we use the word 'happy' to tell someone 'how it is with us' is not to be found in the construction 'I am happy today'. Rather, it is to be located in the change in my privately conceived state that the word 'happiness' signifies. The individuality of the peculiar quality of experience denoted by 'happiness' leaves open the possibility for the individual's experience or reading of happiness. The use of the emotion word 'happiness' in any particular public conversation is always correspondent to the intertextual or private expression of the affective state of happiness for the given individual or reading, when affective states are relevant to the proper use of an emotion word. It is not a space within the text itself but an extra-textual reference, a gap between public and private expression, which is idiosyncratic and entails and idiosyncratic reading of the meaning symbolized by the term 'happiness'—an absence in the text which becomes the direct intentional object of the semantic term 'happiness'.

In the methodology of post-modern social science, intertextuality is substituted for causal explanation. Causality among states and events and prediction using causal laws assumes a stable and independent reality. An interactive intertextuality denies the relevance of the concept of direct causality to an explanation of psychological phenomena. If everything is semantically related to everything else then it is impossible to extract a chain of causality by fixing background conditions in the manner of the physical sciences. Following Latour (1987), the causality that is implied by the view that social science is a human construct is mutually entailed by the reversal that social practices construct human beings. Put in post-modern terms, Latour's argument becomes not one of causality but of intertextuality. The construction of social science as a discursive phenomenon of necessity implies a construction of the self through that process. The thesis of the social construction of emotions in discursive acts, the anthropologist's location of culturally specific emotions in the discourses, and cross-cultural comparative studies of the uses of emotion words, place the study of emotion within this post-modern domain. In this context emotions are not caused by environmental conditions. They are expressions of attitudes to, judgements of and elocutionary acts apropos of how environmental conditions are locally interpreted. And as such they are to be treated as part of discourse.

When post-modernists attempt to construct their own scientific discourses they look to the multiplication of scenarios over the reconciliation of binary oppositions or competing 'truths'. While not seeking modernist 'essences', the post-modernist will seek to place emotion theories in parallel, emphasizing multiple possibilities over single solutions. The text to be interpreted, that is the complex pattern of feeling, display, context, significant others, inherited tendencies, local vocabularies, and so on, is not seen as an independent reality constraining interpretation, but as something many of whose facets become 'visible' only in the light of the interpretation.

In the debate about nature or environment as the overriding cause of emotion however, at some point in the theoretical continuum the two factions can be seen to abandon their positions and seek the shared ground of common discourse. This common ground involves the idea that there are no emotions that are intrinsically meaningful, that is, that could exist *as such* without context. Post-modernists concur with the constructionist view of reality in which the radical distinction between mental states and the 'outside' world is illusory. Emotional context is the same context as that of discursive communication. As Gergen (1986) puts it "... there are no real world objects of study (for psychology) other than those inherent within the make-up of persons" (p141). Post-modernists are also contextualists for whom all knowledge claims are intelligible only within a particular paradigm or interpretative community (Fish, 1989). Post-modernist views of psychological and social reality, like those of social constructionists such as Harré, are dependent on linguistic convention in which the language of social description is not given meaning by independently verifiable, 'real world' referents. Transferring this insight to our knowledge of the physical world, and the ontological status of this world is a delicate and dangerous business which fortunately has no place here.

For social science to have a purpose or project (even if viewed as only one of a number of possible interpretations for the activity) then it must be seen to be more than the exercise of linguistic habit. In this regard, post-modernists have advanced the idea of a *soft* content for social science, with affective content that may be transitory. For any language based discipline content will in part be derived from a plurality of methodologies, just as data replicate theory, by its implicit inclusion in the constructs of language. If post-modern social science draws on local practice, narratives, or folk stories, without just one author representing a particular claim to legitimacy or 'truth', then the content of social science will inevitably broaden. This is consistent with the post-modern acceptance of multiplicity. The successful (but not 'good' or 'bad') social scientist may well then become the individual who is readily equipped to assemble and process the multiplicity of narratives within his or her discursive scientific domain.

The post-modern criterion for evaluation rests on a proliferation of theories rather than on the making of distinctions between good and bad theories or right and wrong descriptions. This, however, is not necessarily to abandon evaluation, but to advance the idea of a scientific practice that questions evaluative norms. Sceptical post-modernists argue against consistency, coherence, and for theory to be liberated necessarily from data (Gergen, 1987). A post-modern social science is, in the present view, more properly to be a 'topographical' exercise (White, 1993) which Toulmin (1983) believes to cover the 'range and scope' of the discursive interpretations that have been concerned with the area under consideration. We have neither better maps nor worse maps, but maps which describe a multiplicity of terrains, or the same terrain from a multiplicity of viewpoints. Which map one chooses to follow will depend on the task in hand.

White's (1993) suggestion to turn emotion thinking 'inside-out' is along these lines when he suggests that the answers to the questions posed by an emotion theory are largely constrained by ethnopsychological assumptions that: "... naturalize emotions by locating them within individual brains and minds, thus privileging psychobiological variables in emotion theory to the detriment of social and semiotic factors, premised on the Western conceptions of the person as individual" (p37). White suggests that this could be corrected by giving equal importance to the study of cognitive, linguistic, and sociohistorical processes that produce culturally meaningful emotions which have the power of influencing people and altering relationships. (Stearns and Stearns, 1988, 1994).

There are at least three themes already existing in theoretical analyses of emotion that can take shelter under a post-modern umbrella.

The role of the lexicon

White cites his work with Lutz (Lutz and White, 1986) proposing discourse-centred approaches to comparative research. This inherently micro-narrative based approach enacts a reversal of the methodological status quo by framing the parameters of emotion in terms of a "set of problems of social relationship or existential meaning that cultural systems often appear to present in emotional terms, rather than a given set of psychological universals. This approach has at the heart of its conception the necessity of avoiding an interpretive apparatus limited to English-language emotion terms and pre-supposed Western models" (1986, p427). Such a relativist and discourse centred, culturally specific approach is inherently post-modern, with its tendency to go from a generalized model of symbolic violation of cultural codes (as with 'anger') to examine the localized manner in which the events or feelings compel a personal response as articulated in the idioms of a given culture.

The focus for post-modern social scientists may well then be that of drawing comparisons and *differances* between the narratives under their attention, claiming 'this version of the truth is like this one which implies another that is absent from both texts', rather than saying 'this text has a better claim to truth than this (other) one which is implicit in modernist methodology'. The successful post-modern social scientist like the successful post-modern social-science text, will be the person who readily contributes to the quality of his or her field. This 'quality' will be an intuitively based 'measure' of contribution to the ongoing and amorphous narrative that comprises that area of discourse, or perhaps even that text, which persuades of its coherence, intuitive appeal and internal consistency through eloquence and simplicity. The aim of a criterion for post-modern social science will be to produce, as Lyotard (1984) puts it, "... not the known, but the unknown" (p60), as post-modernism sets out to change the orientation of discourse-based knowledge.

Following the poststructuralist, deconstructionist lines as suggested by Kemper, for Hochschild (1983), emotion has a signal function and that signifies the discrepancy between what we perceive and what we expected. For example, I expected to succeed, failed and experienced chagrin. Emotion announces "our relation to the world" (p216). But this relation is not complete until the emotion is given full cognitive status through attachment of a name which derives from the culture. However, such emotions are culture-specific. Continuing the example, in some societies chagrin would not be invoked because boasting, or a public declaration of success, entails no commitment to the future. So the word 'chagrin' is not in their lexicons. Thus culture acts so as to influence how we feel and how we name what we feel. Hochschild proposes a perceptual template for forming emotions. She too, argues that emotion is not fixed or frozen nor is it determined by immutable biological factors.

Similarly, Thoits (1985, 1990) views emotions as "complexes of situational cues, physiological changes, expressive gestures, and an emotion label. These are systematically interconnected, so that a change in one inaugurates a change in others" (1990, p329). Thoit's 'systematic interconnection' also shares common ground with post-modern intertextuality, in which everything influences everything else. Kemper, Hochschild, and Thoits demonstrate a marked movement away from positivist modern science to a kind of science in which one discursive avenue connects with another, an intertextual 'body' of theory replaces the mistaken pursuit of 'essence'. The authors are not suggesting that these constructionists are post-modernists but that facets of a post-modern approach to science are located in their conceptualizations of emotion.

A post-modern approach is also reflected in Harré's (1986) claim that: "Psychologists have always had to struggle against a persistent illusion that in such studies as those of the emotions, there is something *there*, the emotion, of which the emotion word is a representation" (p4). The use of the emotion word is part of the whole process of emoting. The concept of representation and its post-structuralist Derridean repudiation (1982) is thus drawn into the psychological debate of emotion. The focus of post-modernist repudiation of representation strikes a parallel with Harré's commentary which centres on the questioning of any attempt to represent the object of study as abstracted from the concrete conditions of its appearance. As Oatley points out (1993), most constructionists allow for the existence of a limited range of natural emotion responses, without which, as Wittgenstein (1958, PI246) states, no affective lexicon could ever be acquired.

Discourse-centred approaches

Recent anthropological, cross-cultural, and discourse-centred approaches to emotion also display features of post-modernism. As White points out (1993), discourse-centred approaches recognize that all language entails culturally specific modes of thought and action which not only express but create the relations they represent. Discourse-centred definitions of emotion have the effect of decoupling emotions from their essential interiority, broadening the focus of emotion research into public arenas, made all the more visible, accessible, and prolific by mass communication. Such cross-cultural anthropological research casts doubts upon the status of institutionalized 'givens' and macro-narratives of modernist science, which try to explain universal, time-independent theories of emotions.

Lutz and Abu-Lughod are anthropological advocates of the discourse-centred, inter-disciplinary approach to emotion. In *Language and the politics of emotion* (1990), they argue that emotion cannot properly be understood without study of the discourse in which it is used: "Paying special attention to the theoretical terms 'discourse' is meant to replace, we argue that the most productive analytical approach to the cross-cultural study of emotion is to examine discourses on emotion and emotional discourses as social practices within diverse ethnographic contexts" (p1). In their introduction to this volume, Lutz and Abu-Lughod acknowledge the post-structuralist, post-modern approach to culture and discourse 'hovers around the edges' of the chapters within it. Lutz and Abu-Lughod claim that: "Emotion can be *created in*, rather than shaped by, speech in the sense that it is postulated as an entity in language where its meaning to social actors is also elaborated" (p12). Sociability, that is the intimacy-formality spectrum, and power relations, that is the powerful-powerless spectrum, are key components of Lutz and Abu-Lughod's analysis of the social relations that are implicated in emotion discourse.

Emotion in experience

Before drawing conclusions, it is important to mention three relatively recent analyses of emotion which at least accord with the post-modern approach which has been explicated here and which have been mentioned previously in this book. What might be termed a post-modern tolerance to the psychological research in emotion is expressed by Oatley and Duncan (1992). They suggest a synthesis and interrelation of folk narratives of emotion and physiological and behavioural observations: "For the foreseeable future, people's understandings of the incidents of emotion in their lives will be important for scientific explanations of emotions, as they are for more personal understandings" (p289).

A more fully worked attempt to deal with emotion in the manner suggested presently is reflected in the work of Crawford, Kippax, Onyx, Gault and Bendon (1992) in their analysis of emotion and gender. See earlier in this chapter for details.

The fullest account of emotion which fits within a post-modern perspective comes from Denzin (1984, 1989, 1990). His work is concerned with an analysis of the significance of emotionality in daily life. He argues that emotionality forms the basis of interpreting and understanding both scientific life and daily life, that it underlies the social and moral foundations of society, that it prompts us to act in particular ways towards other people, and that such actions determine our moral worth and the moral worth of others.

Denzin (1984) emphasizes the hermeneutical study of interactional emotional experience. Concern should centre on interpretation and understanding through linguistic analysis and through attempts to uncover 'inner meanings'. He suggests that the stress should be laid on interpreted understandings of emotionality rather than recording or presupposing prior understandings, which is what traditional researchers in emotion have tended to do. The aim is to search for the meaning of emotional displays.

To allow Denzin to speak for himself:

"Emotionality and its reflections give the everyday world and the ordinary people who live in that world a sense of joy, bewilderment, pain, confusion, satisfaction and pleasure that no other form of conduct can.

For this reason emotionality and its investigation must lie at the heart of the human disciplines; for to understand and reflect on how this being called human is, and how it becomes what it is, it is necessary to understand how emotionality as a form of consciousness is lived, experienced, articulated, and felt by persons." (1984, p278)

Conclusions: post-modern approaches to emotion

The study of emotion might be on the brink of an important post-modern reconceptualization. To call this a 'new paradigm' is to risk perpetuating the system of binary-oppositions of 'before' and 'after', subjectivity/objectivity, that are rife in modernist thinking. The shift in emphasis on the importance of biological and environmental influences on emotion parallels a shift with respect to the prevailing approaches in modern and post-modern approaches to scientific discourse. The suggestion is that facets of the post-modern approach are reflected in the writings of many of the exponents of social constructionism. The location and acceptance of emotion as revealed in narrative, the discourse centred-approach to intentional states, reflected in the anthropological studies of Lutz and Abu-Lughod and White can be seen as aspects of a movement towards a post-modern approach to emotion.

The measure of the significance of these approaches will be the extent to which this proliferation of scientific narratives adds to the quality of knowledge and thinking about human behaviour in the community. It also reflects a wider concern with emotion centredness in the post-modern world.

The problem now becomes that of assembling criteria for the evaluation and assessment of the study of emotion as it approaches a post-modern form that belongs among the sciences. It is possible that the concept of 'quality' will assume a central importance in the plethora of textual narratives, construction, and deconstructions of emotion narrative. If the post-modernist will reduce the social sciences to the status of stories this will not necessarily undermine, but might broaden the concept of social *science*, for there will be some stories that warrant continual re-reading and others that are enduring and have cross-cultural appeal. These will be the more favourable stories of post-modern social science and the stories that will contribute to quality of understanding and act so as to enhance the 'narrative' interchange of personal and community life. As Gergen puts it in 'Warranting voice': "Thus, if psychology is to fulfil its avowed role of benefiting humankind, the doors should be opened to multiplicity in perspective. Rather than singing the same old refrain decade after decade (albeit in different words), a premium should be placed on new songs" (p80). Here it is useful to distinguish between ontological post-modernism which posits no 'essences' and methodological post-modernism with its emphasis on competing but equally legitimate stories. The status of the stories will be determined by a qualitative measure. which may not presuppose a modernist methodological conception, but rather such concepts as intuition, style, irony, contextual appropriateness, and local relevance.

The post-modern view is that our understanding of emotion will never be truthfully and finally expressed because there is nothing determinate to define. Moreover, the search for it is based on a self-deceptive methodology, which is questionable in the light of ever more shifting alternatives. The post-modern concept of emotion will take the shape of a coherent concept of the language, personal and community discourse-centred narratives of emotion, locating public and private displays in characteristic, even particular, episodes of everyday life, and as such will be amorphous, non-temporal and evolutionary. It will be evidenced in societal linguistic construction, and whose 'causality' is to be observed in the aporia of intertextual communication, the dissonance and *differance* between affective stability and instability. Of course, whether this type of approach replaces or simply broadens or merely offers an alternative to that of modernist science (with which most of this book has been concerned) remains to be seen.

Conclusions

As mentioned at the start of this book approximately 150 theories of emotion have been canvassed in it. Why are there so many? Is there any other area of psychology in which so many people have had a go at putting forward a theory? I can think of no other, so perhaps it is the nature of emotion that causes people to have a rush of theory to the head.

Emotion is always there in some form or another, an integral part of existence. Yet, as the plethora of theory attests, it is difficult to define and to distinguish from non-emotion. More than this, because of its ubiquitousness it can be approached from any direction within psychology, and from quite a few in related disciplines.

Whatever the reason, there are many theories of emotion (and it should be pointed out that not all of them have been considered in this book). Which of them may be said to be the best? The answer to this rather significant question depends a little on how one applies the various criteria for judging theory. It also and perhaps inevitably depends on one's particular biases.

It is not a matter of chance that Lazarus's and Oatley and Johnson-Laird's theories are amongst the best. After all, it is these authors that have suggested the criteria that have been mainly used in assessing emotion theory throughout this book. Lazarus's theory is impressively complete and that of Oatley and Johnson-Laird offers a nice *rapprochement* between academic psychology and folk psychology.

Mandler's theory is also wonderfully broad and delightfully bold in the way that it faces difficult issues such as the place of consciousness in emotion. Panksepp's theory goes furthest in the physiological direction, Plutchik's in the evolutionary, and Ekman's from the important perspective of facial expression. Izard's theory is special because it makes a clear distinction between emotion and cognition rather than building cognition into emotion as do most of the other theories. And Izard and Malatesta-Magai's and Lewis's theories are amongst the best of the theories that start from a developmental viewpoint.

Moving outside psychology, there have been some splendid recent theoretical contributions to emotion from sociology, anthropology, cultural studies in general, and to some extent from philosophy and history. Perhaps Kemper's theory should be mentioned in particular. These theories from outside psychology show that emotion is not simply an intra-individual matter. All of the theories just mentioned here have a useful heuristic value.

Of them all, my own biases would prompt me to choose Lazarus's as the best that is currently available. It has been developed over a lifetime of thought and research and is broad enough to embrace almost anything that one might expect of an emotion theory. It treats emotion from every possible angle, has its applied aspects, and is capable of subsuming any new data that one could think of. However, to choose this theory as the best should not be to detract from the others mentioned in this concluding section, nor indeed from the many that are described in this book. They all have a role to play in the understanding of emotion. It is no easy matter to devise a theory that fulfils at least some of the criteria for 'good' theory. So anyone that achieves it is to be congratulated.

Should you be inspired by reading this book to produce your own theory of emotion, what should you be sure to discuss? You must distinguish emotion from non-emotion even if you do not go so far as to define it. You must discuss emotion's possible biological (and hence evolutionary) foundations and its socially constructed aspects. You should consider its development and its role in social interaction and communication. You should consider what happens when it goes wrong or causes distress to the person. Above all you should consider the relationship between emotion and cognition.

Moving outside the person, you should consider emotion in the broader context of language and culture. Of course you should ensure that your theory is devised in such a way that it is internally consistent, can be used to derive testable predictions, can embrace new data, and has heuristic value. You might even wish to see if it could be couched in terms compatible with a postmodern as well as a modernist approach to social science. And of course, there again, you might wish to do none of this.

Having considered so many theories from so many perspectives, it is easy enough to set down conditions that should be fulfilled. However, this says little about the future directions that should be taken by emotion theory. There would be little point in producing another theory which is simply very similar to those already in existence, or is even an amalgam of some of them. What *should* happen next?

I believe that there are clear lessons to be learned from the sheer number and extent of theories of emotion and from the fact that they come from a number of disciplines. In no aspect of the human condition than that of emotional life is it more obvious that those who investigate should be comfortable with a multi-disciplinary approach and with a theoretical pluralism.

Anything else is too simplistic and would not do sufficient justice to the complexities of a fascinating area. Recent developments in feminist thought and in post-modern approaches to social science also point in this direction. Moreover, the increasingly obvious importance of folk psychology or folk theory should also be taken into account. All of these concerns not only suggest the importance of taking a theoretically pluralist approach but also that close attention should be paid to the development of qualitative as well as quantitative research methods.

If this argument has some force, then the politics of the academic world do not bode well for the future development of emotion theory. Academic careers are structured within institutions and are predicated on caution and conservatism. Interdisciplinary research and thinking, not only taking theory into account but also making such theory complex and plural, is decidedly unsafe. To create an emotion theory at all is bold; to create the sort of emotion theory suggested here might be considered by some to be foolhardy.

During the last two decades an enormous amount of thought has been put into gaining an understanding of emotion. This has provided a splendid springboard from which to leap out into the difficult waters of theoretical pluralism that lie between the various shores of some half-a-dozen social sciences. Why not make a splash?

References

Adelmann, P.K. and Zajonc, R.B. (1989). Facial efference and the experience of emotion. *Annual Review of Psychology*, **40**, 249–280.

Amsel, A. (1958). The role of frustrative nonreward in noncontinuous reward situations. *Psychological Bulletin*, **55**, 102–119.

Amsel, A. (1962). Frustrative nonreward in partial reinforcement and discrimination learning: Some recent history and a theoretical extension. *Psychological Review*, **69**, 306–328.

Arnold, M.B. (1945). Physiological differentiation of emotional states. *Psychological Review*, **52**, 35–48.

Arnold, M.B. (1960). *Emotion and Personality* (2 vols.). New York: Columbia University Press.

Arnold, M.B. (1968). *The Nature of Emotion: Selected Readings*. Harmondsworth: Penguin.

Arnold, M.B. (1970a). *Feelings and Emotions: The Loyola Symposium*. New York: Academic Press.

Arnold, M.B. (1970b). Brain functions in emotions: A phenomenological analysis. In P. Black (Ed.) *Physiological Correlates of Emotion*. New York: Academic Press.

Aronfreed, J. (1968). *Conduct and Conscious: The Socialization of Internalized Control over Behavior*. New York: Academic Press.

Averill, J.R. (1982). *Anger and Aggression: An Essay on Emotion*. New York: Springer-Verlag.

Averill, J.R. (1988). A Ptolemaic theory of emotion. *Cognition and Emotion*, **2**, 81–87.

Averill, J.R. and Nunley, E.P. (1988) Grief as an emotion and as a disease: A social-constructionist perspective. *Journal of Social Issues*, **44**, 79–95.

Averill, J.R. and & More, T.A. (1993). Happiness. In M. Lewis and J.M. Haviland (Eds) *Handbook of Emotions*. New York: The Guilford Press, pp.617–632.

Beck, A.T. (1967). *Depression: Clinical, Experimental, and Theoretical Aspects*. New York: Harper & Row.

Berscheid, E. (1983). Emotion. In H.H. Kelley *et al* (Eds) *Close Relationships*. New York: Freeman.

Bertocci, P.A. (1988). *The Person and Primary Emotions*. New York: Springer-Verlag.

Bindra, D. (1968). A neuropsychological interpretation of the effects of drive and incentive-motivation on general activity and instrumental behavior. *Psychological Review*, **75**, 1–22.

Bindra, D. (1969). A unified interpretation of emotion and motivation. *Annals of the New York Academy of Science*, **159**, 1071–1083.

Blanchard, R.J. and Blanchard, D.C. (1990). An ethoexperimental analysis of defense, fear and anxiety. In N. McNaughton and G. Andrews (Eds), *Anxiety*. Dunedin: Otago University Press.

Bousfield W.I. and Orbison, W.D. (1952). Ontogenesis of emotional behavior. *Psychological Review*, **59**, 1–7.

Bower, G.H. (1981). Mood and memory. *American Psychologist*, **36**, 129–148.

Bowlby, J. (1969). Psychopathology of anxiety: The role of affectional bonds. In M.H. Lader (Ed.) *Studies of Anxiety*. Ashford: Headley Bros, pp.80–86.

Bowlby, J. (1973). *Attachment and Loss*, Vol 2, *Separation*. New York: Basic Books.

Bowlby, J. (1980). *Attachment and Loss*, Vol. 3, *Loss*. New York: Basic Books.

Bradbury, T.N. and Fincham, F.D. (1987). Affect and cognition in close relationships: Towards an integrative model. *Cognition and Emotion*, **1**, 59–87.

Braun, E. (1969). *Meyerhold on Theatre*. London: Eyre Methuen.

Bretherton, I. (1985). Attachment theory: Retrospect and prospect. In I. Bretherton & E. Waters (Eds), Growing points in attachment theory research. *Monographs of the Society for Research in Child Development*, **50**, 3–35.

Bridges, K.M.B. (1932). *The Social and Emotional Development of the Pre-School Child*. London: Kegan Paul

Brierly, M. (1937). Affects in theory and practice. *International Psychoanalysis*, **18**, 256–268. (As quoted in Rapaport, 1950.)

Brody, L.R. and Hall, J.A. (1993). Gender and emotion. In M. Lewis and J.M. Haviland (Eds) *Handbook of Emotions*. New York: The Guilford Press, pp.447–460.

Buck, R. (1983). Emotional development and emotional education. In R. Plutchik and H. Kellerman (Eds), *Emotion: Theory, Research and Experience*. New York: Academic Press.

Buck, R. (1985). Prime theory: An integrated view of motivation and emotion. *Psychological Review*, **92**, 389–413.

Buck, R. (1988). *Human Motivation and Emotion*, 2nd edn. New York: Wiley.

Buck, R. (1991). Motivation, emotion and cognition: A developmental–interactionist view. In K.T. Strongman (Ed) *International Review of Studies on Emotion*, Vol. 1. Chichester: Wiley, pp.101–142.

Bull, N. (1951). The attitude theory of emotion. *Nervous and Mental Disorders Monograph, No. 81.*

Buytedjik, F.J.J. (1950). The phenomenological approach to the problem of feelings and emotions. In M.L. Reymert (Ed.) *Feelings and Emotions: The Mooseheart Symposium*. New York: McGraw-Hill, pp.127–141.

Cacioppo, J.T., Klein, D.J., Berntson, G.G. and Hatfield, E. (1993). The psychophysiology of emotion. In M. Lewis and J.M. Haviland (Eds) *Handbook of Emotions*. New York: The Guilford Press, pp.119–142.

Campos, J.J., Campos, R.G. and Barrett, K.C. (1989). Emergent themes in the study of emotional development and emotion regulation. *Developmental Psychology*, **25**, 394–402.

Camras, L. (1991). A dynamical systems perspective on expressive development. In K.T. Strongman (Ed.) *International Review of Studies on Emotion*, Vol. 1. Chichester: Wiley, pp.16–28.

Camras, L.A. (1992). Expressive development and basic emotions. *Cognition and Emotion*, **6**, 269–283.

Camras, L.A., Holland, E.A. and Patterson, M.J. (1993). Facial expression. In M. Lewis and J.M. Haviland (Eds), *Handbook of Emotions*. New York: The Guilford Press, pp.199–208.

Cannon, W.B. (1915) *Bodily Changes in Panic, Hunger, Fear and Rage* (2nd edn, 1929). New York: Appleton-Century.

Cannon, W.B. (1927). The James–Lange theory of emotion: A critical examination and an alternative theory. *American Journal of Psychology*, **39**, 106–124.

Cannon, W.B. (1931). Again the James–Lange and the thalamic theories of emotions. *Psychological Review*, **38**, 281–295.

Cannon, W.B. (1932). *The Wisdom of the Body* (2nd edn, 1939). New York: Norton.

Cichetti, D and Hesse, P. (1983). Affect and intellect: Piaget's contributions to the study of infant emotional development. In R. Plutchik and H. Kellerman (Eds), *Emotion: Theory, Research and Experience*, Vol 2. New York: Academic Press.

Clifford, S. and Marcus, G. (Eds) (1986). *Writing Culture: The Poetics and Politics of Ethnography*. Berkeley: University of California Press.

Collins, R. (1990). Stratification, emotional energy, and the transient emotions. In T.D. Kemper (Ed), *Research Agendas in the Sociology of Emotions*. Albany: State University of New York Press, pp.27–57.

Cornelius, R.R. (1991). Gregorio Marañon's two-factor theory of emotion. *Personality and Social Psychology Bulletin*, **17**, 65–69.

Cotton, J.L. (1981). A review of research on Schachter's theory of emotion and the misattribution of arousal. *European Journal of Social Psychology*, **11**, 365–397.

Crawford, J., Kippax, S., Onyx, J., Gault, U. and Benton, P. (1992). *Emotion and Gender*. London: Sage.

Darwin, C.R. (1872) *The Expression of the Emotions in Man and Animals*. London: Albemarle.

Davitz, J.L. (1969). *The Language of Emotion*. New York: Academic Press.

Davitz, J.L. (1970). A dictionary and grammar of emotion. In M.L. Arnold (Ed.), *Feelings and Emotion: The Loyola Symposium*. New York: Academic Press, pp.251–258.

Denzin, N.K. (1984). *On Understanding Human Emotion*. San Francisco: Jossey-Bass.

Denzin, N.K. (1985). Emotion as lived experience. *Symbolic Interaction*, **8**, 223–240.

Denzin, N. (1990). On understanding emotion: The interpretative-cultural agenda. In T.D. Kemper (Ed.) *Research Agendas in the Sociology of Emotions*. Albany: State University of New York Press.

de Rivera, J. (1977) *A Structural Theory of the Emotions*. New York: International Universities Press.

de Rivera, J. (1992) Emotional climate: Social structure and emotional dynamics. In K.T.Strongman (Ed.), *International Review of Studies on Emotion*, Vol 2. Chichester: Wiley, pp.197–218.

de Rivera, J. and Grinkis, C. (1986). Emotions as social relationships. *Motivation and Emotion*, **10**, 351–369.

Derrida, J. (1982). Sending: On representation. *Social Research*, **49**, 294–326.

Diener, E. and Larsen, R.J. (1993). The experience of emotional well-being. In M. Lewis and J.M. Haviland (Eds), *Handbook of Emotions*. New York: The Guilford Press, pp.405–416.

Dollard, J. and Miller, N. (1950). *Personality and Psychotherapy*. New York: McGraw-Hill.

Duffy, E. (1934). Emotion: An example of the need for reorientation in psychology. *Psychological Review*, **41**, 184–198.

Duffy, E. (1941). An explanation of 'emotional' phenomena without the use of the concept 'emotion'. *Journal of General Psychology*, **25**, 283–293.

Duffy, E. (1962). *Activation and Behavior*. New York: Wiley.

Durkheim, E. (1954). *The Elementary Forms of the Religious Life*. New York: Free Press.

Eibl-Eibesfeldt, I. (1970). *Ethology—The Biology of Behaviour*. New York: Holt, Rinehart & Winston.

Ekman, P. (1972). Universals and cultural differences in facial expressions of emotions. In J. Cole (Ed.), *Nebraska Symposium on Motivation*, **19**, 207–283. Lincoln: University of Nebraska Press.

Ekman, P. (1982). *Emotion in the Human Face*, 2nd edn. Cambridge: Cambridge University Press.

Ekman, P. (1992). An argument for basic emotions. *Cognition and Emotion*, **6**, 169–200.

Ekman, P. (1992). Facial expressions of emotions: New findings, new questions. *Psychological Science*, **3**, 34–38.

Ekman, P and Friesen, W.V. (1969). Non-verbal leakage and clues to deception. *Psychiatry*, **32**, 88–106.

Ellsworth, P.C. (1991). Some implications of cognitive appraisal theories of emotion. In K.T. Strongman (Ed.), *International Review of Studies on Emotion*, Vol 1. Chichester: Wiley, pp.143–160.

Epstein, S. (1993) Emotion and self-theory. In M. Lewis and J.M. Haviland (Eds), *Handbook of Emotions*. New York: The Guilford Press.

Eysenck, H.J. (1957). *The Dynamics of Anxiety and Hysteria*. New York: Praeger.

Eysenck, H.J. (1976). The learning theory model of neurosis—a new approach. *Behavior Research and Therapy*, **14**, 251–267.

Eysenck, M.W. (1988). Trait anxiety and stress. In S. Fisher and J. Reason (Eds), *Handbook of Life Stress, Cognition and Health*. Chichester: Wiley.

Federn, P. (1936) Zur Unterscheidung des gesunden und krankhaften. *Narzimus*, **22**, 5–39. (As quoted by Rapaport, 1950.)

Fehr, F.S. and Stern, J.A. (1970). Peripheral physiological variables and emotion: The James–Lange theory revisited. *Psychological Bulletin*, **74**, 411–424.

Fell, J.P. (1977). The phenomenological approach to emotion. In D.K. Candland, J.P. Fell, E. Keen, A.T. Leshner, R.M. Tarpy and R. Plutchik, *Emotion*. Monterey: Brooks/Cole.

Fischer, K.W. (1980). A theory of cognitive development: The control and construction of hierarchies of skills. *Psychological Review*, **87**, 477–531.

Fischer, K.W., Shaver, P. and Carnochan, P. (1988). From basic- to subordinate-category emotions: A skill approach to emotional development. In W. Damon (Ed.), *Child Development Today and Tomorrow*. San Francisco: Jossey-Bass.

Fischer, K.W., Shaver, P. and Carnochan, P. (1990). How emotions develop and how they organize development. *Cognition and Emotion*, **4**, 81–127.

Fischer, W.F. (1970). *Theories of Anxiety*. New York: Harper & Row.

Fish, S. (1989). *Doing What Comes Naturally*. Durham, NC: Duke University Press.

Fisher, G.A. and Chon, K.K. (1989). Durkheim and the social construction of emotions. *Social Psychology Quarterly*, **52**, 1–9.

Fitness, J. and Strongman, K.T. (1991). Affect in close relationships. In G.J.O. Fletcher and F. Fincham (Eds) *Cognition in Close Relationships*. Hillsdale: Erlbaum.

Freud, S. (1917). *Introductory Lectures on Psychoanalysis*. In the standard edition of the complete psychological works of Sigmund Freud, 1975. London: Hogarth Press.

Freud, S. (1926). *Inhibitions, Symptoms and Anxiety*. In the standard edition of the complete psychological works of Sigmund Freud, 1975. London: Hogarth Press.

Fridlund, A.J. (1992) Darwin's anti-Darwinisms in the *Expression of the Emotions in Man and Animals*. In K.T. Strongman (Ed.), *International Review of Studies on Emotion*, Vol 2. Chichester: Wiley, pp.117–138.

Frijda, N.H. (1969). Recognition of emotion. In L.Berkowitz (Ed.), *Advances in Experimental Social Psychology*, **4**, 167–223.

Frijda, N.H. (1986). *The Emotions*. Cambridge: Cambridge University Press.

Frijda, N.H. The laws of emotion. *American Psychologist*, **43**, 349–358.

Frijda, N.H. (1992b). The empirical status of the laws of emotion. *Cognition and Emotion*, **6**, 467–477.

Frijda, N.H. (1993). Moods, emotion episodes, and emotions. In M. Lewis and J.M. Haviland (Eds), *Handbook of Emotions*. New York: The Guilford Press.

Gellhorn, E. (1964). Motion and emotion: The role of proprioception in the physiology and pathology of the emotions. *Psychological Review*, **71**, 457–472.

Gellhorn, E. & Loufbourrow, G.N. (1963). *Emotions and Emotional Disorders*. New York: Hoeber.

Gergen, K.J. (1986). Correspondence versus autonomy in the language of understanding human action. In D.W. Fiske and R.A. Schneider (Eds), *Metatheory in Social Science*. Chicago: University of Chicago Press.

Giblin, P.T. (1981). Affective development in children: An equilibrium model. *Genetic Psychology Monographs*, **103**, 3–30.

Gibson, J.J. (1979). *An Ecological Approach to Visual Perception*. Boston: Houghton-Mifflin.

Gilligan, S.G. and Bower, G.H. (1984). Cognitive consequences of emotional arousal. In C. Izard, J. Kagan and R. Zajonc (Eds), *Emotions, Cognition and Behavior*. New York: Cambridge University Press.

Giorgi, A. (1970) *Psychology as a Human Science: A Phenomenologically Based Approach*. New York: Harper & Row.

Goffman, E. (1967). *Interaction Ritual*. Garden City: Doubleday/Anchor.

Griffiths, P.E. (1989). The degeneration of the cognitive theory of emotions. *Philosophical Psychology*, **2**, 297–313.

Gray, J.A. (1971). *The Psychology of Fear and Stress*. London: Weidenfeld & Nicolson.

Gray, J.A. (1982). *The Neuropsychology of Anxiety: An Enquiry into the Functions of the Septo-hippocampal System*. Oxford: Oxford University Press.

Gray, J.A. (1987). *The Psychology of Fear and Stress*, 2nd edn, Cambridge: Cambridge University Press.

Greenwood, J.D. (1992). The social constitution of emotion. *New Ideas in Psychology*, **10**, 1–18.

Hammond, L.J. (1970). Conditioned emotional states. In P. Black (Ed.), *Physiological Correlates of Emotion*. New York: Academic Press, pp.245–259.

Harlow, H.F. and Stagner, R. (1933). Psychology of feelings and emotions. 2. Theory of emotions. *Psychological Review*, **40**, 84–194.

Harré, R. (Ed.) (1986). *The Social Construction of Emotions*. Oxford: Blackwell.

Harris, P. (1993). Understanding emotion. In M. Lewis and J.M. Haviland (Eds), *Handbook of Emotions*. New York: The Guilford Press, pp.237–246.

Haviland, J.M. and Goldston, R.B. (1992). Emotion and narrative: The agony and the ecstasy. In K.T. Strongman (Ed.), *International Review of Studies on Emotion*, Vol 2. Chichester: Wiley, pp.219–248.

Haviland, J.M. and Kahlbaugh, P. (1993). Emotion and identity. In M. Lewis and J.M. Haviland (Eds), *Handbook of Emotions*. New York: The Guilford Press, pp.327–340.

Heise, D.R. and O'Brien, J. (1993). Emotion expression in groups. In M. Lewis and J.M. Haviland (Eds), *Handbook of Emotions*. New York: The Guilford Press, pp.489–498.

Hillman, J. (1960). *Emotion*. London: Routledge & Kegan Paul.

Hochschild, A.R. (1983). *The Managed Heart: The Commercialisation of Human Feeling*. Berkeley: University of California Press.

Hochschild, A.R. (1990). Ideology and emotional management: A perspective and path for future research. In T.D. Kemper (Ed.), *Research Agendas in the Sociology of Emotions*. Albany: State University of New York Press, pp.117–142.

Husserl, E. (1913). *Ideas* (1962 edition). New York: Collier Books.

Izard, C.E. (1972) *The Face of Emotion*. New York: Appleton-Century-Crofts.

Izard, C.E. (1977). *Human Emotions*. New York: Plenum.

Izard, C.E. (1990). The substrates and functions of emotion feelings: William James and current emotion theory. *Personality and Social Psychology Bulletin*, **16**, 626–635.

Izard, C.E. (1991). *The Psychology of Emotions*. New York: Plenum.

Izard, C.E. (1992). Basic emotions, relations among emotions, and emotion–cognition relations. *Psychological Review*, **99**, 561–565.

Izard. C.E. (1993). Four systems for emotion activation: Cognitive and noncognitive processes. *Psychological Review*, **100**, 68–90.

Izard, C.E. and Malatesta, C. (1987). Perspectives on emotional development: 1, Differential emotions theory of early emotional development. In J.D. Osofsky (Ed.), *Handbook in Infant Development*, 2nd edn. New York: Wiley, pp.494–554.

James, W. (1884). What is an emotion? *Mind,* **9**, 188–205.

Johnson-Laird, P.N. and Oatley, K. (1989). The language of emotions: An analysis of a semantic field. *Cognition and Emotion,* **3**, 81–123.

Johnson-Laird, P.N. and Oatley, K. (1992). Basic emotions, rationality, and folk theory. *Cognition and Emotion,* **6**, 201–223.

Kemp, S. and Strongman, K.T. (1995). Anger theory and management: A historical analysis. *American Journal of Psychology,* **108**, 397–417.

Kemper, T.D. (1978). *A Social Interactional Theory of Emotions.* New York: Wiley.

Kemper, T.D. (1987). A Manichaean approach to the social construction of emotions. *Cognition and Emotion,* **1**, 353–365.

Kemper, T.D. (1991). An introduction to the sociology of emotions. In K.T. Strongman (Ed.), *International Review of Studies on Emotion,* Vol. 1, Chichester: Wiley, pp.301–349.

Kemper, T.D. (1993). Sociological models in the explanation of emotions. In M. Lewis and J.M. Haviland (Eds) *Handbook of Emotions.* New York: The Guilford Press, pp.41–52.

Kemper, T.D. and Collins, R. (1990). Dimensions of micro-interaction. *American Journal of Sociology,* **96**, 32–68.

Kiesler, C.A. (1982). Comments. In W.S. Clark & S.T. Fiske (Eds.), *Affect and Cognition.* Hillsdale: Erlbaum.

Kirkegaard, S.A. (1844). *The Concept of Dread,* 2nd edn. Princeton: Princeton University Press.

Kreitler, H. and Kreitler, S. (1972). *Psychology of the Arts.* Durham: Duke University Press.

Lacey, J.I., Kagan, J., Lacey, B.C. and Moss, H.A. (1963). The visceral level: situational determinants and behavioural correlates of autonomic response patterns. In P.H. Knapp (Ed.), *Expressions of the Emotions in Man.* New York: International University Press.

Lader, M.H. (1972). Psychophysiological research and psychosomatic medicine. In M.H. Lader (Ed.), *Studies of Anxiety.* Ashford: Headley, pp.53–61.

Lakatos, I. (1978). *The Methodology of Scientific Research Programmes: Philosophical Papers* Vol.1. J. Worrall and G. Currie (Eds), Cambridge: Cambridge University Press.

Lange, C.G. (1885). *The Emotions* (English transl. 1922). Baltimore: Williams & Wilkins.

Lazarus, R.S. (1966). *Psychological Stress and the Coping Process.* New York: McGraw-Hill.

Lazarus, R.S. (1968). Emotions and adaptation: Conceptual and empirical relations. In W.J. Arnold (Ed.), *Nebraska Symposium on Motivation.* Lincoln: University of Nebraska Press, pp.175–266.

Lazarus, R.S. (1982). Thoughts on the relation between emotion and cognition. *American Psychologist,* **37**, 1019–1024.

Lazarus, R.S. (1984). On the primacy of cognition. *American Psychologist,* **39**, 124–129.

Lazarus, R.S. (1991a). *Emotion and Adaptation.* New York: Oxford University Press.

Lazarus, R.S. (1991b). Progress on a cognitive-motivational-relational theory of emotion. *American Psychologist,* **46**, 819–834.

Lazarus, R.S., Averill, J.R. and Opton, E.M. Jr. (1970) Towards a cognitive theory of emotion. In M.B. Arnold (Ed.), *Feelings and Emotions: The Loyola Symposium.* New York: Academic Press, pp.207–232.

Lazarus, R.S. and Smith, C.A. (1988). Knowledge and appraisal in the cognition–emotion relationship. *Cognition and Emotion,* **2**, 281–300.

Le Doux, J.E. (1987). Emotion. In F. Plum and V. Mountcastle (Eds), *Handbook of Physiology, Nervous System,* Vol. 5, *Higher Function.* Washington: American Physiological Society, pp.419–459.

Le Doux, J.E. (1989). Cognitive-emotional interactions in the brain. *Cognition and Emotion*, **3**, 267–289.

Le Doux, J.E. (1992). Brain systems and emotional memory. In K.T. Strongman (Ed.), *International Review of Studies on Emotion*, Vol. 2. Chichester: Wiley, pp.23–30.

Le Doux, J.E. (1994). Emotion, memory and the brain. *Scientific American*, **June**, 32–39.

Leeper, R.W. (1948). A motivational theory of emotion to replace 'emotion as disorganized response'. *Psychological Review*, **55**, 5–21.

Leeper, R.W. Feelings and emotions. In M.D. Arnold (Ed.), *Feelings and Emotions The Loyola Symposium*. New York: Academic Press, pp.151–168.

Lemerise, E.A. and Dodge, K.A. (1993). The development of anger and hostile interactions. In M. Lewis and J.M. Haviland (Eds), *Handbook of Emotions*. New York: The Guilford Press, pp.537–546.

Leventhal, H. (1974). Emotions: A basic problem for social psychology. In C. Nemeth (Ed.), *Social Psychology: Classic and Contemporary Integrations*. Chicago: Rand-McNally, pp.1–51.

Leventhal, H. (1982). The integration of emotion and cognition: A view from the perceptual motor theory of emotion. In M.S. Clark and S.T. Fiske (Eds), *Affect and Cognition*. Hillsdale: Erlbaum.

Leventhal, H. and Patrick-Miller, L. (1993). In M. Lewis and J.M. Haviland (Eds), *Handbook of Emotions*. New York: The Guilford Press, pp.365–380.

Leventhal, H. and Scherer, K. (1987). The relationship of emotion to cognition: A functional approach to a semantic controversy. *Cognition and Emotion*, **1**, 3–28.

Leventhal, H. and Tomarken, A.J. (1986). Emotion: Today's problems. *Annual Review of Psychology*, **37**, 565–610.

Lewis, M. (1992). *Shame, the Exposed Self*. New York: Free Press.

Lewis, M. (1993). Self-conscious emotions: Embarrassment, pride, shame and guilt. In M. Lewis and J.M. Haviland (Eds), *Handbook of Emotions*. New York: The Guilford Press, pp.563–574.

Lewis, M. and Saarni, C. (Eds). (1992). *The Socialisation of Emotion*. New York: Plenum Press.

Lewis, M. and Michalson, L. (1983). *Children's Emotions and Moods: Developmental Theory and Measurement*. New York: Academic Press.

Lindsley, D.B. (1950). Emotions and the electroencephalogram. In M.L. Reymert (Ed.), *Feelings and Emotions: The Mooseheart Symposium*. New York: McGraw-Hill.

Lindsley, D.B. (1951). Emotion. In S.S. Stevens (Ed.), *Handbook of Experimental Psychology*. New York: Wiley, pp.473–516.

Lindsley, D.B. (1957). Psychophysiology and emotion. In M.R. Jones (Ed.), *Nebraska Symposium on Motivation*. Lincoln: University of Nebraska Press, pp.44–105.

Lindsley, D.B. (1970). The role of nonspecific reticulothalamocortical systems in emotion. In P. Black (Ed.), *Physiological Correlates of Emotion*. New York: Academic Press.

Lutz, C. (1988). *Unnatural emotions: Everyday Sentiments on a Micronesian Atoll and their Challenge to Western Theory*. Chicago: University of Chicago Press.

Lutz, C. and Abu-Lughod, L. (Eds). *Language and the Politics of Emotion*. Cambridge: Cambridge University Press.

Lutz, C. and White, G.M. (1986). The anthropology of emotions. *Annual Review of Anthropology*, **15**, 405–436.

Lyons, W. (1980). *Emotion*. Cambridge: Cambridge University Press.

Lyons, W. (1992). An introduction to the philosophy of the emotions. In K.T. Strongman (Ed.), *International Review of Studies on Emotion*, Vol. 2. Chichester: Wiley, pp.295–314.

Lyotard, J.-F. (1984). *The Post-modern Condition: A Report on Knowledge*. Transl. G. Bennington and B. Massouri. Minneapolis: University of Minnesota Press.

McDougall, W. (1910). *Introduction to Social Psychology.* Boston: Luce.
McDougall, W. (1923). *Outline of Psychology.* New York: Scribner.
McDougall, W. (1928). Emotion and feeling distinguished. In M.L. Reymert (Ed.), *Feelings and Emotions.* Worcester: Clark University Press.
McGuire, T.T. (1993). Emotion and behavior genetics in vertebrates and invertebrates. In M. Lewis and J.M. Haviland (Eds), *Handbook of Emotions.* New York: The Guilford Press.
MacLean, P.D. (1970). The limbic brain in relation to the psychoses. In P.D. Black (Ed.), *Physiological Correlates of Emotion.* New York: Academic Press.
MacLean, P.D. (1993). Cerebral evolution of emotion. In M. Lewis and J.M. Haviland (Eds), *Handbook of Emotions.* New York: The Guilford Press, pp.67–86.
McNaughton, N. (1989). *Biology and Emotion.* Cambridge: Cambridge University Press.
McNaughton, N. (1995). Brain mechanisms of anxiety. *New Zealand Journal of Psychology,* 24, 2, 11–18.
Magai, C and Hunziker. J. (1993). Tolstoy and the riddle of developmental transformation: A lifespan analysis of the role of emotions in personality development. In M. Lewis and J.M. Haviland (Eds), *Handbook of Emotions.* New York: The Guilford Press, pp.247–260.
Malatesta, C.Z., Culver, C., Tesman, J.R. and Shepard, B. (1989). The development of emotion expression during the first two years of life. *Monographs of the Society for Research in Child Development,* 54, 1–138.
Malatesta, C. and Wilson, A. (1988). Emotion/cognition interaction in personality development: A discrete emotions, functionalist analysis. *British Journal of Social Psychology,* 27, 91–112.
Malatesta-Magai, C., Izard, C.E., Camras, L. (1991). Conceptualizing early infant affect: Emotions as fact, fiction or artifact? In K.T. Strongman (Ed.), *International Review of Studies on Emotion,* Vol. 1. Chichester: Wiley, pp.1–36.
Mandler, G. (1962). Emotion. In *New Directions in Psychology, 1.* New York: Holt, Rinehart & Winston, pp.269–353.
Mandler, G. (1976). *Mind and Emotion.* New York: Wiley.
Mandler, G. (1982). The structure of value: Accounting for taste. In M.S. Clark and S.T. Fiske (Eds), *Affect and Cognition.* Hillsdale: Erlbaum.
Mandler, G. (1984). *Mind and Body: Psychology of Emotion and Stress.* New York: Norton.
Mandler, G. (1990). A constructivist theory of emotion. In N.S. Stein, B.L. Leventhal and T. Trabasso (Eds), *Psychological and Biological Approaches to Emotion.* Hillsdale: Erlbaum.
Mandler, G. (1992). Emotions, evolution and aggression: Myths and conjectures. In K.T. Strongman (Ed.), *International Review of Studies on Emotion,* Vol. 2. Chichester: Wiley, pp.97–116.
Maranon, G. (1924). Contribution a l'étude de l'action émotive de l'adrenoline. *Revue Francaise d'Endocrine,* 21, 201–205.
Marks, J. (1982). A theory of emotion. *Philosophical Studies,* 42, 227–242.
Mehrabian, A. and Russell, J.A. (1974). *An Approach to Environmental Psychology.* Cambridge, MA: MIT Press.
Michalos, A.C. (1985). Multiple discrepancies theory (MDT). *Social Indicators Research,* 16, 347–413.
Michalos, A.C. (1986). Job satisfaction, marital satisfaction, and the quality of life. In F.M. Andrews (Ed.), *Research on the Quality of Life.* Ann Arbor: University of Michigan, Institute for Social Research, pp.57–84.
Millenson, J.R. (1967). *Principles of Behavioural Analysis.* New York: Macmillan.
Miller, G.A., Galanter, E.H. and Pribram, K.H. (1960). *Plans and the Structure of Behavior.* New York: Holt.

Mowrer, O.H. (1953). A stimulus response analysis of anxiety and its role as a reinforcing agent. In L.M. Stolurow (Ed.), *Readings in Learning*. Englewood Cliffs: Prentice Hall.

Mowrer, O.H. (1960a). *Learning Theory and Behavior*. New York: Wiley.

Mowrer, O.H. (1960b). *Learning Theory and the Symbolic Processes*. New York: Wiley.

Neill, A. (1993). Fiction and the emotions. *American Philosophical Quarterly*, **30**, 1–13.

Nesse, R.M. (1990). Evolutionary explanations of emotions. *Human Nature*, **1**, 261–289.

Nisbett, R. and Ross, L. (1980). *Human Inference: Strategies and Shortcomings in Social Judgement*. Englewood Cliffs: Prentice Hall.

Oatley, K. (1992). *Best Laid Schemes*. Cambridge: Cambridge University Press.

Oatley, K. (1993). Social construction in emotion. In M. Lewis and J.M. Haviland (Eds), *Handbook of Emotions*. New York: The Guilford Press, pp.341–352.

Oatley, K. and Duncan, E. (1992). Structured diaries for emotions in daily life. In K.T. Strongman (Ed.), *International Review of Studies on Emotion*, Vol. 2. Chichester: Wiley, pp.249–294.

Oatley, K. and Jenkins, J.M. (1992). Human emotions: Function and dysfunction. *Annual Review of Psychology*, **43**, 55–85.

Oatley, K. and Johnson-Laird, P.N. (1987). Towards a cognitive theory of emotions. *Cognition and Emotion*, **1**, 29–50.

Oatley, K. and Johnson-Laird, P.N. (1990). Semantic primitives for emotions: A reply to Ortony and Clore. *Cognition and Emotion*, **4**, 129–143.

Öhman, A. (1993). Fear and anxiety as emotional phenomena: Clinical phenomenology, evolutionary perspectives, and information-processing mechanisms. In M. Lewis and J.M. Haviland (Eds), *Handbook of Emotions*. New York: The Guilford Press, pp.511–536.

Ortony, A. (1987). Is guilt an emotion? *Cognition and Emotion*, **1**, 283–298.

Ortony, A. and Clore, G.L. (1989) Emotions, moods, and conscious awareness. *Cognition and Emotion*, **3**, 125–137.

Ortony, A, Clore, G.L. and Collins, A. (1988) *The Cognitive Structure of Emotions*. New York: Cambridge University Press.

Ortony, A. and Turner, T.J. (1990). What's basic about basic emotions? *Psychological Review*, **97**, 315–331.

Ostwald, P.F. (1966). Music and human emotions—discussion. *Journal of Music Therapy*, **3**, 93–94.

Panksepp, J. (1981). Toward a general psychobiological theory of emotion. *The Behavioral and Brain Sciences*, **5**, 407–467.

Panksepp, J. (1989) The neurobiology of emotions: Of animal brains and human feelings. In H. Wagner and T. Manstead (Eds), *Handbook of Social Psychophysiology*. Chichester: Wiley, pp.5–26.

Panksepp, J. (1991). Affective neuroscience: A conceptual framework for the neurobiological study of emotions. In K.T. Strongman (Ed.), *International Review of Studies on Emotion*, Vol. 1. Chichester: Wiley, pp. 59–100.

Panksepp, J. (1992). A critical role for 'affective neuroscience' in resolving what is basic about basic emotions. *Psychological Review*, **99**, 554–560.

Panksepp, J. (1993). Neurochemical control of moods and emotions: Amino acids to neuropeptides. In M. Lewis and J.M. Haviland (Eds), *Handbook of Emotions*. New York: The Guilford Press.

Papez, J.W. (1937). A proposed mechanism of emotion. *Archives of Neurological Psychiatry*, **38**, 725–743.

Papez, J.W. (1939). Cerebral mechanisms. Research Publication, *Association for Research in Nervous and Mental Disorders*, **89**, 145–159.

Parrott, W.G. and Sabini, J. (1989). On the 'Emotional' qualities of certain types of cognition: A reply to arguments for the independence of cognition and affect. *Cognitive Therapy and Research*, **13**, 49–65.

Pennebaker, J.W. (1982). *The Psychology of Physical Symptoms.* New York: Springer-Verlag.

Pervin, L.A. (1993). Affect and personality. In M. Lewis and J.M. Haviland (Eds), *Handbook of Emotions.* New York: The Guilford Press, pp.301–312.

Peters, R.S. (1969). Motivation, emotion and the conceptual schemes of common sense. In T. Mischel (Ed.), *Human Action.* New York: Academic Press, pp.135–165.

Peters, R.S. (1970). The education of the emotions. In M.B. Arnold (Ed.), *Feelings and Emotions: The Loyola Symposium.* New York: Academic Press, pp.187–204.

Pittam, J. and Scherer, K.R. (1993). Vocal expression and communication of emotion. In M. Lewis and J.M. Haviland (Eds), *Handbook of Emotions.* New York: The Guilford Press, pp.185–198.

Plutchik, R. (1962). *The Emotions: Facts, Theories and a New Model.* New York: Random House.

Plutchik, R. (1980). *Emotion: A Psychoevolutionary Synthesis.* New York: Harper & Row.

Plutchik, R. (1989) Measuring emotions and their derivatives. In R. Plutchik and H. Kellerman (Eds), *Emotion: Theory, Research and Experience.* Vol. 4, *The Measurement of Emotion.* San Diego: Academic Press.

Plutchik, R. (1991). Emotions and evolution. In K.T. Strongman (Ed.), *International Review of Studies on Emotion*, Vol. 1. Chichester: Wiley, pp.37–58.

Plutchik, R. (1993). Emotions and their vicissitudes: Emotions and psychopathology. In M. Lewis and J.M. Haviland (Eds), *Handbook of Emotions.* New York: The Guilford Press.

Popper, K.R. (1945). *The Open Society and its Enemies*, Vol. 1. *Plato.* London: Routledge.

Pradines, M. (1958). *Traite de Psychologie*, 6th edn, Vol. 1. Presses Universitaires de France. Transl. Y. Begin and M.B. Arnold. Excerpts reprinted in M.B. Arnold (Ed.), (1968), *The Nature of Emotion.* Harmondsworth: Penguin, pp.189–200.

Pratt, M. (1986). Fieldwork in common places. In J. Clifford and S. Marcus (Eds), *Writing Culture: The Poetics and Politics of Ethnography.* Berkeley: University of California Press.

Pribram, K.H. (1970). Feelings as monitors. In M.B. Arnold (Ed.), *Feelings and Emotions: The Loyola Symposium.* New York: Academic Press, pp.41–53.

Rapaport, D. (1950). *Emotions and Memory.* New York: International Universities Press.

Ratner, C. (1989). A social constructionist critique of the naturalistic theory of emotion. *The Journal of Mind and Behavior,* **10**, 211–230.

Reisenzein, R. (1983). The Schachter theory of emotion: Two decades later. *Psychological Bulletin,* **94**, 239–264.

Reisenzein, R. and Schönpflug, W. (1992). Stumpf's cognitive-evaluative theory of emotion. *American Psychologist,* **47**, 34–45.

Robinson, R.J. and Pennebaker, J.W. (1991). Emotion and health: Towards an integrative approach. In K.T. Strongman (Ed.), *Internatioinal Review of Studies on Emotion*, Vol. 1. Chichester: Wiley.

Rolls, E.T. (1990). A theory of emotion, and its application to understanding the neural basis of emotion. *Cognition and Emotion,* **4**, 161–190.

Roseman, I. (1991). Appraisal determinants of discrete emotions. *Cognition and Emotion,* **5**, 161–200.

Rosenberg, M. (1990). Reflexivity and emotions. *Social Psychology Quarterly,* **53**, 3–12.

Rosin, P., Haidt, J. and McCauley, C.R. (1993). Disgust. In M. Lewis and J.M. Haviland (Eds), *Handbook of Emotions.* New York: The Guilford Press, pp.575–594.

Russell, J.A. (1991). Culture and categorization of emotions. *Psychological Bulletin,* **110**, 426–450.

Ryle, G. (1948). *The Concept of Mind.* London: Hutchinson.

Sartre, J.-P. (1948). *The Emotions.* New York: Philosophical Library.

Schachter, S. (1959) *The Psychology of Affiliation.* Stamford: Stamford University Press.

Schachter, S. (1964). The interaction of cogntive and physiological determinants of emotional state. In L. Berkowitz (Ed.), *Mental Social Psychology*, Vol. 1. New York: Academic Press, pp.49–80.

Schachter, S. (1970). The assumption of identity and peripheralist–centralist controversies in motivation and emotion. In M.B. Arnold (Ed.), *Feelings and Emotion: The Loyola Symposium.* New York: Academic Press.

Schachter, S. and Singer, J. (1962). Cognitive, social and physiological determinants of emotional state. *Psychological Review, 69*, 370–399.

Scheff, T. (1990). Socialisation of emotions: Pride and shame as causal agents. In T.D. Kemper (Ed.), *Research Agendas in the Sociology of Emotions.* Albany: State University of New York Press, pp.281–304.

Scherer, K. (1986) Vocal affect expression: A review and a model for future research. *Psychological Bulletin, 99*, 143–165.

Scherer, K. (1992). On social representations of emotional experience: Stereotypes, prototypes, or archetypes? In M. Von Cranach, W. Doise, and G. Mugny (Eds), *Social Representations and the Social Bases of Knowledge.* Berne: Huber, pp.30–36.

Scherer, K.R. (1992). Emotions are biologically and socially constituted: A response to Greenwood. *New Ideas in Psychology, 10*, 19–22.

Scherer, K. (1993). Neuroscience projections to current debates in emotion psychology. *Cognition and Emotion, 7*, 1–41.

Schneirla, T.C. (1959). An evolutionary and developmental theory of biphasic processes underlying approach and withdrawal. In M.R. Jones (Ed.), *Nebraska Symposium on Motivation.* Lincoln: University of Nebraska Press, pp.1–42.

Seligman, M.E.P. (1971). Phobias and preparedness. *Behavior Therapy, 2*, 307–320.

Seligman, M.E.P. (1975). *Helplessness.* San Francisco: Freeman.

Shibbles, W. (1991). Feminism and the cognitive theory of emotion: Anger, blame and humor. *Women and Health, 17*, 57–69.

Shields, S.A. (1991). Gender in the psychology of emotion: A selective research review. In K.T. Strongman (Ed.), *International Review of Studies on Emotion*, Vol. 1. Chichester: Wiley, pp.227–246.

Shott, S. (1979). Emotion and social life: A symbolic interactionist analysis. *American Journal of Sociology, 84*, 1317–1334.

Shweder, R.A. (1993). The cultural psychology of the emotions. In M. Lewis and J.M. Haviland (Eds), *Handbook of Emotions.* New York: The Guilford Press, pp.417–434.

Siminov, P.V. (1970). The information theory of emotion. In M.B. Arnold (Ed.), *Feelings and Emotions: The Loyola Symposium.* New York: Academic Press, pp.145–149.

Singer, J.A. and Salovey, P. (1988). Mood and memory: Evaluating the network theory of affect. *Clinical Psychology Review, 8*, 211–251.

Smedslund, J. (1992) Are Frijda's 'Laws of emotion' empirical? *Cognition and Emotion, 6*, 435–456.

Smith, C.A. and Ellsworth, P.C. (1985). Patterns of cognitive appraisal in emotion. *Journal of Personality and Social Psychology, 48*, 813–838.

Smith, C.A. and Ellsworth, P.C. (1987). Patterns of appraisal and emotion related to taking an exam. *Journal of Personality and Social Psychology, 52*, 475–488.

Smith, R.H., Kim, S.H. and Parrott, W.G. (1988). Envy and jealousy: Semantic problems and experiential distinctions. *Personality and Social Psychology Bulletin, 14*, 401–409.

Solomon, R.C. (1976). *The Passions: The Myth and Nature of Human Emotions.* Notre Dame: University of Notre Dame Press.

Solomon, R.C. (1988). The rediscovery of philosophy in emotion. *Cognition and Emotion*, **2**, 105–113.

Solomon, R.C. (1993) The philosophy of emotions. In M. Lewis and J.M. Haviland (Eds). *Handbook of Emotions.* New York: The Guilford Press, pp.3–15.

Solomon, R.C. (1994). *About Love: Reinventing Romance for our Times.* Lanham, MD: Rowman & Littlefield.

Sroufe, L.A. (1979). Socioemotional development. In J.D. Osofsky (Ed.), *Handbook of Infant Development.* New York: Wiley.

Staats, A.W. and Eifert, G.H. (1990). The paradigmatic behaviorism theory of emotions: Basis for unification. *Clinical Psychology Review*, **10**, 539–566.

Stanislawski, C. (1929). Direction and acting. *Encyclopaedia Britannica*, 14th edn, Vol. 22.

Stearns, C.Z. (1993). Sadness. In M. Lewis and J.M. Haviland (Eds), *Handbook of Emotions.* New York: The Guilford Press, pp.547–562.

Stearns, P.N. (1986). Historical analysis in the study of emotion. *Motivation and Emotion*, **10**, 185–193.

Stearns, P.N. (1993). Girls, boys and emotions: Redefinitions and historical change. *The Journal of American History*, **80**, 36–74.

Stearns, P.N. and Knapp, M. (1993). Men and romantic love: Pinpointing a 20th-century change. *Journal of Social History*, **26**, 769–795.

Stearns, P.N. and Stearns, D.C. (1994). Biology and culture: Toward a new combination. *Contention*, **3**, 29–53.

Stein, N.L., Trabasso, T. and Liwag, M. (1993). The representation and organization of emotional experience. In M. Lewis and J.M. Haviland (Eds), *Handbook of Emotions.* New York: The Guilford Press, pp.279–300.

Sternberg, R.J. (1986). A triangular theory of love. *Psychological Review*, **93**, 119–135.

Sternberg, R.J. (1987). Liking versus loving: A comparative evaluation of theories. *Psychological Bulletin*, **102**, 331–345.

Stocker, M. (1987). Emotional thoughts. *American Philosophical Quarterly*, **24**, 59–69.

Strongman, K.T. (1990). Evaluating emotional theory. A review of *The Person and Primary Emotions. Cognition and Emotion*, **4**, 375–380.

Strongman, K.T. (1993). Emotion theory and cognitive behaviour therapy. *Behaviour Change*, **10**, 141–153.

Strongman, K.T. (1995). Theories of anxiety. *New Zealand Journal of Psychology*, 24, 2, 4–10.

Strongman, K.T. (1996). Emotion and Memory. In C. Malatesta-Magai & S.H. McFadden (Eds), *Handbook of Emotion, Adult Development and Aging.* New York: Academic Press.

Strongman, L., Strongman, K.T. and Harré, R. (1996). Post-modern aspects of contemporary accounts of emotion. Submitted for publication.

Stumpf, C. (1899). Über den Begriff der Gemüthsbewegung (On the concept of emotion). *Zeitschrift für Psychologie und Physiologie der Sinnesorgane*, **21**, 47–99.

Sullivan, H.S. (1953). *The Interpersonal Theory of Psychiatry.* New York: Norton.

Thelen, E. (1989). Conceptualizing development from a dynamical systems perspective. In B. Berenthal, A. Fogel, L. Smith and E. Thelen (Chairs), Dynamical Systems in Development. Society for Research in Child Development, pre-Conference Workshop, Kansas City. (Quoted in Camras, 1991.)

Thoits, P.A. (1985). Self-labelling processes in mental illness: The role of emotional deviance. *American Sociological Review*, **91**, 221–249.

Thoits, P.A. (1990). Emotional deviance: Research agendas. In T.D. Kemper (Ed.), *Research Agendas in the Sociology of Emotions.* Albany: State University of New York Press, pp.180–203.

Tinbergen, M. (1963). On the aims and methods of ethology. *Zeitschrift Tierpsychologie*, **20**, 410–433.

Tomkins, S.S. (1962). *Affect, Imagery and Consciousness*, Vol. 1, *The Positive Affects.* New York: Springer.

Tomkins, S.S. (1963). *Affect, Imagery and consciousness*, Vol. 2, *The Negative Affects.* New York: Springer.

Toulmin, S. (1983). The construct of reality: Criticisms in modern and post-modern science. In W. Mitchell (Ed.), *The Politics of Interpretation.* Chicago: University of Chicago Press.

Turner, M.B. (1967). *Philosophy and the Science of Behaviour.* New York: Appleton-Century-Crofts.

Turner, T.J. and Ortony, A (1992). Basic emotions: Can conflicting criteria converge? *Psychological Review*, **3**, 566–571.

Ulrich, R.S. (1983). Aesthetic and affective response to natural environment. In I. Altman and J.F. Wohlwill (Eds.), *Human Behavior and Environment, Vol. 6, Behavior and the Natural Environment.*

Watson, J.B. (1929). *Psychology. From the Standpoint of a Behaviorist.* (3rd edn, revised). Philadelphia: Lippincott.

Watson, J.B. (1930). *Behaviorism* (revised edn). Chicago: University of Chicago Press.

Watson, J.B. and Raynor, R. (1920). Conditioned emotional reactions. *Journal of Experimental Psychology*, **3**, 1–14.

Watts, F.N. (1992) Applications of current cognitive theories of the emotions to the conceptualisation of emotional disorders. *British Journal of Clinical Psychology*, **31**, 153–167.

Waynebaum, L. (1907). *La Physionomie humaine: Son mécanisme et son rôle social.* Paris: Alcan. (As quoted in Zajonc, 1985.)

Weiskrantz, L. (1968). Emotion. In L. Weiskrantz (Ed.), *Analysis of Behavioural Change.* New York: Harper & Row, pp.50–90.

Wenger, M.A. (1950). Emotion as visceral action: An extension of Lange's theory. In M.L. Reymert (Ed.), *Feelings and Emotions: The Mooseheart Symposium.* New York: McGraw-Hill.

White, G.M. (1993). Emotions inside out: The anthropology of affect. In M. Lewis and J.M. Haviland (Eds), *Handbook of Emotions.* New York: The Guilford Press, pp. 29–40.

Wierzbicka, A. (1992). Talking about emotions: Semantics, culture, and cognition. *Cognition and Emotion*, **6**, 285–319.

Wittgenstein, L. (1958). *Philosophical Investigations.* Transl. G.E.M. Anscombe. Oxford: Blackwell.

Young, P.T. (1961). *Motivation and Emotion.* New York: Wiley.

Zajonc, R.B. (1980). Feeling and thinking: Preferences need no inferences. *American Psychologist*, **35**, 151–175.

Zajonc, R.B. (1984). On the primacy of affect. *American Psychologist*, **39**, 117–123.

Zajonc, R.B. (1985). Emotion and facial efference: A theory reclaimed. *Science*, **228**, 15–21.

Zajonc, R.B., Murphy, S.T. and Inglehart, M. (1989). Feeling and facial efference: Implications of the vascular theory of emotion. *Psychological Review*, **96**, 395–416.

Author index

Subject index

Related titles of interest from Wiley...

Handbook of Personal Relationships
2nd Edition
Theory, Research and Interventions
Edited by **Steve Duck**
A thoroughly revised second edition which adds a new section on family studies and sociology, and updates sections on developmental, social, clinical and community psychology and communication.
0-471-95913-8 825pp 1996 Hardback

Disorders of Personality
2nd Edition
DSM-IV and Beyond
Theodore Millon with **Roger D. Davis**
Brings the previous edition up-to-date, incorporating changes in the new DSM and reviewing all relevant research.
0-471-01186-X 832pp 1996 Hardback

Personality Disorders
Clinical and Social Perspectives
Assessment and Treatment Based on DSM-IV and ICD-10
Jan J.L. Derksen
Describes the diagnosis and treatment of each DSM-IV and ICD-10 personality disorder in detail, illustrated by the use of case examples.
0-471-94389-4 374pp 1995 Hardback
0-471-95549-3 374pp 1995 Paperback

Temperament in Childhood
Edited by **G.A. Kohnstamm, J.E. Bates** and **M.K. Rothbart**
"[a book]... which all clinicians who work with children will find of great interest, and one well worth dipping into. ... throughout, the relevance of the work presented, to real children and their families, is readily apparent." **Child: Care Health and Development**
0-471-95583-3 660pp 1995 Paperback